STELLICKTRICITY

STELLICKTRICITY

Stories, Highlights, and Other Hockey Juice from a Life Plugged into the Game

Gord Stellick

John Wiley & Sons Canada, Ltd.

Library and Archives Canada Cataloguing in Publication
Stellick, Gord
   Stellicktricity : stories, highlights, and other hockey juice from a life plugged into the game / Gord Stellick.

Includes index.
Issued also in electronic formats.
ISBN 978-1-118-07610-1

   1. Stellick, Gord.   2. National Hockey League— Anecdotes.   3. Hockey—Anecdotes.   4. Toronto Maple Leafs (Hockey team)—Anecdotes.   5. Sports executives—Canada— Biography.   6. Sportscasters—Canada—Biography.   I. Title.

GV848.5.S84A3 2011   796.962092   C2011-901793-8

ISBN 978-1-118-07610-1 (hardcover); 978-1-118-07844-0 (ePDF); 978-1-118-07842-6 (Mobi); 978-1-118-07843-3 (ePub)

Production Credits
Cover Design: Soapbox Design
Cover Photo Credit: Lorella Zanetti
Composition: Thomson Digital
Printer: Friesens Printing Ltd.

Editorial Credits
Executive Editor: Karen Milner
Production Editor: Pauline Ricablanca

John Wiley & Sons Canada, Ltd.
6045 Freemont Blvd.
Mississauga, Ontario
L5R 4J3

Printed in Canada

1 2 3 4 5 FP 15 14 13 12 11

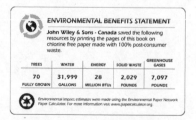

ENVIRONMENTAL BENEFITS STATEMENT

John Wiley & Sons - Canada saved the following resources by printing the pages of this book on chlorine free paper made with 100% post-consumer waste.

TREES	WATER	ENERGY	SOLID WASTE	GREENHOUSE GASES
70 FULLY GROWN	31,999 GALLONS	28 MILLION BTUs	2,029 POUNDS	7,097 POUNDS

Environmental impact estimates were made using the Environmental Paper Network Paper Calculator. For more information visit www.papercalculator.org.

CONTENTS

PROLOGUE

Stellicktricity is the term I have used to describe the phone-in portions of my shows on the Toronto sports radio station The Fan 590 and on the NHL Home Ice XM/Sirius network.

I like the term because it emphasizes fun: though professional sports has become a big business, we should never lose sight of the fun. Being a sports fan involves no heavy lifting, we are not attempting to split the atom, and one sports fan's passionate and insightful opinions are just as good as another's.

I have been extremely fortunate to have been involved in the game for over 35 years, beginning with a chance to work Leafs game nights in the Maple Leaf Gardens press box in 1975, when I was still a high school student at Georges Vanier Secondary School in North York.

Because of that job, I had an opportunity to work part-time in the Maple Leafs executive offices in 1977 while attending the University of Toronto. I began working full-time for the

Leafs in 1979 as an assistant to the general manager. I still hold the distinction of being named the youngest general manager in NHL history when in April, 1988, at the age of 30, I assumed that position with the Maple Leafs. I like to joke that 16 months later I also became the youngest ex-general manager in NHL history when I left the Leafs to work with the New York Rangers for a brief time.

I never even dreamed of the possibility of working for the Toronto Maple Leafs or any other NHL team when I was a young boy. I did harbour dreams of actually playing in the NHL, though that was tempered by my mostly house-league-calibre career as a player.

To be involved in sports media was my ultimate fantasy, however. I would devour the *Globe & Mail* sports section first thing in the morning before anyone else was up. I would do the same thing in the afternoon when the *Toronto Star* was delivered, and also try my best to find a *Toronto Sun* box, so I could read all three papers' sports sections from stem to stern.

I listened each morning to the 8:00 a.m. newscast on CKEY radio at 590 AM, so I wouldn't miss the start of Jim Hunt's morning sports report. Twenty or so years later, I would be broadcasting on that same frequency, which would by then belong to Canada's all-sports radio station, The Fan 590. Jim Hunt was among those whom I would work with on-air at The Fan from time to time.

I have enjoyed my involvement with The Fan 590 since it launched in September 1992. I hosted a show called *The Big Show* in the afternoons for 11 years and then partnered with Don Landry to co-host the *Morning Show* for six years. Most recently I have hosted the *Blue & White Tonight* pre-game show for Toronto Maple Leafs games.

Through it all, it has been a pleasure to talk sports, whether with our loyal listeners or with some of the biggest names in the sports world. My number one sports topic and passion remains the Maple Leafs, as it has been for all of my life. It is an unshakable addiction. When someone I don't know recognizes me and opens with a line that includes "I know you are tired of talking about this, but . . ." I assure them I never get tired talking about our shared passion.

After 35 years in the business, I believe I've figured out what people like to hear from me when it comes to the Leafs and the NHL. They like to hear stories. Fun stories, not just the ones laden with statistical analysis or controversy. They like to hear what really happened behind the scenes—what it was like to actually be there.

They like to hear about the people in hockey, and I love to talk about them, the great friends that I have been so fortunate to meet and in some cases work with.

I appreciate the opportunity to share.

DRAFT DAY
SCOUTING HIGHS AND LOWS

The Entry Draft kicks off the season each year and provides a key opportunity for teams to augment their rosters. Here's a look at noteworthy picks.

The average hockey fan is intrigued about what goes on at the draft tables of NHL teams on draft day. It's a day of optimism for all 30 NHL teams, the one day they can honestly say that they feel they have improved their teams with the addition of new young players. That enthusiasm can be dampened somewhat a few months later as training camp begins, but draft day is one that leaves all NHL teams in great spirits.

So, what are the last-minute discussions and arguments that determine if a team ends up with a Mario Lemieux, a Claude Lemieux, or a Jocelyn Lemieux? One was a superstar, one a quality player, and one a journeyman.

The 1987 Entry Draft was the first to be hosted by an American city. Mike Ilitch had brought the Entry Draft and

NHL meetings to Detroit; Joe Louis Arena would be the site of the actual draft. It was an enthusiastic crowd that immersed themselves in the opportunity to see the top junior and college talent connect with their first NHL destination.

They cheered loudly as the Red Wings made their selection in the first round, 11th overall, and took defenceman Yves Racine from Longueuil, of the Quebec Major Junior Hockey League. It was a few hours later, as the Red Wings were about to make their second-round pick, 32nd overall, that the Joe Louis crowd became even more opinionated. The loud chant of "Adam, Adam" enveloped the building as Red Wings fans clamoured for the hometown boy to be picked by his home team. Detroit native Adam Burt was a defenceman with the North Bay Centennials, of the Ontario Junior League.

The Red Wings ignored the advice of their newest, most vocal "scouts" and selected Gord Kruppke, a defenceman from Prince Albert, of the Western Junior Hockey League. Kruppke was welcomed to the Red Wings organization with a mixed reaction from the hometown crowd—thunderous booing competed with the cheers. When Adam Burt was selected nine picks later by the Hartford Whalers, he received an ovation far surpassing Kruppke's welcome to the Red Wings and comparable to the top selections in the first round.

Hindsight would prove that the Red Wings' management would have fared better had they listened to the crowd. Adam Burt played a steady 11 years as a valued member of the Carolina Hurricanes' defence corps before brief stints in Philadelphia and Atlanta during the final two years of his NHL career. Gord Kruppke became a career minor-leaguer who played in only 23 NHL games with the Detroit Red Wings.

That 1987 draft in Detroit also stands out for its humorous moments. One such moment involved Gilles Leger, the assistant general manager of the Quebec Nordiques. He had a unique fashion sense, and on that particular day he wore a white jacket, one befitting a struggling Bohemian artist. Although draft day is one of the busiest days of the year for the scouting staff, the coaching staff have plenty of idle time—they're just there to greet the players. Bob McCammon, a member of the Vancouver Canucks' coaching staff, grabbed a similar looking white jacket from one of the many food and beverage servers. Putting on the jacket, he headed toward the Quebec Nordiques' table, cleaning up empty cups and garbage as he went. Speaking loudly in the direction of Leger, he said, "Quit goofing off and get up and help clear the tables." This brought no shortage of laughter from everyone within earshot—McCammon and Leger were two of the best liked and most respected NHL executives.

Then there was the time one of the NHL teams used the phone sitting on their draft table to successfully pull off the oldest prank in the books. They ordered 10 pizzas from Domino's Pizza, the archrival and fierce competitor of Mike Ilitch and his Little Caesars franchises. The pizzas were delivered to the Red Wings' draft table on the floor of Joe Louis Arena. Even Mike Ilitch had to laugh at the practical joke. I never did find out if they tipped the Domino's delivery guy. I do think a couple of the Red Wings management team did actually partake of a slice or two from the Little Caesars archrival!

Management and scouts always lobby hard for their favourites, but the best last-minute argument I witnessed was at the Toronto Maple Leafs' draft table. Unfortunately, it didn't work out well for the blue and white in the long run, and their mistake ended up helping the Colorado Avalanche win two Stanley Cups. I was seated at the Leafs' table in Joe Louis Arena as we waited to make the seventh overall selection. (The one upside to all those losing seasons in the 1980s was that we were always one of the first teams to draft!) The Leafs entourage included President Harold Ballard, General Manager Gerry McNamara, Head Coach John Brophy, Chief Scout Floyd Smith, and me, then the assistant general manager. Other members of the scouting staff, coaching staff, and front office filled out the remaining seats at our table, about 16 of us altogether.

The first six selections of the Entry Draft went as forecast: Pierre Turgeon to Buffalo, Brendan Shanahan to New Jersey, Glen Wesley to Boston, Wayne McBean to Los Angeles, Chris Joseph to Pittsburgh, and Dave Archibald to Minnesota. This left our target for the seventh position still available—defenceman Luke Richardson from the Peterborough Petes was our consensus pick. It seemed like it would be quick and easy—until Floyd Smith derailed us at the last second. Smith felt strongly that a young centre named Joe Sakic from the Swift Current Broncos was far and away the best player available.

John Brophy was apoplectic. He wanted size and toughness, and Richardson could provide that to his defence corps. Brophy wanted no part of another smallish centre when the Leafs already had Russ Courtnall, Dan Daoust, Ed Olczyk, and Tom Fergus—none of whom was known for their physical prowess. Besides, Brophy felt the pick had already been decided and that no further debate was warranted.

The conversation between Smith and Brophy, who at the time weren't on the best of terms anyway, grew louder and even a bit mean-spirited. A defiant Floyd Smith was adamant in his opinion about Sakic. John Brophy's face turned beet red with anger, and it seemed as if he was going to explode. Brophy knew he had a trump card in his favour: he was a favourite of Ballard's and that would carry some clout as the Leafs owner watched the escalating argument with interest. We used our time out as the heated debate continued. After a few minutes, it was time to make the pick. Gerry McNamara made the final decision, sticking with the original plan: Luke Richardson was drafted by the Leafs.

One might wonder why Floyd Smith waited until what seemed like the last second to make his passionate argument. Well, Smith had made his case in scouts meetings before the draft, but we had opted to focus on a defenceman, and Richardson was the consensus pick. Smith waited at the draft table, hoping that Richardson would be picked by one of the six other teams ahead of us, which would have given him a stronger case for drafting Sakic.

As it was, Joe Sakic was selected by the Quebec Nordiques with their second first-round pick (15th overall). They had used their ninth overall pick to choose Bryan Fogarty from Kingston. And the rest is history. While Richardson had a solid NHL career, Sakic retired with 1,641 points (625 goals, 1,016 assists) in his 20 seasons and no doubt will be inducted into the Hall of Fame as soon as he's eligible.

I always give Floyd Smith credit for sticking to his convictions and fighting the good fight. Unfortunately for Leafs fans that year, he didn't win the argument.

There have been instances where a team has been "stuck" with a player who wasn't their first choice, but ultimately things worked out rather well. The Boston Bruins' 1979 selection might just be the best example of a Plan B you'll find anywhere.

The year 1979 was the year of the NHL-WHA (National Hockey League–World Hockey Association) merger, which meant that the draft had to wait until final details were worked out. Once the merger was finalized, the new NHL grew to include Edmonton, Winnipeg, Quebec, and Hartford. The delay pushed back the draft into July. And because of these unusual events, it was held by conference call, with the 21 NHL teams using their offices or a hotel suite as their home base. This gave an impersonal feel to what was usually the most personal of events. But, for that year only, NHL teams were in their own little sphere.

Although the Boston Bruins had finished the season in first place in the Adams Division and had made it to the NHL semifinals, they held the eighth overall selection. This was because their general manager, Harry Sinden, had traded goaltender Ron Grahame to the Los Angeles Kings for that position a year earlier.

While the Kings staff sat in Los Angeles, quietly lamenting what they had given up, the Bruins staff were almost giddy about the prospect of drafting a player they felt would have a true impact on their defence and who they hoped would still be available at eighth overall.

That coveted player wasn't selected in the first five selections, and now only the Chicago Black Hawks (known as the Blackhawks before 1986) stood in the way of Boston being able to select this potential franchise player who could single-handedly change the team's fortunes. Those on the conference line then heard Black Hawks general manager Bob Pulford announce in his distinctive drone the selection of Keith Brown from the Portland Winterhawks.

After a second of disbelief, there was anger and disappointment in the Bruins' room. A few fists pounded the table loudly, and one scout threw his binder against the wall in frustration. They had come so close to being able to draft the franchise player they had held in such high esteem.

But they had to compose themselves and get back to business. Because they'd been so focused on Brown, they had not thought too much about a Plan B. They decided to stick with selecting a defenceman, and after a short debate, announced the player they had chosen as their runner-up: Raymond Bourque from Verdun.

It turned out that they had selected their franchise player after all; it just happened through unexpected circumstances.

Raymond Bourque entered the Hall of Fame in 2004 as the epitome of a franchise player, while Keith Brown was a solid presence on the Chicago Black Hawks' defence for 14 seasons. He finished his NHL career with two seasons with the Florida Panthers and retired in 1995 after playing in 876 NHL regular-season games.

Bourque's statistics don't tell the full story. Though a different personality than Bobby Orr, he filled the superstar-defenceman void Orr had left. He won the Calder Trophy as the NHL's Rookie of the Year in 1980. He was named to the NHL First All-Star team on a remarkable 13 occasions and to the NHL Second All-Star team six times. He won the Norris Trophy as the best defenceman five times (1987, 1988, 1990, 1991, and 1994).

I had the opportunity to chat with Bourque at a Raleigh, North Carolina–area hotel at the time of the 2004 NHL Draft, along with my colleague Nick Kypreos of Sportsnet. Bourque looked like a normal-sized guy—until you looked closely and saw the thickness of his legs and chest. Kypreos spoke for all NHL players of his time when he said, "When he hit you, it was like running into a fire hydrant. You never forgot the feeling of taking a Ray Bourque hit."

And Ron Grahame, the goalie who had been the catalyst for the Bourque trade, lasted four very ordinary seasons with the Los Angeles Kings. As another twist in the tale, years later, his son John Grahame would be drafted by the Bruins in 1994, going on to spend six seasons in the Bruins organization.

Like the movie *The Accidental Tourist*, Raymond Bourque was in some ways *The Accidental Franchise Player.*

The 1979 NHL Entry Draft would have been very different with the inclusion of one more player: a young player named Wayne Gretzky was 18 years old and this was the year he was eligible for the draft. However, one provision of the NHL-WHA merger a few weeks earlier had been that each of the four WHA teams got to keep their rights to two players of their choice from their roster. Typically, veterans were protected, but the Oilers wisely made Gretzky one of their protected players. This was really a no-brainer, as Gretzky had starred as a 17-year-old with 110 points (46 goals, 64 assists) in his one season in the World Hockey Association.

If it weren't for that provision, we could envision that Gretzky would have been the first overall selection by the Colorado Rockies, meaning his first-ever NHL coach would have been none other than Don Cherry. Can you imagine weekly *Coach's Corner* segments with the man who coached not only Bobby Orr but also Wayne Gretzky? Or maybe Gretzky would have brought so much success to the Colorado Rockies that Cherry would have remained an NHL coach for life and never entered the world of broadcasting. This would have been the scenario had the Edmonton Oilers not taken the most logical action and made Wayne Gretzky one of their two protected skaters.

With the 1979 Entry Draft being "Gretzky-less," Colorado's first overall pick was Rob Ramage. The St. Louis Blues had the second overall pick. If Gretzky had been eligible, it is likely Ramage would have been drafted by the St. Louis Blues. As it was, Ramage was traded by Colorado to the St. Louis Blues three years later, and that was where he enjoyed his best NHL seasons.

And who is to say what the trickle-down effect would have been had Gretzky been included? There would have been at least a decent chance that the much-coveted Keith Brown would still have been available when the Bruins selected eighth. Would that have meant that the next team would have drafted Raymond Bourque? We will never know the answer to that question, but we do know that the next team in the order was the Toronto Maple Leafs, who used the ninth overall pick for Laurie Boschman, from the Brandon Wheat Kings.

Boschman had a solid NHL career with 577 points (229 goals, 348 assists) in 1,009 career NHL regular-season games with Toronto, Edmonton, Winnipeg, New Jersey, and Ottawa. Nevertheless, Leafs fans are left to wonder about what could have been if Wayne Gretzky had entered the draft as scheduled. He would have obviously gone to Don Cherry and his Colorado Rockies. This might have left Ray Bourque available to be drafted by the Toronto Maple Leafs.

"Where's Gerry? This contract is just bullshit!" was how the red-headed man with fiery eyes and an obvious temper greeted me when I delivered an NHL player's contract to his room at the Sheraton hotel in downtown Montreal during the 1986 NHL Entry Draft.

The contract was for a late-round pick named Cliff Abrecht, who had an outside chance at best of making it to the NHL and wasn't a sure thing for the American Hockey League either. His player agent, whom I had never met before, was Bob Goodenow. I handed Goodenow the envelope containing Abrecht's contract and told him that he could get hold of Leafs general manager Gerry McNamara at our hotel if he wanted to talk further.

"Geez, this Goodenow guy is all riled up about a contract that he had already agreed to; he must be something to negotiate with," I thought as I left him. Abrecht did end up signing that contract, though he never established himself in the American Hockey League or even came close to the NHL.

I had very little to do with Goodenow over the next two years as I continued to work in the Leafs front office. About a month after I became the Leafs' general manager, in April 1988, I sent out qualifying NHL contract offers to all Leafs-affiliated players where required. We had selected a goaltender named Dean Anderson in the now-discarded NHL Supplemental Draft, another player who was a long shot to make the NHL. I sent Anderson a minimal qualifying offer.

About a week later, Anderson's agent called to advise me that he didn't think much of the contract offer and was prepared to have his client take our team to arbitration. It was Bob Goodenow. I recalled our meeting two years earlier, and his angry eyes as he bristled at me. I braced myself for the verbal onslaught that was to come but was pleasantly surprised when his demeanour changed after I told him that we had sent out only a minimal offer to retain his client's rights for our team and that we would begin negotiating further in good faith. The month of July was a quiet month, good for negotiating any player contractual business. While my negotiation with agent Don Meehan over his client Wendel Clark's new contract was getting a bit testy, it was a different story with the talks with Bob Goodenow. It was a different man I was dealing with now—he was nothing like he had been during our brief initial meeting.

We had maybe three conversations in total. He was visiting his mother in rural Michigan, where he usually spent a week or so each summer doing odd jobs to help her out. When I called, he would take a break from his chores and we would talk about Anderson's contract, everything else in the world of sports, and just life itself. Goodenow was then a passionate Tigers fan and so talked about his baseball team and their rivalry with the Blue Jays, as well as his concern for the health and welfare of Tigers manager Sparky Anderson. Through these chats we amicably came to terms on the other Anderson, and Dean Anderson signed an NHL contract with the Toronto Maple Leafs.

A little over a year later, my professional life changed when I resigned as the general manager of the Toronto Maple Leafs on August 11, 1989, and three days later was hired as the assistant general manager of the New York Rangers.

On a Friday in late October 1989, I made my first trip to Flint, Michigan, where the Flint Spirits, the top minor league affiliate for the New York Rangers, played in the International Hockey League. It was my first in-person glimpse of Rangers' prospects like Mike Richter, Peter Laviolette, and others doing battle. A few NHL scouts, a few media people, and at least one player agent were part of the spirited crowd of about five thousand that night: Bob Goodenow had made the 90-minute drive from Detroit to watch his client Kevin Miller play for our Flint team.

After the game, Flint GM Don Waddell took me to the best watering hole in the area, the Grand Blanc Inn, where we were soon joined by Goodenow. This happened a few times during the season, and in this very relaxed environment, I again found a very different man from the public Goodenow. Yet, over the next 20 years, the public would continue to see that fire that remains a large part of the Goodenow persona.

An ongoing conversation these evenings was the upcoming contract negotiation of Brett Hull, Goodenow's most significant client. Hull was in the process of playing out his option with the St. Louis Blues, and Goodenow continually talked about the price escalating for Hull's next contract. Back then, playing out your option was not often the best contractual move for a player to make. The player would become a restricted free agent at the end of the season, and other NHL teams had been reluctant in the past to sign these players, given the significant compensation that was usually required in the form of players and/or draft selections. Goodenow was confident that Hull was going to be the exception to that unspoken rule and that there would be no shortage of suitors from the other NHL teams (he felt Detroit was one possibility). Hull was worth the risk of whatever compensation might be required.

Goodenow cut his teeth on this deal, taking on NHL owners with a firm, hardline stance, becoming a guy who was used to doing whatever it took to get his way. Hull (and Goodenow) ended up playing their cards perfectly by having Hull play out his option, forcing the Blues to sign Hull to a hefty new contract that made him one of the very few players drawing a million-dollar salary. Interestingly, Hull had originally been a client of Brian Burke, now the president and general manager of the Toronto Maple Leafs. Burke was a player agent until 1987, when he became a member of management with the Vancouver Canucks.

A few months before the Hull deal was completed, Bob Goodenow's career took a somewhat surprising turn in a meeting room at the Westin William Penn in Pittsburgh, during the weekend of the NHL All-Star Game in January 1990. That meeting was about who would be named the new deputy director of the NHL Players' Association under Alan Eagleson. The thinking was that whoever was chosen would become the next executive director. Goodenow's was one of five names on the final shortlist, along with fellow player agents Anton Thun and Steve Bartlett, lawyer Kevin O'Shea, and businessman Lyman MacInnis. One rumour was that Gerry Meehan had discussed the possibility of leaving his post as general manager of the Buffalo Sabres to take the NHLPA post, but the Sabres' owners would not give their blessing.

I saw Goodenow in the hotel lobby on the Saturday afternoon, the day before the game. He thought his meeting with the NHLPA selection committee had gone well. He told me that he planned to head back to Detroit later that night if he didn't get the job—he wasn't going to stay for the game the next day. The next morning I learned that Goodenow had been selected for the job. I was pleased for him, yet a bit surprised by the news, as the general perception was that he had more of an outside chance than some of the other contenders. As I was heading out of the Westin William Penn to make the short walk over to the Civic Arena for the All-Star Game that afternoon, I bumped into him and stopped to offer my congratulations.

The jubilant Goodenow could hardly contain his excitement, but did have one question. "Where can I get a ticket for the game?" He really had been expecting to be home in Detroit by puck drop. He knew I could direct him to a contact, but as luck would have it, I could go even one better: I happened to have an extra ticket and had been looking for someone who was in need of one. I had had no idea that the seat would end up being filled by a person who would soon become one of the most powerful and influential men—for better or worse—in the world of hockey for the next two decades.

At the first intermission, I ran into Steve Dryden of the *Hockey News*. "Any idea where Bob Goodenow is?" Dryden asked, wondering aloud where the subject of the big hockey story of the day was. "I can do one better, not only do I know where he is but I'll go get him to talk to you," I replied to a surprised Dryden, and went back to our seats to fetch Goodenow. Though he wasn't always media friendly, on this occasion he was, agreeing to talk to Dryden. As I led him up the steps to the concourse, a number of other media had joined Dryden, and an informal press conference took place as the puck dropped for the second period. I watched the last two periods without Goodenow. That was the beginning of his new life, his new career, and a new way of doing business for the NHLPA.

Goodenow became a great friend to me over the next two decades. We would meet for lunch a couple of times a year, and, reminiscent of the Grand Blanc Inn days, occasionally at a watering hole to talk about life and hockey. He brought unparalleled success to the cause of the NHL players and their association, and he was a chief architect of the NHL lockout in the 2004–05 season.

But the job took its toll—Goodenow thinks of his 15-year run as leader of the NHLPA as the equivalent of 30 years in any other position. Now, though, he enjoys a more relaxed and anonymous life between Michigan and Florida. But even today, when talking about the business of hockey over the phone, his voice rises an octave or two, and in my mind's eye I can see the fire in his eyes.

Strength down the middle, from the goaltender to the centre, is the credo of most successful NHL teams. These are the two key positions on the team. What should have ranked as the greatest example ever of strength and depth at the centre ice position for the Toronto Maple Leafs existed for about two weeks in the summer of 1996, but unfortunately proved not to be anything beyond that, as the team never got the opportunity to hit the ice intact.

After two successful playoff runs in 1993 and 1994, the Leafs had not enjoyed anywhere near the same success the following two seasons. But they did have veteran star centre 33-year-old Doug Gilmour and a young star centre in 25-year-old Mats Sundin, both of whom gave significant strength down the middle. And Cliff Fletcher was about to dwarf those two big names with an even bigger and greater name.

My wife, Lisa, and I were among the hundreds of guests at Wendel Clark's wedding in Saskatoon on June 26, 1996. We were seated at a table with Leafs general manager Cliff Fletcher and his companion and future wife, Linda; Leafs assistant general manager Bill Watters and his wife, Naddie; and Fletcher's administrative assistant, Shelly Usher, and her boyfriend at the time, Gord Miller of TSN. Fletcher quickly won the friendly "what's-new?" contest among the eight of us. Fletcher could barely contain his enthusiasm about his piece of breaking news: the anticipated landing of Wayne Gretzky in a Toronto Maple Leafs uniform.

Wayne Gretzky had finished the season with the St. Louis Blues after joining them in a mid-season trade with the Los Angeles Kings. The Great One was an unrestricted free agent and at 35 years of age was looking to come home and finish his NHL career as a Maple Leaf. He was willing to play for a salary in the $3.5 million range, less than other teams like the New York Rangers were offering, and less than half of the top bid from the Vancouver Canucks.

The exciting and shocking news made an already enjoyable evening even more enjoyable. Denise and Wendel Clark put on a fun, first-class event with a down-home and personal feel that reflected Wendel's small-town Canadian roots. NHL players like Joe Sakic, Doug Gilmour, Tie Domi, Kirk Muller, Kelly Chase, and Dave Ellett mixed easily with the other guests. The only hint that NHL players were among the guests was a small note on the wedding program asking that no autographs be requested.

One of the more memorable moments was when Wendel's father, Les, had a special dance with his mother, Wendel's

Draft Day | 17

grandmother. Wendel's parents, Les (who died in 2009) and Alma, remain two of my all-time favourite people. I was also surprised that the main entree was salmon (which was delicious), as I was expecting a big slab of beef, given Clark's dietary habits when he joined the Leafs. Denise, it seemed, had influenced Wendel's healthier diet.

Heading back to Toronto the next day, I thought about the pleasant time we had enjoyed. I also looked forward to what I understood was about to unfold in Toronto. Wayne Gretzky would formally become an unrestricted free agent about a week later, on July 1. Gretzky, Gilmour, and Sundin: strength down the middle, unlike in any other period in the history of the Toronto Maple Leafs.

Arriving back home from the wedding was like coming back to reality, and for Cliff Fletcher, that reality was of a fiscal sort. The unthinkable, or maybe the thinkable but certainly the unfortunate, happened: money reared its ugly head. Almost 25 years earlier, owner Harold Ballard had been unable or perhaps just unwilling to pay enough to keep the likes of Bernie Parent, Jim Harrison and Rick Ley, so let them jump to the World Hockey Association. Now, once again, a cash crunch was going to cost the Leafs. And this time, it cost them a chance at the Great One.

A few weeks earlier, Fletcher had witnessed Wendel and Denise Clark say, "I do." Now, owner Steve Stavro gave Fletcher a "No, you don't" when it came to signing Gretzky. Stavro was feeling the pressure to find funds for the building of the new Air Canada Centre and had grudgingly paid funds to the charities that were benefactors of Harold Ballard's will. As the executor of Harold Ballard's will, Stavro had successfully used this power to gain control of the Toronto Maple Leaf hockey team. The millions in cash that he had to pay to the charities was financed by Maple Leaf Gardens Ltd., which meant mostly him. The top man in the Leafs ownership structure, he struggled daily to keep financially solvent and keep his position as top man. Even a reasonable $3.5 million was too rich for his bleeding finances.

Stavro would continue to struggle with his finances and later lose control at the top of the Leafs ownership structure to the wealthier Larry Tanenbaum (with the Ontario Teachers' Pension Plan remaining the top equity partner). With the powers he had gained from being Ballard's executor, Stavro had established a structure whereby he retained the most power at Maple Leaf Gardens Ltd. (later known as Maple Leaf Sports and Entertainment) even though he wasn't the top equity stakes holder.

Ultimately, Stavro lost his power in the boardroom, but in early July 1996, it was the Leafs and their fans who lost out on the chance to acquire Wayne Gretzky. Just three years later, the new ownership structure (and no longer cash-poor) Maple Leaf Sports and Entertainment paid Lenny Wilkens what was the going NBA rate of $5 million per season to coach the Toronto Raptors of the National Basketball Association. The owners of the Toronto Maple Leafs now had money to spend, but it was three years too late for Cliff Fletcher and his grand plan.

How can anyone possibly put a positive spin on the way in which Darryl Sittler left the Toronto Maple Leafs in 1982 and what little the Leafs got back in return? Well, I doubt I can explain the unexplainable, but I believe I can soften the blow.

Not to go over all the not-so-pleasant details of why Sittler left in the first place, but the Leafs captain, their best forward and future Hall of Famer, had been continually at odds with Leafs general manager George "Punch" Imlach from the moment Imlach began his second reign as GM in 1979.

Three years later, even though Imlach had been fired months earlier, it was mutually decided that too many hard feelings remained and it was best if the Leafs and the 31-year-old Sittler parted company. Sittler had a no-trade clause in his NHL contract and consented to being traded to just two other NHL teams, the Philadelphia Flyers and the Minnesota North Stars, so the Leafs knew they lacked the leverage to get fair market value for Sittler in a trade. And that is precisely what happened on January 20, 1982, when Sittler was traded to Philadelphia for two prospects, Rich Costello and Ken Strong, and a second-round draft choice in the 1982 draft. That draft selection was used to select Peter Ihnacak from Czechoslovakia.

How can one possibly make this deal look any better for the Leafs? The fact is that the Leafs had two consecutive selections in the second round. Their own pick was 24th overall, while the pick they had acquired from Philadelphia (which originally had belonged to Hartford) was 25th overall. The 25-year-old Ihnacak was the Leafs' target all along, and the Leafs were, quite frankly, worried whether he would still be available in the second round. For the other second-round pick, they would see what was available and decide on that selection at the draft table.

The thinking was that Ihnacak was ready, and old enough, to break into the NHL immediately and possibly pick up where Sittler left off (at least to some degree) as a top NHL centre. For this reason, the Leafs used the pick they acquired from

Philadelphia to select Ihnacak, in the hopes that it would make the Sittler trade to Philadelphia look better in the eyes of hockey revisionists. Ihnacak would have his best season that first year, 1982–83, with 66 points (28 goals, 38 assists), but would ultimately have a seven-year NHL journeyman career.

Who did the Leafs choose with their 24th pick? None other than Gary Leeman, who the Leafs drafted from the Regina Pats. Although the course of his career was somewhat volatile, he did score at least 30 goals on three occasions and became the second Leaf in team history to score 50 goals when he scored 51 in 1989–90.

Ultimately, Leeman's greatest value came two years after his 51-goal season, when he was the key component (from the Calgary Flames' point of view) in a 10-player blockbuster trade with the Leafs that saw Leeman and four others head to Calgary while Doug Gilmour and four others headed to Toronto. Now that trade is difficult for anyone from Calgary to put a positive spin on.

So, Darryl Sittler to Philadelphia for Rich Costello, Ken Strong, and Gary Leeman—and, ultimately, Doug Gilmour! Isn't that a tad better? Well, that might be a bit of a stretch, but it is true.

Okay, fact or fiction? On the surface it was a pretty simple trade involving one of the Sudbury Five (Randy Carlyle, Ron Duguay, Dave Farrish, Rod Schutt, and Dale McCourt—all from the Sudbury area). Montreal traded Rod Schutt to the Pittsburgh Penguins on October 18, 1978, in exchange for a first-round pick in the 1981 Entry Draft. A little less than three years later, the Canadiens would use that pick (seventh overall) to select Mark Hunter.

At the time of the trade, Schutt had played two years with the Canadiens organization but, except for two NHL games, had played with the Nova Scotia Voyageurs in the American Hockey League. At the start of the 1978–79 season, he was ticketed for Nova Scotia once again. A first-round pick seemed a bit of a steep price for Pittsburgh to pay, even though Schutt did become a 20-goal scorer twice in his six seasons with the Penguins. Urban myth has it that one person who signed off on the trade on behalf of Pittsburgh was under the impression that it was Steve Shutt, not Rod Schutt, who they were acquiring. Steve Shutt had slipped to "just" 49 goals the previous year with the Canadiens, after scoring 60 the year before that. As nice a guy as Rod Schutt is, apparently it was a nightmare for one Penguins executive when he met his newest player, Shutt . . . uh, that is, Schutt. I can just hear him muttering to himself, "Oh, shit!"

2 FUN AND GAMES
THE GAMES WITHIN THE GAMES

*Put a bunch of guys together, pay them to play a game they love,
and there are bound to be high spirits and shenanigans from time to
time. Even in the NHL—boys will be boys!*

I've always viewed Eddie Olczyk as one of the really bright students of the game of hockey when he was playing, coaching,
and, especially, as a broadcaster. He joined the Toronto Maple
Leafs via a trade from the Chicago Blackhawks in 1986, and his
hockey smarts and thirst for knowledge about the game were
immediately apparent. Morning skates, he would watch the
opposing team and quickly absorb the line combinations and
other subtleties of their game. He was our first active player
to have a satellite dish installed at his home in Unionville,
just north of Toronto, to feed his insatiable appetite for all the
NHL action.

Al Iafrate was our first-round pick in 1984 and, in hindsight, we rushed him to the NHL too early at the age of 18 to

begin his career as a Leaf that year. Talking to Iafrate this past year in a radio interview, he stated the obvious: that he regrets missing a year playing in the Ontario Hockey League (with Belleville, which had his rights) to grow up and mature more both on and off the ice. He was a player with natural skills and a great sense of humour but was unfairly viewed as a loose cannon personality-wise. He was bright in his own way, but he wasn't a student of the game like Olczyk was.

Olczyk was selected third overall in the first round in 1984, one ahead of Iafrate's selection, by the Chicago Black Hawks. He was traded to the Toronto Maple Leafs in 1987 along with Al Secord in exchange for Rick Vaive, Steve Thomas, and Bob McGill. More mature than Iafrate, Olczyk scored 20 goals his rookie season with the Black Hawks in 1984–85 and was far readier to accelerate his development to the NHL.

In the year leading up to Olczyk and Iafrate being the two top Americans selected in the 1984 NHL Draft, the two had been teammates on the U.S. Olympic team and ultimately played in the 1984 Winter Olympics in Yugoslavia. Warming up for the Winter Olympics, the U.S. team had a challenging schedule of games facing professional and college teams, as well as some international games. Being just 17, and the two youngest players on the team, Iafrate and Olczyk saw stretches of very limited ice action. This gave them an opportunity to use their creativity off the ice while still sitting on the Team USA bench. They were both still students, just teenage kids, and in an attempt to alleviate boredom, they developed a game within the game: Clock Poker. Each time the clock stopped for a whistle, the digit of the last second was the card for either Olczyk or Iafrate. Next whistle, the other player would get the card. Their goal was to make a pair, three of a kind, a straight, or a full house—while their teammates focused on beating the opposition.

"Sometimes we were more focused on the clock than the game," recalled Olczyk. "Every now and then when a play was whistled and one of us got a card that gave us a great hand, we would let out a yell of joy, and a couple of times, the coaches looked at us from the end of the bench, wondering what the hell was going on."

A much more mature, wiser, and less sensitive Al Iafrate has long ago dealt with the issue of losing his hair with the modern-day fashion statement of a shaved head. But the younger Iafrate in his first few years in the NHL lacked that confidence when he experienced the not uncommon problem among males of losing his hair. Even though he was just 18 years old, he was losing his hair at an alarming rate. And, understandably, he was very sensitive about it: each year meant less hair.

Iafrate typically arrived at the arena a couple of hours before a game. A few minutes later, he'd be in his pre-game garb of underwear and helmet, quite often a cigarette dangling from his lips, which he would light with a blowtorch used to modify hockey sticks. He seemed to act like James Dean in the classic movie *Rebel Without a Cause* but he was really just an 18-year-old kid not really ready for the adult environment that had embraced him.

Even though just 18 years old, he had outstanding hockey skills, and within a year or two he was one of our top two defencemen. That meant he was often slated to open the game on the first line, since we liked to open with our "best" players. This put pressure on Iafrate that we were initially unaware of but that, during the course of the season, we learned about from his agent. Starting for a game meant taking your helmet off during the playing of the national anthems, something that caused Iafrate acute embarrassment, feeling as he did that the entire crowd was staring at him and his bald head.

We appreciated the insight and immediately revised the starting line-up. The best starting five (which at that time included Iafrate) would still start the game, except we would substitute another defenceman in Iafrate's place. At the first whistle or opportunity to change on the fly, we would get Iafrate onto the ice. It often seemed strange when there was a whistle a few seconds after the puck was dropped and Iafrate would be the one lonely player emerging from the Leafs bench while the player he replaced would skate off by himself.

In one memorable game, Iafrate took a hit that sent him headfirst into the stantion at the end of the players' benches—similar to the controversial hit Max Pacioretty of Montreal suffered at the hands of Zdeno Chara of Boston in 2011. Fortunately, Iafrate wasn't seriously injured. Though in a daze, Iafrate instinctively looked around for his dislodged helmet, grabbed it, and put it back on his balding head before skating, winded and woozy, the few strides to the bench.

Now involved in the world of computer technology and other businesses, and well over the insecurities of his youth, Iafrate looks comfortable and confident with his fashionable hairstyle. He has also evolved as a coach to Midget hockey players with elite hockey programs in the United States.

In the early 1980s, I had seen the red light go on against us for a goal by Al Secord of the Chicago Black Hawks far too many times. Secord played on their first line with Hall of Famer Denis Savard and another great player, Steve Larmer, and his best three goal totals were 54, 44, and 40 over that period, many with the Toronto Maple Leafs as his victims. But it was as a new Leaf that I saw him red-faced—the one and only occasion.

The trade that made Ed Olczyk a Maple Leaf in the summer of 1986 also delivered Al Secord to the team in exchange for Rick Vaive, Steve Thomas, and Bob McGill. In his prime, Secord had that combination of scoring ability and physical prowess coveted by all NHL teams. Secord had played that role for Boston (and was loved by Don Cherry for it) and Chicago. That is why the Leafs had given up significant players in a trade to acquire Secord.

However, he would not enjoy anywhere near that level of success or be able to sustain that successful style of play during his stay in Toronto. But Secord remained an honest player both on and off the ice, his northern Ontario roots, rather than the bright lights of Boston, Chicago, or Toronto, apparent in his personal makeup.

We prepared for our final pre-season home game for the 1986–87 season. The Leafs' training camp itinerary showed that the organized stretching session the morning before one particular skate had been cancelled. Then, at the last minute, the team was advised that there would be a group stretching session after all, with a new instructor. So, slowly and with some squawking, the players made their way up one storey to the concourse level of the Maple Leaf Gardens, to where the red seats were—the area closest to the dressing room that could comfortably accommodate that number of people. I had initially found it surreal to see all those Leafs greats and non-greats spread out in the hallway where I had lined up for concessions for so many years.

The team arrived, spreading out on the floor, giving the supposedly new instructor some space. She was attractive, and when she took off her sweats, her skimpy attire revealed the body of a beautiful exotic dancer. The players' puzzlement over the impromptu session turned to surprise and intrigue.

Unbeknownst to most of the other players, a few of the veterans had been to one of the finer exotic dancing establishments the previous evening. This woman, who had been one of the performers, had the title of Miss Nude Manitoba, or something along those lines. They thought it would be a great practical joke to have her show up as the stretching instructor the next morning. She agreed to do it, wanting, of course, the cash up front.

Those who had chipped in the few hundred dollars wondered if she would be a no-show, given that she already had their cash. But she proved to be a good sport and, true to her word, showed up at the appointed time. The players, who had been scattered around the concourse, quickly moved in closer so they could get a better view of their new dream instructor.

After leading the team through a few well-received and enthusiastic stretching exercises, she told the players that she needed an assistant. As she had been prompted, rather than asking for a volunteer she asked Al Secord to come forward and help her out. As the team pushed the veteran but new Leaf forward, cheering him on, a flushed and visibly nervous Secord obligingly partnered her for the next few "demonstrations." When she bent forward, her barely covered chest was right in Secord's face. When she turned around to demonstrate other stretches, her butt was also strategically placed in Secord's face.

When they had finished their series of stretches—to a rousing ovation—the team was let in on the joke. It had played itself out to perfection. And, newcomer Al Secord, for perhaps the only time in his life, didn't seem to mind being made the butt of the joke.

I like bets that are original and creative. And, in 1977, five young players from the Sudbury, Ontario, area shook hands on one such bet. Randy Carlyle, Ron Duguay, Dave Farrish, Rod Schutt, and Dale McCourt were enjoying the off-season and a time in life when they all had the world by the tail. They had made it to the "show"—the NHL—Carlyle and Farrish with the Toronto Maple Leafs, Duguay with the New York Rangers, Schutt with the Montreal Canadiens, and McCourt with the Detroit Red Wings—all Original Six NHL teams to boot.

Because of the competition from the World Hockey Association, salaries for professional hockey players had never been greater. And the five of them, all around 20 years of age, were living the dream of playing in the NHL, making six-figure salaries.

The subject of women and girlfriends came up. Great to partake in and great to enjoy, but, why would any man in their position want to get tied down at that stage in their lives? The good-natured needling continued all summer as they teased one another about being on the verge of marriage.

So they decided to put their money where their mouths were. I'm not sure who thought of the bet, but all five Sudbury hockey success stories pledged $2,000, to be given to the guy who got married last. They all went on to varying degrees of success in their National Hockey League careers, the pledge continuing as one by one the Sudbury natives marched down the aisle, knowing the trip would cost him $2,000 somewhere down the road.

About 10 years after the pledge was first made, Dave Farrish walked down the aisle with his lovely bride, Roxanne. The $8,000 from his friends made for welcome spending money on their honeymoon in Hawaii.

Today, Farrish is an assistant coach to Carlyle with the Anaheim Ducks.

Wendel Clark had never been mistaken for one of those great NHL players who develops a swelled head. And, in one incident, two future teammates made sure that wasn't going to happen.

The 1987 tryouts for Team Canada for the Canada Cup international tournament, as always, included one or two controversial last cuts. Steve Yzerman had the distinction of being a last cut in both 1987 and 1991, and in 2002 a knee injury meant that he played basically on one leg to help Canada win Olympic gold in Salt Lake City. In 2010, as general manager of the Canadian Olympic team, he was the one making the decision on those final cuts.

After two outstanding first seasons in the NHL, Wendel Clark was also among the last cuts for Team Canada in 1987. He was a sentimental favourite for Leafs fans and made it as far as the last cuts because of his work ethic, his character, his ethos of putting the team first, and the respect his older teammates had for the then 21-year-old.

The greatest practical jokes are those that are executed slowly so as to not be detected, and two of Clark's Team Canada teammates were having fun with the popular Leaf. Doug Gilmour of the St. Louis Blues and Kirk Muller of the New Jersey Devils took turns every morning tightening Wendel's helmet by just a half turn. Gilmour and Muller figured that by the end of the tryout camp, Clark must have been competing with a constant headache—his helmet had been tightened by five complete turns on each side by then. "Lucky he didn't make the team because if we kept it up, his head would have exploded in a few more days," kidded Gilmour. Clark would later be teammates of Gilmour and Muller (at separate times) with the Leafs.

Not that Wendel Clark was a slouch himself in the practical jokes department. I was a victim of one occasion, though he may have had the help of a henchman or two.

The 1987–88 season was the first of two where Wendel missed significant time due to a chronic back problem, playing in just 43 of the 160 regular-season games over those two seasons. A major portion of Clark's day comprised afternoon sessions of treatment and rehabilitation exercises at Maple Leaf Gardens. It was a slow, often boring, process to work at solving his mysterious back ailment.

Sometimes at the end of the business day, I was fortunate to be able to use the Leafs weight room to work out. On this one occasion, I changed in the empty dressing room before walking across the hall to the very cramped weight room. There, I ran into Clark, who was just finishing his afternoon treatment. We greeted each other, and there may have been some verbal jousting involved, I can't remember exactly. Clark went on his way and I began my workout, finishing about an hour later. When I returned to the dressing room, my business clothes—jacket, pants, shirt, tie, socks, and shoes—were nowhere to be found, even after a thorough search.

I located one of the Leafs' trainers, who told me to look up. Puzzled, I went back to the dressing room. There on the ceiling was something comparable to a *CSI* crime scene, my dress clothes the victim.

It was actually difficult to see the clothes. There were just a few small bulges—everything had been thoroughly and efficiently wrapped with hockey tape and attached to the ceiling. It took a few minutes getting it all down, with the help of a hockey stick. Then came the hard part, unwrapping the tape. Certainly Clark, and a possible crony, had done excellent work.

Finally freed from their hockey-tape shackles, my items of clothing were accounted for, with one small modification. When I put my underwear on, I could feel a breeze where one's protective cup would be. Figuring the "modifications" could have been much worse, I finished getting dressed and then headed back upstairs to the executive offices.

This was usually a good time to get a few hours of administrative work done and phone calls made in the quiet that came with the dinner hour. I was still chuckling to myself about Clark's mischievous work. When I got to my office, the door was closed, an inter-office envelope pinned to it. Inside was the missing piece of my undergarment.

A job well done, but obviously by a player who had a bit too much time on his hands.

We had a fun-loving Leafs team in the late 1970s that worked hard and played hard. The line-up included the likes of Darryl Sittler, Lanny McDonald, Tiger Williams, Borje Salming, and Mike Palmateer. There was a pretty established line-up of veterans who used training camp to prepare for the start of the regular season, with very few spots on the Leafs roster truly open for competition.

For a few years, Ken "Gunnar" Garrett assisted at training camp for a few weeks before heading to Saginaw, Michigan, for his full-time job as trainer for the Saginaw Gears, of the International Hockey League, at that time two levels below the NHL. Garrett would later move up one rung when, in 1982, he became the trainer for the Leafs' American Hockey League team in St. Catharines, which moved to Newmarket in 1986.

He was a classic and vocal minor league legend. There was no sacred cow for Garrett's constant barbs and insults, and he could take it as well as he could dish it out. It didn't matter if you were a minor league journeyman or an NHL star, no player or topic was off-limits for Garrett. "There's a graveyard full of hockey players like you," was one of Garrett's favourite comebacks.

At the end of each camp, the players would throw together a collection of about $2,000 to show their appreciation for his work. It was huge money for Garrett, who at the time was making only about $10,000 for his duties in Saginaw.

At the end of one of the Leafs training camps, one veteran came up with a novel idea. The players could reward Garrett for his tireless work—and constant chatter—during training camp *and* make one last attempt at getting even with him. The veteran collected the cash for Garrett in a box, which he then stashed in a hidden spot in the Leafs dressing room. For the next three days, whenever a player wanted to clear his throat or nose, he did so into the box.

After a few days, the box was presented in a show of appreciation. Garrett didn't miss a beat, just muttered a quick thanks, picked up the box of cash covered with the slimy film, and was gone. No word on the bank teller who had to ultimately deal with the "unlaundered" money.

Years later when Garrett was with the Newmarket Saints, I had to chuckle at the innovativeness of one of the Saints players. Knowing Garrett's fondness for his beloved Boston cream doughnuts, this player spent a few minutes tampering with one left in the box. With great precision, he inserted a drinking straw into the doughnut and sucked out most of the cream. Next he dipped the straw into a jar of Vaseline, then pushed as much Vaseline into the doughnut as he could without it being noticeable.

The unsuspecting target let out a yell after a not-so-delicious bite, angry but also amused. I only wish the journeyman player was as driven and innovative on the ice as he had been with that doughnut in the team dressing room!

Our trainers with the Toronto Maple Leafs in the 1970s and 1980s got along well enough but couldn't be considered best friends.

As we were getting ready to land in Vancouver one day, one of the trainers was searching through his carry-on bag for something to give to a player who had an upset stomach. He found some Ex-lax, which looks and tastes like pieces of chocolate, and passed a few squares to the queasy player. One of the other trainers put his hand out for a share of the "sweet" and received a generous portion.

After the plane landed, the trainers went first to the Vancouver arena to get the Leafs equipment and supplies in order. Then they headed to the hotel downtown to freshen up before meeting the team in the lobby.

It was a beautiful Vancouver evening as the trainer waited for his colleague. Twenty minutes soon turned into 30, then 40. He called his colleague's room on the house phone but there was no answer. Finally, his colleague joined him, his face ashen. "You won't believe what happened to me," he relayed. He had just stepped into the elevator to come down to the lobby when the Ex-lax kicked in full throttle. Such was his anxiety about an accident that he stayed in the elevator with his butt firmly pushed against the wall, fearful that any move would be catastrophic. He stayed that way for about 20 minutes, riding up and down in the elevator as people entered and left. Only when the elevator was finally empty did he have the confidence to move slightly to push the button for his floor. He made it to his room just in the nick of time.

It was only days later that he learned the ingredients of his chocolate treat.

Paul Maurice is not just a successful NHL coach; he's also one of those people who make the game of hockey so rewarding to be a part of. The same goes for Harry Neale, who not only had a long and at times successful coaching career in the WHA and NHL but also earned even more success and notoriety in his career as a broadcaster.

Neale tells a good story about how Paul Maurice acted quickly to alleviate what could have been an embarrassing situation. It was at an NHL All-Star Game. A fellow broadcaster relied on Neale to give him the heads-up about the various players and team personnel that they would come in contact with during the weekend of festivities. When it's just two NHL teams competing, it's fairly simple to keep track of who is who, but in an All-Star Game, it's much more difficult.

Walking around the dressing room area just outside the actual dressing room after the game, Neale's colleague saw Maurice off in the distance with what proved to be his parents and other family members. He asked Neale who it was. "Teemu

Selanne" Neale replied, mistaking Maurice for the player with whom he bore a strong resemblance. Although Neale quickly realized that it was not Selanne, it was too late—his colleague was full-bore chatting with the "Selanne" group. Because the broadcaster was in so deep, Maurice chose to accept for that brief period that he was Selanne, and offered his opinions on what it was like to play in Anaheim and other things pertinent to Teemu Selanne.

The broadcaster finished his visit and carried on his way, satisfied that he had had a nice chat with Teemu Selanne and his family. Maurice's parents said little but were aware that they had played the role of Selanne's parents for a brief period. Paul Maurice likes to keep this story quiet, but I think it reflects that he is a class act and remains so even in unusual circumstances.

Harry Neale became more familiar with Paul Maurice a few years later when Maurice was head coach of the Toronto Maple Leafs and Neale the colour commentator on their TV broadcasts. Maurice's tenure with the Leafs certainly would have been more successful had he had a player like Teemu Selanne in the Leafs line-up.

Few fans likely remember what dire straits the Red Wings franchise was in when Mike Ilitch bought the team from Bruce Norris in 1982. Detroit was a far cry from "Hockeytown" in those days, and the Red Wings were a long, long way away from the four Stanley Cup championships that ultimately came their way. With the downtown core of Detroit collapsing and the economy suffering the ravages of the downturn that continues to plague both the city and state, season ticket sales were down to about three thousand.

One bright spot from Ilitch's first season as owner was a promotion unlike any other I have seen. The Red Wings joined with Chrysler to produce the fan giveaway that remains unmatched today. It was actually quite simple, but the payoff was huge. At each and every one of the Red Wings 40 home games, some lucky fan won a brand new Chrysler automobile: 40 games, 40 Chrysler automobiles. An improving product on the ice, and a promotion like this off the ice was also seeing more fans attending Red Wing games.

During the first intermission, the Chrysler car that was the evening's prize was driven around the rink of Joe Louis Arena before the machine came on to recondition the ice. In the first stoppage of play in the second period, the section the winner of the car was seated in was announced. A buzz would emerge from that section, and the rest of the crowd would keep one eye on the excitement there and one eye on the ice as the play continued.

After the second stoppage of play, the row in which the winner was seated was announced. The giddiness was apparent as the 20 or so fans seated in that row high-fived each other and waited excitedly for the next whistle.

At the next whistle, the announcer slowly and dramatically revealed the winning seat. The crowd would erupt, the lucky patron reacting as if he or she had won the final showcase on *The Price Is Right*. This was 30 years ago, and I have never seen any promotion come close to this one.

Years later, in 2003, when I was doing work for the Hockey Hall of Fame during its annual Induction Weekend, I was fortunate to chat with Mike Ilitch, who was fittingly being inducted as a Builder. He shared with me stories of his younger days—how as a minor league baseball player he was already plotting the development of what became the Little Caesars Pizza empire. "With a minor league team, when the bus went to a new town, the first thing the players wanted to see was the stadium where they would be playing. While we drove by the stadium, I was looking around the town and scouting out ideal pizza locations," Ilitch told me. Nothing like developing one's entrepreneurial acumen along with one's baseball skills!

I told him my recollections of that great giveaway in his first year of ownership of the Wings and asked how it had come about. The big smile on Ilitch's face made it obvious it was a fond memory of his. "I knew we had to do something big, so I cold-called Lee Iacocca at Chrysler," Ilitch told me. "I was put right through to his office and he took my call. I was calling him Lee and he was calling me Mr. Ilitch. It was that straightforward." At the time, Iacocca was a high-profile CEO who earned legendary status for his efforts in taking Chrysler from a position of near bankruptcy to being a significant player in the automobile industry.

The Chrysler giveaway was a one-year phenomenon, but it remains unmatched in the National Hockey League. And the reason the Ilitch family is worth a fortune is not just luck. It can be partly explained by Ilitch's gumption to do what many of us dread—making that cold call.

When Ilitch purchased the Detroit Red Wings in 1982, the deal included the new Joe Louis Arena. Even though it was a newer arena, Joe Louis was not state-of-the-art. It was built on the cheap and had many flaws when it opened. The concrete stairs outside leading up to the building are but one example: many of them often had to be chained off because they were far too dangerous in inclement weather.

Another flaw was that a press box had not been included in the original design. In a last-minute scramble, the builder turned a few of the back rows on one side into a makeshift press box. To get there, you had to walk through the seats in the upper bowl. I remember saying to the press box attendant the first time I was at the arena with the Leafs, in 1980, that I must have come the wrong way but that I couldn't find a direct route or elevator to the press box, like there was in every other NHL building. He told me about the construction oversight and that the circuitous route I had taken was indeed the only way there.

As the assistant to the general manager from 1980 to 1987 overseeing all travel and administrative matters, one of my assignments was to compile team statistics during the game, including scoring chances, hits, giveaways, turnovers, and faceoffs. Today, they're all compiled and stored on computers and included in the stats package given to the media. But back in the early 1980s, I was the compiler of our internal team statistics, which meant I had to make a hasty visit to the Leafs dressing room between periods to drop off the stats.

It proved to be a daunting task at Joe Louis Arena to navigate through the fans and make it to the dressing room and then back to the press box in time for the puck drop of the next period. After a game or two, I figured out a better route: the stairwell via a fire-exit door at the back wall adjacent to the press box. It was kept propped open, as it could only be opened from inside the arena. If you happened to get locked out, you were dependent on someone hearing you knocking and opening the door. But it meant I could hurry down the stairs to the dressing room area, getting a bit of exercise as I hustled back up to the press box.

Insufficient washroom facilities were another flaw in the design of Joe Louis Arena. This flaw was especially apparent when there was a full house of beer-consuming fans: the odd patron would slip out the door to relieve himself at the top of the stairs—another of the occupational hazards that made for an challenging journey to and from the dressing room.

Nowadays, all NHL teams travel to their long-distance NHL games by private chartered jet. When I was with the Toronto Maple Leafs, however, NHL players flew strictly economy on regularly scheduled flights with Air Canada, American Airlines, or an other commercial carrier if they needed to travel any significant distance. (For the bulk of the shorter flights, we used our somewhat antique Convair 580 turboprop, which we jokingly called "Treetops" because the airplane flew at such a low altitude that you could see the ground during the entire flight.)

And unlike baseball players, who booked a set of three seats for every two players, keeping the middle seat empty, on crowded flights, the middle seats were occasionally included in our seat allocation. When that occurred, it was the rookie or those without seniority who dealt with the discomfort.

I always enjoyed watching the young hockey fans who happened to be on our flights. Imagine the looks of disbelief on their faces when they saw the entire Toronto Maple

Leafs team in the departure lounge. It must have been like a dream for them to be able to walk about the plane, meet the players, and get their autographs in the captive, though always friendly, environment.

Falling asleep on a commercial flight often brought out the high school prankster in a teammate. Often the dozing player had his head covered with shaving cream, much to the delight of the other passengers. An unlit cigarette in the mouth completed the amusing picture—fortunately for the victim of the prank, this was in the days before cell phone cameras! Once in a while the player's shoes would disappear too, not turning up until later in the day. I can still remember Jim Korn walking shoeless through the Minneapolis airport on a frigid January day.

The team's competitive zeal really shone as they waited for their luggage at the carousel. One of the team leaders would holler, "Buck a bag!" and $1 bills would be quickly pulled out of wallets. The pot was to go to the team member whose luggage came down the carousel first. As each piece of luggage came down the ramp onto the carousel, it would be met with cheers, groans, play-by-play commentary, and humorous remarks by a player who thought it might be his. When the first piece of luggage belonging to a team member appeared, it would be greeted by a loud hurrah from the wealthier (by about $23) player and a chorus of boos from his teammates—and good-natured laughter from the rest of the passengers.

One of my favourite travel stories is of a flight that I wasn't on. But, knowing the late Carl Brewer, I can clearly envisage it.

Although there were many sides to Carl Brewer, most people saw only the serious and principled side. But on this occasion, he displayed his great sense of humour.

It was the mid-1970s, and Brewer was with the Toronto Toros, in the World Hockey Association. On one of the team's commercial flights to California, the airline had room to bump a few of the team executives into first class. It also had seats for a couple of players up at the front of the plane. Brewer, being the senior player on the team, was one of the fortunate ones.

Halfway through the flight, Brewer took an item out of his carry-on bag and slipped into the first-class washroom, exiting moments later wearing only his skimpy Speedo bathing suit. For good measure, he had splattered water over himself, paying special attention to his head and hair.

He made a dramatic entrance through the dividing curtain into the economy section of the plane, where most of his teammates sat with the other hundred or so passengers. "Hey, guys," Brewer yelled out, commanding total attention with his appearance. "You've got to see the swimming pool they have up here in first class. It's unbelievable!" With that, Brewer turned and disappeared back behind the curtain.

Like a few of his teammates, Brewer packed his bathing suit in his carry-on so that he could hit the hotel pool as soon as he checked in. This time, it had come in handy even before arrival.

The Leafs team made the playoffs in 1987, and our first-round opponents were the St. Louis Blues. We were scheduled to leave on a chartered flight at about 3 p.m. the day before the first game when I received a call from the charter company about mechanical problems that put our departure time in doubt. It was decided that we would take commercial flights to St. Louis instead. There were no direct flights, so we connected through Detroit, still making it in good time.

The change in travel plans obviously hadn't dampened the mood of the players. My brother Bob had just completed his second year working full-time in the Leafs office as the head of public relations, and this was one of the few occasions he was included in the team's travelling entourage. The players wasted few opportunities to make him feel welcome. On the team bus from the St. Louis airport, one player yelled out, "Watch out . . . hot news . . . hot news!" Bob was oblivious to the commotion as he sat intently reading his newspaper—until flames erupted at the bottom of the paper and raced toward his hands. Bob hardly had time to react as the flame quickly spread upward and the paper was in small ashes and the flame died as fast as it had arrived.

Arriving at the hotel a few minutes later, the players quickly headed one by one to the front desk to pick up their room keys—all efficiency and order. Bob's turn came, and that's when the efficiency stopped: someone had clipped the snap from the velvet ropes on the queue stantion to Bob's belt. As he walked forward, the velvet ropes caved in behind him and the metal stabilizers fell noisily to the ground in a domino effect.

The next day was game day and the high mood continued. Bob was awakened by a loud knock at his door at 6 a.m. "Room service," a voice called out. Bob opened the door to find enough of the hotel's famed Ozark sausage to feed the entire floor. Which player had taken the liberty of completing the extensive breakfast order card and placing it on the doorknob of his hotel room—with early-morning delivery to boot—we never did find out.

At the team and staff lunch, I was sitting beside Bob when I heard the cry of "shoe check" from one of the players. As inevitably happened, others echoed him, creating a verbal barrage. I had a sinking feeling for Bob, the travelling rookie. And, sure enough, he was once again the victim of a prank. A player had snuck under our table and placed a few scoops of sour cream on top of Bob's shoes. Once the player had returned to his seat, the chant of "shoe check" began, protecting the identity of the perpetrator (though, of course, there were many accomplices).

The Leafs won that first game in St. Louis and went on to win the series in six games. Which just goes to show you that you can be successful and have your fun and games too.

3 BUILDING THE BLUE AND WHITE

Building a team involves good drafts and good trades. Every team has their successes and failures in this department, and the Leafs are no exception. Bricks, mortar, blood, sweat, and tears—a continual work in progress for Leafs fans.

As recent Stanley Cup champions like the Pittsburgh Penguins and Chicago Blackhawks have illustrated, the key to rebuilding a team is getting the opportunity to pick early in the draft and score potential superstars like Sidney Crosby and Jonathan Toews.

The New York Islanders won four straight Stanley Cups to start the 1980s, and they benefited from being able to draft high to select Denis Potvin (first overall in 1973) and Clark Gillies (fourth overall in 1974). But generally, to win it all, you also have to have acquired quality players beyond the first round. As the Islanders' improving on-ice success saw them no longer have the benefit of the very high draft position, excellent scouting allowed them to continue to build their dynasty with later-round picks like Bob Nystrom (third round in 1972), Ken Morrow (fourth round in 1976), Garry Howatt (ninth round in 1972), and John Tonelli (second round in 1977). They especially struck drafting gold with a second-round draft choice named Bryan Trottier, in 1974.

The final piece of the Islanders personnel puzzle was the selection of Mike Bossy in the 15th overall pick in the first round of the 1977 Entry Draft. This would complete the foundation for the Islanders dynasty of four consecutive Stanley Cup championships in the early 1980s. As for their 1977 Entry Draft, Bossy's Hall of Fame career would far and away surpass that of any of the 14 players selected ahead of him.

You might wonder what Mike Bossy has to do with the Leafs' story. The connection is that although the Leafs owned the 11th and 12th overall selections in the 1977 Entry Draft, they had overlooked Bossy. Word was as well that legendary and long-retired Toronto Maple Leafs and Montreal Canadiens executive Frank Selke Sr. had offered his opinion that this "kid" Bossy, playing in the Quebec Major Junior Hockey League, was going to be something special. Selke's opinion quickly proved prophetic.

The Leafs elected instead to use both of their selections close to home, with picks from the Toronto Marlboros in right winger John Anderson and defenceman Trevor Johansen. In defence of the Leafs, the next two teams selecting also passed on the opportunity to take Bossy: the New York Rangers took Ron Duguay and the Buffalo Sabres, Ric Seiling.

Though Anderson and Johansen were quality prospects, why would the Leafs or any other team overlook Bossy, who, after four seasons in Laval, had scored 70, 84, 79, and 75 goals? A significant factor was a popular theory back in the 1970s that, in the era of the Broad Street Bullies in Philadelphia and the Big Bad Bruins in Boston, players from the Quebec Major Junior Hockey League in general, and a player like Bossy in particular, would not stand up to the rigours of the physical play of the National Hockey League. The Quebec Major Junior Hockey League was then the least physical junior league in Canada.

That said, the Leafs had not selected a very physical player in Anderson either, and Johansen was a somewhat surprising selection in comparison with the option of a player who averaged scoring 77 goals per season in his junior career. Well, like in life, timing is everything, and in this case, it didn't work in the Leafs' favour. Or the New York Rangers' or the Buffalo Sabres', for that matter.

Denis Potvin, Bryan Trottier, Mike Bossy, and Clark Gillies have all been inducted into the Hockey of Hall of Fame to add another ring to the four reflecting the consecutive Stanley Cup championships they won from 1980 to 1983.

The period of the 1977 Entry Draft was a very unsettled time in the Toronto Maple Leafs front office. After the 1976–77 season ended and just a few weeks before the draft, the Leafs decided to part company with Red Kelly, their coach for the previous four seasons. The legendary former Leafs captain George Armstrong was Ballard's choice for the next Leafs coach. Armstrong had coached some impressive Toronto Marlboro teams for the previous six seasons while also serving as a scout for the NHL team. As would be the case 12 years later, Armstrong was reluctant to take over the head coaching job.

Nevertheless, at the time of the Entry Draft, it looked like Armstrong, in spite of his initial reluctance, was going to be the next Leafs coach. He naturally felt loyalty to his Marlie players and was comfortable with the choices of Anderson and Johansen, whom he had coached for a number of years. A few weeks after the draft, however, the prospective plan for Armstrong coaching the Leafs fell apart over differences in salary expectations and Armstrong's supporting managers. In the end, Armstrong remained as a Leafs scout for a few more months and then left the organization, after a 30-year career. He worked as a scout for the Quebec Nordiques for several years, before being welcomed back to the Leafs organization with open arms by Ballard in 1988.

With Armstrong out of the picture, the Leafs turned to general manager Jim Gregory's initial plan, an innovative idea to bring Roger Neilson to the NHL as the team's coach. Neilson had coached the Leafs' Central Hockey League affiliate in Dallas the previous year, 1976, after a successful junior coaching career with the Peterborough Petes. Neilson proved to be successful with the Leafs in his two seasons. Though never a favourite of Ballard's, he would make a lasting imprint on modern-day coaching.

We will never know if or how the drafting order might have changed had Neilson been hired a month earlier. Odds are that Roger Neilson wouldn't have advocated for a player like Bossy either. The New York Islanders certainly benefited from others not heeding the advice of Frank Selke Sr.—Mike Bossy scored 53 goals for the Islanders in his rookie season, the first of nine consecutive 50+ goal seasons.

George Armstrong's backing out of the Leafs coaching job naturally didn't sit well with the Leafs owner. I happened to be in the Leafs offices that Friday afternoon in November when Armstrong surprisingly left the organization, the only one he had ever been associated with. He sat at his desk taking company keys off his key ring as he waited to see Jim Gregory to finalize details about his departure.

I don't remember what was said, but do remember that I enjoyed chatting with him that day. For someone who was always joking, he was in an exceptionally serious mood. He spoke in a quiet voice with great clarity and great conviction about why it was time to move on. I felt sad but I also thought his actions admirable.

Although I ran into Armstrong quite a bit over the next few years in his role as scout for the Nordiques, it was that last meeting in the Leafs offices that made the most lasting impression on me. That was why I led the movement to bring Armstrong back to the Leafs' front office staff in 1988 after he was let go by Quebec.

Just one year later, Armstrong having reluctantly accepted the position of interim coach for the Leafs, I found myself doing the very same thing: taking the keys off my ring and visiting Harold Ballard to say goodbye.

"I've had it with this guy. You've got to get me out of here."

Russ Courtnall stood beside me at the Zamboni entrance in the old Chicago Stadium. We had just arrived for a game—my third as general manager of the Leafs—at the start of the 1988–89 season, and Courtnall had discovered that Coach John Brophy had made him a healthy scratch in favour of Dan Daoust.

It was no secret that Courtnall was not a favourite of the Leafs coach, who liked his players, whether they were skilled or not, big and physical. There had also been a constant clash of attitudes between the confident, cocky Courtnall and the old-school coach in Brophy.

Brophy had been the unofficial head of our general manager triumvirate, which included Dick Duff and me and which finished off the previous season, 1987–88, after Ballard fired Gerry McNamara on February 7. Brophy had been anxious to trade Courtnall by the March 1988 deadline, but nothing had worked in making the right deal. The fact that our triumvirate was unwieldy and dysfunctional certainly inhibited our ability to achieve a consensus to successfully execute a satisfactory trade.

Though we liked each other personally, the three months of our triumvirate were a disaster. Brophy and Duff were old school, I wasn't. Of the three, I had the administrative background and mostly stuck to that. I was usually the point man at the office fielding all the calls. In their haste and excitement and eagerness to make trades, we seemed to continually go in a circle. We couldn't get on the same page to work a consensus to make any trades.

A few days before the 1988 trade deadline, I found myself standing next to Vancouver Canucks' general manager Pat Quinn as we both waited for our luggage at the Saskatoon airport. A great many hockey executives and scouts were travelling to nearby Prince Albert to watch a key junior game between the top two upcoming draft prospects—Mike Modano of the Prince Albert Raiders and Trevor Linden of the Medicine Hat Tigers. I began making small talk with him. After a few minutes of pleasantries, Quinn's demeanour changed suddenly as he said,

"I better tell you this, since I've already sent you a letter." He went on to vent his anger at our organization for apparently spreading rumours about a Russ Courtnall trade to Vancouver for defenceman Garth Butcher, and about how unprofessional he felt we had been and how it was causing his team unnecessary problems. Once Quinn's rant was over, I assured him that we weren't in the rumour-spreading business—though I could never be sure of what Brophy might have inadvertently told someone in the media as he was close friends with a couple of members of the Toronto media.

When I returned to my Toronto office a few days later, I was greeted as expected by Quinn's scathing letter. As well, there was a message to call player agent Herb Pinder. I did just that and quickly discovered his concern was about a client of his, one Garth Butcher. He echoed what Quinn had said a few days earlier and wanted to make it clear that Butcher had no interest in playing for the Toronto Maple Leafs. He softened it with, "This is one of the challenges you are going to face in trying to win the respect and the confidence back around the league and your organization." I thanked him for his call and again assured him that we hadn't thrown Butcher's name out in trade conversations.

I didn't have to clear any trade discussions about Butcher with Pinder—that wasn't his business—but I did want to emphasize that I wasn't a guy who would publicly throw a player's name out in what was an internal matter. Interestingly, Butcher would finish his NHL career with the team he didn't want to play for, the Toronto Maple Leafs, in 1994–95. Quinn would join the Leafs organization in 1998 for a much longer period. We learned more about how prickly he could be with and about the media during that reign.

Now, standing with Courtnall at that Zamboni entrance in Chicago Stadium, I was the general manager, and no longer a secondary member of a triumvirate. I had made a lot of headway with Brophy, a man I truly liked but who I differed with on many of his coaching philosophies and how they applied to the NHL compared with the minor leagues. Courtnall wasn't one of the matters I had made headway with. And sitting him out in the third game of the season was Brophy's message about where Courtnall stood.

I realized over those next few minutes that the situation would have to be resolved by one of them leaving. I felt like a deflating wave of negative energy was consuming me. Since I was committed to the owner's choice of Brophy as our coach, it looked like I would have to find an alternative for Courtnall. I asked Courtnall to keep his frustration and anger to himself and told him that I would endeavour to find a place for him to play where he would be appreciated, if the situation in Toronto didn't change in the near future. To Courtnall's credit, he did just that.

It was a heady start to what turned out to be my brief reign as Leafs general manager and Courtnall's final weeks as a Leaf. We opened the season with an 8-3-1 record in our first 12 games and stood in first place in the Wales Conference. The month of October would end with a 3–2 loss in St. Louis, and the following month wouldn't be pleasant at all. In fact, it was quite the opposite.

We opened November 1988 with a game against the tough Boston Bruins, who beat us decisively, 7–2, at Maple Leaf Gardens. We were now a very respectable 8-5-1 in our first 14 games. But beyond the good record, things were beginning to crumble internally. Brophy was getting impatient and was apoplectic about the way the Bruins had manhandled us in our own building. His fuse got even shorter a few days later when Marty McSorley bullied us as the Los Angeles Kings beat us 6–4, again in our own building. That game was less about Wayne Gretzky's Maple Leaf Gardens' debut as a Los Angeles King and more about how McSorley and a few others had been especially tough on Borje Salming. (McSorley is now a media colleague at Rogers' Sportsnet. I often kid him that his actions in that game were the beginning of the end for the early hope we had held for that 1988–89 season.)

I agreed with Brophy that our team could use more of a physical presence. We had traded for Brian Curran the previous March and drafted Tie Domi the previous June, but he still had a year of junior hockey eligibility left with Peterborough and I wasn't interested in continuing what had been our recent pattern of fast-tracking players to the NHL line-up. We had made what proved to be a solid move in claiming Brad Marsh off Philadelphia in the Waiver Draft to start the season. I hoped to incorporate more toughness into the line-up as we moved forward.

We had several players who were skilled but not too physical, like Ed Olczyk, Gary Leeman, Vincent Damphousse, Daniel Marois, Dave Reid, and Russ Courtnall. Brophy, however, was focused on the immediate picture: his team was getting beaten physically and he wanted a presence then and there. Brophy's primary interest was in adding John Kordic from Montreal. "Number one, the top heavyweight bar none," was how Brophy assessed Kordic's potential value to us.

Brophy had been coaching in the Montreal organization with the Nova Scotia Voyageurs when Kordic had enjoyed his greatest NHL success, helping the Canadiens in the playoff run toward their Stanley Cup victory in 1986. Kordic had played in 11 of those playoff games and had been a strong physical presence. He had even scored two playoff goals, one a game winner.

So, contrary to rumour, it wasn't that Serge Savard was pursuing Courtnall on behalf of the Montreal Canadiens but the other way around. After our loss to Los Angeles, I made the call to Savard about Kordic. I was aware that Kordic was a problem for Montreal management—that their relationship was strained—and that Savard wouldn't be unhappy about the possibility of moving him. As we were to soon discover, much had changed over the two years since that heady Stanley Cup championship spring of 1986. Where and when Kordic's battles with alcohol and drugs began is unclear, but it would soon become evident to us that his problems went beyond a simple falling out with the Montreal Canadiens management and coaches.

In return for Kordic, Savard wanted one of our younger players, like Courtnall or Todd Gill. We had played 15 games, and Courtnall had been a healthy scratch for 6 of them, scoring two points (one goal, one assist) in the 9 games he had played. Savard was a bit more interested in Courtnall and we were in the position where Courtnall was a spare part, whereas Gill was playing regularly on the Leafs defence. As well, I had promised Courtnall an opportunity elsewhere should the appropriate deal arise.

So, I bartered with Savard to add a draft choice. The best I could get was a sixth-round pick. We made the trade on November 7, 1988. I can't even save this one by adding that the sixth-round pick (Michael Doers) was a diamond in the rough. No, Doers never played a single game of professional hockey.

Though at times a fan favourite and effective on the ice, John Kordic was sinking into a deeper abyss, both on and off the ice. An intermission tongue-lashing from Brophy shortly after Kordic's arrival in Toronto sent an angry Kordic back onto the ice for a game against the Edmonton Oilers. His sticking the butt end of his stick into the mouth and face of Oiler Keith Acton (recently a long-time Leafs assistant coach) earned Kordic a 10-game suspension.

Many people wanted to help him, but Kordic's substance abuse and subsequent downward spiral would continue after he left Toronto, in his stops in Washington, Quebec City, and Edmonton. Ultimately, it was the cause of his death, in a Quebec City hotel room, on August 8, 1992, at the age of 27.

Despite being the "winner" of the trade that defines the most negative move of my brief career as general manager, Serge Savard remains one of my favourite people in the business and a class act. Although Paul Henderson and Phil Esposito stood out as the stars of the Canadian team of the century, Team Canada 1972, Savard was the underrated anchor of the Team Canada defence. A Hall of Fame player, he took those skills to achieve success as the GM of the Montreal Canadiens (beyond just the Courtnall-Kordic trade) and also has had incredible success as a businessman.

When I chatted with him at a Hall of Fame event in Toronto a few years ago, Savard remained a supportive colleague. "The Courtnall-Kordic trade," he said, "that's what happens when you listen to the coach." To commiserate with me, he claimed that he made an even worse deal because of *his* coach. "I couldn't get my coach [Jacques Demers] to play John LeClair," Savard said, "and I had to move him to Philadelphia in what wasn't a very good deal. I told Reggie Houle not to listen to the coach [Mario Tremblay] when he convinced him to bring Stephane Richer back, which turned out to be a bad idea."

LeClair was traded to Philadelphia in early 1995 along with Eric Desjardins and Gilbert Delorme in exchange for Mark Recchi and a third-round draft choice. Richer had a second whirl with Montreal for a season and a half beginning in 1996. Classy and generous of Serge Savard to attempt to put a positive spin on our one trade, but in the end, Savard's positive moves far outweigh any negative moves he may have made on and off the ice in the National Hockey League, as well as in the business world.

Actually, if truth be told, if the 1983 NHL Entry Draft had been held six weeks earlier than its usual June date, Russ Courtnall wouldn't even have been our target. At the time we were leaning toward Cam Neely of the Portland Winterhawks.

Leafs management, our scouting staff, and coaches Mike Nykoluk and Dan Maloney spent most of the Memorial Cup week in early May 1983 in beautiful Portland, Oregon. It was the first Memorial Cup to be elevated to a higher stature on and off the ice. And it was the first year that the host city's team, in this case the Portland Winterhawks, was included along with a representative team from the three Canadian junior hockey leagues. This made for a four-team tournament rather than what had been a three-team tournament. With the host city team assured a spot, it increased crowd interest, media profile, and marketing opportunities significantly.

I remember a number of enjoyable things about that week. I met Ken Wregget for the first time when we invited our 1982 draft choice, and goaltender for the Lethbridge Broncos, to dinner. Wregget was injured and unable to play for the Broncos, which was a blow to their Memorial Cup chances. He proved to be a really funny and great kid that first evening, one who blossomed into a really funny and great adult.

All of the teams were allowed to bring a third goaltender from another team in their league, in case of emergencies or injuries. The Ontario Hockey League champion Oshawa Generals added Allan Bester from the Brantford team to their roster. Bester was a short, personable, talkative kid who you couldn't seem to shake. Not dressed for the games, Bester seemed to always be just hanging around wherever we were in the Portland arena. He obviously made a great impression, as we ended up drafting him in the third round of the NHL Entry Draft six weeks later.

Cam Neely's play for the hosting Portland Winterhawks in that tournament was ordinary for him, and he had the disadvantage of playing with both of his eyes somewhat bruised and blackened from an earlier mishap during a game. With hindsight and given the career Neely went on to have, our mistake as an organization was to involve people in the decision-making process who had not seen Neely play throughout the season. Their interest in Neely, based solely on his Memorial Cup play, was lukewarm. As all hockey fans soon became aware, "lukewarm" was just about the least appropriate description of how Cam Neely played hockey during his Hall of Fame NHL career.

As part of the scouting process, Gerry McNamara and Mike Nykoluk headed out one morning to visit with one of the draft prospects. They met with Russ Courtnall somewhere between Portland and his hometown of Victoria, British Columbia. It's tough for me to think of a person who can make a better first impression than Russ Courtnall, and that was certainly the case on that day in the idyllic West Coast setting. Upon their return to Portland for some more Memorial Cup action, McNamara and Nykoluk made it obvious that Courtnall had caught their attention over the two black eyes that Neely sported.

It was Russ Courtnall who we used as our seventh overall pick in the 1983 NHL Entry Draft six weeks later. The Vancouver Canucks used the ninth overall pick to take Cam Neely, who was an excellent choice. But what happened later to Neely makes the Courtnall-Kordic trade look like a minor mistake.

Three years later, just prior to the 1986 Entry Draft, the Canucks traded Neely to the Boston Bruins along with their first-round choice in the 1987 Entry Draft in exchange for Barry Pederson. That pick would end up being third overall, and Boston would add a quality defenceman in Glen Wesley (also from Portland) as a result.

But Glen Wesley isn't who Canuck fans remember and lament. After three NHL seasons with 16, 21, and 14 goals in Vancouver, Neely blossomed into a scoring superstar with goal totals of 36, 42, 37, 55, and 51 in his first five seasons in

Beantown. After two seasons cut short by injury, he would save his finest play for the 1993–94 season, when he scored 50 goals in just 49 games. Beyond his goal-scoring acumen, Neely was the star prototype of that endangered NHL species, the elite power forward. They did and still do exist few and far between in the National Hockey League, but Neely knew no peer in that department.

Two years after the 1993–94 season, like another Bruins legend, Bobby Orr, Neely was out of the NHL at the age of 31 thanks to chronic hip problems. And as with Orr, the Hockey Hall of Fame selection committee had seen enough in a short period to induct Neely in 2005. It was my good fortune to be involved as MC for the Hall of Fame Induction Weekend, and it was a pleasure to talk with Neely. I also remember actor Michael J. Fox being part of that weekend as a close friend of his.

I also vividly remember chatting with Neely for several minutes on an unlikely subject—John Kordic. Neely remembered his troubled Portland teammate with fondness and sadness. He talked about how Kordic had been an all-star defenceman in the Western Junior Hockey League before becoming an enforcer forward when he turned pro. Neely had spent a week at his junior teammate's home in Edmonton one summer. They were both sent by their Portland Winterhawks junior team to attend a week-long power-skating course in Kordic's home city. After seeing first-hand the difficult relationship that Kordic had with his father, Neely could empathize more with his teammate's struggle off the ice.

I recall Kordic being quite upset when his father had passed away in 1990. It seemed like there had been a great deal of love between them, but it was in a difficult and, at times, toxic environment. It seems to me, in hindsight, a precursor to Kordic's future. He had a surprising (to those who didn't know him) number of admirable personal qualities but lacked the ability to form and develop positive relationships. That he gravitated to enablers of his substance and alcohol problems, a group that grew larger as he became a better-known NHL hockey player, facilitated his continued professional and personal demise.

The drafting of Luke Richardson ahead of Joe Sakic in 1987 is obviously one scenario that didn't play out in the Leafs' favour. But it wasn't always like that. The previous year, the Leafs actually caught a bit of luck in how the draft unfolded.

Sitting at our table in Montreal for the 1986 Entry Draft as we waited to make the sixth overall pick, there seemed to be a consensus as to how the draft would play out at the top, with the top five players being Joe Murphy from Michigan State, Jimmy Carson from Verdun, Vincent Damphousse from Laval, and two members from the Canadian National Team, Zarley Zalapski and Shawn Anderson. Our choice would likely be a winger from the Western Junior Hockey League, Pat Elynuik (Prince Albert) or Dan Woodley (Portland). Our hope was that one of the first five teams would go off the board and take a player outside those five consensus picks and we would take whichever of the top-rated five fell to us in the sixth slot.

After Detroit selected Murphy and Los Angeles selected Carson, the New Jersey Devils were next up. This was a year before Lou Lamoriello began his 25-year run as general manager, but the Devils' scouting staff were advocates of psychological testing and placed a heavy emphasis on a tool that, at the time, was used by few NHL teams. They ended being the team that went off the board when they chose centre Neil Brady from Medicine Hat as the third overall pick.

Not a big scorer in junior hockey, Brady would record just nine career NHL goals in 89 NHL games with New Jersey, Ottawa, and Dallas. It's not really fair to be overly critical of the New Jersey Devils staff, as their somewhat unique style of player evaluation would pay more dividends than misses in the long run. But on that day, we at the Toronto Maple Leafs table felt we had been offered a huge break.

So we sat back and waited our turn. Pittsburgh selected Zalapski and Buffalo took Anderson. We felt fortunate that Damphousse fell into our laps, and his selection for us was a no-brainer. His NHL career was far and away greater than that of the five players picked ahead of him and that of Elynuik and Woodley, who were picked right after him.

Damphousse would crack the Leafs line-up as a rookie in 1987 and have five very solid seasons with impressive offensive stats. Four of those seasons he scored over 20 goals, and his best offensive performance was in 1989–90 with 94 points (33 goals, 61 assists). Some within the Leafs organization questioned his abilities as a "money" player in the Stanley Cup playoffs. This opinion was mostly based on his playoff statistics, which weren't nearly as successful, as he scored only one playoff goal in 23 playoff games while with the Leafs. That aside, Damphousse was the key player in Cliff Fletcher's first bold move as the Leafs general manager in 1991, when Damphousse, Peter Ing, Scott Thornton, and Luke Richardson were traded to Edmonton for Grant Fuhr, Glenn Anderson, and Craig Berube.

A year later he played for his hometown Montreal Canadiens, and quieted critics of his playoff performance with 23 points (11 goals, 12 assists) in 20 playoff games as the Canadiens hoisted the Stanley Cup in 1993, the last Canadian-based NHL team to do so.

After their selections of great player Damphousse and decent player Richardson, the Leafs have had little to show for their first-round selections. Scott Pearson, Drake Berehowsky, Brandon Convery, Grant Marshall, Kenny Jonsson, Landon Wilson, Eric Fichaud, Jeff Ware, Nik Antropov, Brad Boyes, Luca Cereda, Jiri Tlusty, Carlo Colaiacovo, Alexander Steen, Tuukka Rask, Luke Schenn, and Nazem Kadri are a rather pathetic sum total of Leafs first-round picks over a span of 24 years. To add insult to draft injury, the Leafs have traded away their first-round pick on eight occasions (1991, 1996, 1997, 2003, 2004, 2007, 2010, and 2011).

The one year I need to include in this list is the 1989 Entry Draft, where it seems my choice of three players from the same Ontario Hockey League team was another notorious blot (along with the Courtnall-Kordic trade) on my brief career as general manager.

The actual trade to acquire the additional first-round selections was received very well. On March 6, 1989, just a day before the NHL trade deadline, I completed a deal on behalf of the Leafs with Bob Clarke of the Philadelphia Flyers. They coveted our goaltender Ken Wregget, who, at the time, was sharing goaltending duties with Allan Bester. We were able to receive two first-round selections in the 1989 draft in exchange for Wregget, the Flyers' pick and the Calgary Flames' pick who the Flyers had acquired in an earlier trade.

The thought of having three first-round selections prompted immediate excitement within the organization and among our fans. At the time of the trade, the Flyers' pick stood as 10th overall and the Flames were 19th overall. Over the final 15 games, both the Flyers and Flames finished strongly, so we would end up drafting 12th overall with the Flyers' pick and 21st overall with the Flames' pick to go with our pick at third overall.

So when June 20—draft day in Minneapolis—arrived, how did all three of our first-round picks come from one team and one team only, the Belleville Bulls, of the Ontario Hockey League? Trust me, that was never the plan. It wasn't even said in jest at any of our scouting meetings or within the organization. It's just how the cards played out.

We knew that the first round of the 1989 draft was viewed as one of the weaker drafts because of the calibre of the talent pool. While Mike Modano, Trevor Linden, Jeremy Roenick, Rod Brind'Amour, and Teemu Selanne had been picks in the top 10 the previous year, this draft lacked the same wow factor.

Still, the goal is always to get the best player available regardless of the calibre of the draft. And Bull number one, Scott Thornton, was somewhat expected. Mats Sundin went first overall to the Quebec Nordiques, which was expected, as was Dave Chyzowski of Portland going second to the New York Islanders. Like many teams, we also had Chyzowski ranked right behind Sundin. If he had been available at third overall, we would have selected him.

The night before the draft we debated extensively the merits of taking Thornton or Stu Barnes of the Tri-City Americans with our third overall pick. We even had another Smythe Division team general manager calling in to offer his opinion, as the better the choice we made, the weaker a player would go to his divisional rival, the Winnipeg Jets, who were selecting fourth overall. We ended the night by agreeing on Thornton, who, by the way, was whom the Smythe Division team's scouting staff had ranked.

As we headed to the 12th overall pick, we had to let the draft play itself out. We planned to take a defenceman with one of our three picks, and we felt we would make that choice at 12th overall. When it came time for our pick, the two defencemen we hoped might be available, Jason Herter of North Dakota and Adam Bennett of Sudbury, had already been selected. Our staff really liked the play of Rob Pearson. As one scout said, "He is one of their leading scorers and leads the league in spearing goalies." Even though John Brophy was no longer the coach, we still knew our Leafs team needed to acquire players who were tough and more physical, just not with the single-minded focus of Brophy. This was one of the attributes we saw in Rob Pearson. We valued Pearson's physical presence, nastiness, and edge, along with his scoring ability. He became Bull number two.

For the 21st overall pick, we were very focused on a defenceman. The New York Rangers' selection of Steven Rice of Kitchener took away the top forward on our draft wish list. The next available forward on our Leafs team draft list was Kent Manderville of Cornell University who we were not nearly as high on as we had been with Rice. With our choice for forward gone, it was easier for us to focus on defencemen.

This was the first time we discussed drafting the three Belleville Bulls in one round. And, as a matter of fact, our concern was that it would be perceived negatively if we made such a move. In the end, our philosophy was to take who we felt was the best player available, and we held firm on our decision.

A surprising number of defencemen (eight) had already been taken with the first 20 selections, a number a bit higher than usual. Our top two names were Steve Bancroft from Belleville and Dan Ratushny, like Manderville, from Cornell.

There had been a strong consensus for selecting Pearson, but that wasn't the case for the 21st overall pick. One of our Ontario scouts just loved Bancroft as a player, and his persuasive arguments were probably the deciding factor. Steve Bancroft became Bull number three.

And now you know the story . . . well, at least the background of how we made the three first-round selections from the same junior hockey team—for the first and still only time in National Hockey League history.

In fairness, the end product was not a complete bust. Scott Thornton (an older cousin to current NHL star Joe Thornton with the San Jose Sharks) enjoyed a 17-year NHL career with Toronto, Edmonton, Montreal, Dallas, San Jose, and Los Angeles before retiring to the Collingwood, Ontario, area. He evolved as more of a defensive, checker-type player with 285 points in 941 regular-season NHL games.

Rob Pearson actually had a strong start to his NHL career. He had 23 goals in 78 regular-season games and added the toughness with 211 penalty minutes in his memorable first full season with the Toronto Maple Leafs, in 1992–93. Pearson added four points (two goals, two assists) and 31 penalty minutes in 14 playoff games that spring. Injuries helped cut his NHL career short and he retired before the age of 30, after playing in 269 career NHL games with Toronto, Washington, and St. Louis.

Steve Bancroft capably plied his trade as a career minor league defenceman in the second tier of professional hockey in the American Hockey League and International Hockey League.

Over 14 seasons he had stops in Newmarket, Maine, Indianapolis, Moncton, Cleveland, Detroit, Fort Wayne, St. John's, Los Angeles, Chicago, Las Vegas, Saint John, Providence, Cincinnati, Houston, Kentucky, Cleveland, Worcester, and Binghamton.

Bancroft made only two appearances in the National Hockey League and they were almost 10 years apart. In 1992–93, he played in one game for the Chicago Blackhawks. He wasn't recalled to the NHL again until 2001–02, when he played in five games for the San Jose Sharks.

As we got set to announce Steve Bancroft as the 21st and final pick of the first round, millions of hockey fans across Canada watched with interest. Many with vested interests were passionately hoping that a relative or close friend would be drafted early and that they could share the excitement.

A loyal group of Adam Foote's friends were gathered in Whitby, Ontario, as we got set to make that last pick in the first round. A Whitby native, Foote was playing for the Sault Ste. Marie Greyhounds and had been considered a likely second-round pick.

Still, his many friends and family knew he had an outside chance at going in the first round and were especially excited about the possibility of Foote wearing the blue and white of the local Toronto Maple Leafs. They were disappointed in our selection and further disappointed when television coverage abruptly ended after the first round. With the termination of the coverage, they were unaware that their guy, Adam Foote, was selected as the first pick in the second round, 22nd overall, by the Quebec Nordiques. With Sundin in the first round and Foote in the second round, this draft ranks as strong a first two picks as an NHL team has ever made.

Nine defencemen were drafted before Foote (Adam Bennett, Doug Zmolek, Jason Herter, Jason Marshall, Lindsay Vallis, Kevin Haller, Jason Soules, Jamie Heward, and Steve Bancroft) and none came anywhere close to having the successful NHL career that Foote achieved. (Nor was Foote the first defence-man drafted that year from the Ontario Hockey League with the first name Adam. That distinction went to Adam Bennett of Sudbury, who went sixth overall to the Chicago Blackhawks.)

One of that group sitting around the TV on that June after-noon was Foote's best friend, Bob Torrens. As fate would have it, Torrens has been one of my many bosses over the past decade as one of the producers of NHL hockey at Rogers' Sportsnet. He is a great friend and a very personable guy, but don't think I don't hear the draft legacy story from time to time.

As time marches on, I take in stride jokes of our drafting of three Belleville Bulls (that the Leafs were so cheap that they only allowed their scouts to travel as far as Belleville). I'm more bothered by whom we missed who went 22nd overall . . . and so are 19 other NHL teams!

Eighteen years after that memorable drafting of three Belleville Bulls in the first round, the Stellick connection was rekindled. My 16-year-old nephew, Robert, the youngest of two sons of my brother Bob, was set to be a probable middle-round pick in the 2007 Ontario Hockey League Draft.

As projected, he was selected in the sixth round—by the Belleville Bulls. Robert played two seasons for a very successful Bulls team with the likes of P.K. Subban and Shawn Mattias. He got to enjoy the Memorial Cup experience when the Bulls qualified in 2008.

His two years in Belleville were made even more enjoyable by his being billeted with the Cook family. They have been long-time fans of the Bulls team and have billeted junior players for over two decades. Their nephew Matt Cook is an NHL player who has gained a degree of notoriety recently thanks to his tendency to create controversy and draw NHL suspensions for a few of his illegal hits. Wouldn't you know that the Cooks were the same family that Steve Bancroft billeted with when he played for the Bulls almost 20 years earlier?

A year earlier, at the 1988 NHL Entry Draft, we made what proved to be our most successful selection in my two years as Leafs general manager—and it wasn't among those most scrutinized players who were selected in the first round.

After having selected Scott Pearson in the first round in 1988, we were looking to go a bit outside the consensus rankings with our second-round pick. Watching the Peterborough Petes in the Ontario Hockey League in the last part of their season and in their playoffs, two things became apparent to us. The first was that a 16-year-old rookie from Toronto, Mike Ricci, was going to be an impact junior hockey player and an early draft pick when he was eligible in two years. (He went fourth overall to the Philadelphia Flyers in 1990.)

The second was the improving play of a young man named Tie Domi. With just one goal in 18 games a year earlier, Domi had really blossomed in his second year in junior hockey. Though not big in stature, he had embraced the role as protector and enforcer for Ricci and the rest of the Petes. What further impressed us was that he had scored 22 goals to go along with his 292 penalty minutes.

Domi wasn't even ranked in the first three rounds by the NHL Central Scouting Bureau. Since Domi was flying under the radar with most NHL teams, we wondered if we should wait until the third round to draft him, since we were picking in the early part of each round, or whether he was worth that early second-round pick, 27th overall.

I have always tried to hold to the philosophy that if you really like a player, don't gamble that he will last another round—take him. And we really liked Domi. So we used our second-round pick. Over a year later, when I was working with Neil Smith at the New York Rangers, he told me that the Detroit Red Wings team (who he was working for at the time of the 1988 Entry Draft) would have used their second-round pick (38th overall) to select Domi, meaning that Domi wouldn't have made it to the third round.

Domi's selection was the last live coverage shown on TSN for the 1988 Entry Draft. Tie's brother, Dash, and other family members and friends were able to celebrate the Domi selection being higher than anticipated and his going to the Toronto Maple Leafs that they had just watched broadcast live on TV. His parents were among the crowd at the Montreal Forum that day.

Domi was actually traded away from the Leafs in 1990 (to the New York Rangers) and then acquired in another trade from the Winnipeg Jets in 1995. Most of his 1,020 career NHL regular-season games were played with the Toronto Maple Leafs, and for most of the years he combined an appropriate balance and good measure of playing skill, offence, and toughness.

Always a fan favourite, he is considered among the most popular Toronto Maple Leafs players in the past two decades. That day on the draft floor in Montreal in 1988, he was just a kid experiencing a dream and sharing it with his family. As his career continued, I would often kid him, "Tie, you're all I've got left; you are my complete and total NHL general manager legacy."

Professional sports leagues have become more "scientific" and business-like in their approach to their organizations—the expression "due diligence" has gained a prominent place in the vocabulary. But on occasion, timing, perhaps along with a dose of good old-fashioned luck, plays a huge role and offers all of us in professional sports a lesson.

Years ago, in July 1989, the NFL owners gathered at an O'Hare airport hotel in Chicago to vote on who would be their new commissioner. It was thought a slam dunk for respected NFL executive Jim Finks. Well, as often happens, poor weather resulted in the delay of many flights, and the watershed meeting was three hours late in starting.

Although the Young Turk owners like Jerry Jones of the Dallas Cowboys and Pat Bowlen of the Denver Broncos preferred NFL legal counsel Paul Tagliabue, they had been prepared to vote with the wishes of old guard owners like Dan Rooney of the Pittsburgh Steelers and Art Modell of the Cleveland

Browns. But for Jim Finks, those three hours changed everything. The bloc of the younger, newer owners used the three
hours of pre-voting discussion to forge ahead with a new plan.
They had paid higher prices for their franchises than some of
the veteran owners, who had gained entry in the NFL decades
earlier for next to nothing.

Finally, the vote was taken. The coronation of Finks as new
commissioner was not to be. Finks had 16 votes to Tagliabue's
12—three votes shy of the two-thirds majority required.

The Young Turks spent the next few weeks actively
campaigning for their choice. Another vote, three weeks later,
had Tagliabue leading 15 to 13—not enough to make him
commissioner, but he was obviously gaining momentum with
the NFL owners. A few weeks later, Tagliabue had enough votes
to become commissioner of the National Football League.

When Paul Tagliabue retired in 2006, there were very few
complaints about his 17-year tenure from either Young Turk
or old guard owners. But without that severe weather pattern
over Chicago that July afternoon in 1989, Tagliabue may never
have ascended to the commissioner's chair.

There were certainly times when timing and just being in
the right place at the right time were big factors in NHL decisions. It was the difference between seizing and not seizing a
window of opportunity.

The Toronto Maple Leafs organization was the beneficiary
of fortuitous timing as we opened the 1985–86 season with our
first game in Boston, on October 10. After the morning skate,
a visibly angry Bruins general manager Harry Sinden chatted
with Gerry McNamara. He was livid because one of his young
players, Tom Fergus, was refusing to play until he got a satisfactory new contract. "I'm going to trade that greedy bastard,"
Sinden told McNamara.

McNamara jumped at the opportunity, and the next day Fergus came to the Toronto Maple Leafs in exchange for Bill Derlago in a trade that seemingly came out of nowhere. Not a single discussion had been held prior to Sinden's tirade the previous day. It was a clean and easy one-for-one transaction. Fergus even wore Derlago's old number 19 with the Leafs.

Sinden soon admitted that he regretted acting in such an uncharacteristically rash manner and taking his contract dispute with Fergus personally. Tom Fergus was a solid top-six forward for the Leafs and averaged 23 goals and 57 points for the Leafs over the next five seasons. Derlago, on the other hand, wouldn't last the season with the Bruins and would be out of the NHL completely two years later.

July 1, 1998: the first day of the summer free-agent period in the NHL. This was in the pre–salary cap era, before the NHL lockout in 2004, when big signings were often executed and announced in the first hours of Canada's birthday celebrations. It was a time when anything could happen. The salary cap not a factor, teams could throw whatever money they wished at a desirable unrestricted free agent.

Edmonton Oilers goaltender Curtis Joseph was coveted as an available top unrestricted free agent. It was felt that a natural fit for Joseph would be the Philadelphia Flyers, who seemed to be in the market for a big-name goaltender after struggling for seasons with lesser names like Garth Snow, Dominic Roussel, Brian Boucher, Tommy Soderstrom, and Roman Cechmanek.

Another big goaltending name was Mike Richter. He was the star goaltender for archrival New York Rangers, but he was also a Philadelphia native. The prevailing sentiment was that the Flyers would get the goaltending free agent carousel going by signing either Joseph or Richter.

However, despite the typical public outcry for action in the free agent signings, Leafs president and general manager Ken Dryden appeared to be satisfied with the status quo. In goal the Leafs still had Felix Potvin as their number one goaltender, even though his play seemed to be getting worse each season. It appeared unlikely that Dryden would make a bold move signing a big-name unrestricted free agent, and even less likely that it would be a goaltender.

It was indeed the Philadelphia Flyers that set the goaltending carousel in motion, but with a less expensive acquisition. As often happens, the unexpected resulted in shaking up the expected. Philadelphia signed a goaltender, but it was neither Joseph nor Richter. Instead, they opted to sign John Vanbiesbrouck from the Florida Panthers for a lower salary ($3.2 million) than Joseph and Richter were demanding.

Over the next two days, with the Flyers now out of the goaltending picture, the agents for Joseph and Richter had to come up with a new plan. It appeared to be set that Joseph would head to the New York Rangers, and Richter, sensing it was time to move on from the Rangers, would sign with Florida to replace his old Ranger teammate Vanbiesbrouck.

But a funny thing happened the night before this was all to be finalized. Ken Dryden stopped at a downtown Toronto convenience store to buy some ice cream to cool himself down in the sweltering July heat. Joseph's agent, Don Meehan, had the same idea and quite by coincidence stopped in at the same convenience store at the same time as the Leafs president and general manager.

It was there they talked, while their ice cream melted, and forged the parameters of a deal for Joseph that would, once again, change the landscape of the NHL. The next day, with clean hands, Dryden and Meehan agreed to a contract to bring Joseph to Toronto. Curtis Joseph inked a four-year contract with the Leafs at $5 million per season. That completed, Mike Richter would cancel his plans to fly to Florida and re-sign with the New York Rangers.

The next April, 1999, the Leafs won their first-ever playoff series at Air Canada Centre—Curtis Joseph and his Leafs over John Vanbiesbrouck and the Philadelphia Flyers. It would be the only playoff action Vanbiesbrouck would see in his two unappreciated years in Philadelphia. Joseph would enjoy a great four-year run as a Leaf. Twice he backstopped the team to the second round of the Stanley Cup playoffs and twice to the third round (the Conference Final), the best four-year run since the period when the Leafs won three consecutive Stanley Cups in the early 1960s.

Who would have thought that the addition of Curtis Joseph to the Leafs would come about because two of the NHL's most powerful figures were each in search of some ice cream on a hot summer's evening.

After a rather successful first year at the helm as Leafs general manager in 1989–90, Floyd Smith looked forward to more of the same in his second season.

He did make a couple of moves with his coaching staff. He fired Paul Gardner, who had been the head coach of the Leafs' American Hockey League affiliate, the Newmarket Saints. He made one switch to the staff of assistants in Toronto for head coach Doug Carpenter. He retained Mike Kitchen but fired Garry Lariviere. Tom Watt was brought in as Lariviere's replacement.

For the job in Newmarket, Smith was after two of the biggest names seeking coaching employment. Bryan Murray was looking for work after a successful tenure with the Washington Capitals. Beyond those qualified with NHL experience Bob Gainey had returned from a few years of coaching in Europe and was anxious to coach an NHL team.

As the summer weeks wore on, two NHL coaching vacancies remained, with the Detroit Red Wings and the Minnesota North Stars. Both Murray and Gainey were actively pursuing those jobs. Since Floyd Smith viewed those two as his absolute ideal candidates, he was willing to wait a few weeks, as he hoped one or both would still be available when those two NHL coaching positions were filled.

Smith felt it was important to have a big coaching name and experienced hockey person in place in Newmarket, and Murray and Gainey were by far the top candidates in that department. He also wanted to hire someone who would be a quick replacement in assuming NHL duties during the season should he ever have to make a change with Doug Carpenter at the NHL level. Both these two were perfect for that potential scenario.

As luck would have it—for Murray and Gainey anyway, if not for Smith—they would be the successful candidates for the last two NHL coaching positions. Murray was named coach and general manager of the Detroit Red Wings, and Gainey was appointed coach of the Minnesota North Stars.

Now Smith had to look elsewhere for his new head coach in Newmarket. He settled on a very different choice in U.S. college coach Frank Anzalone, who had been head coach of Lake Superior State. Anzalone proved to be different in many ways. His year in Newmarket was a disaster both on and off the ice for all parties. After just one season, he returned to where he felt most comfortable, coaching U.S. college hockey.

Meanwhile, that worst-case scenario for Smith reared its ugly head. The 1990–91 season was anything but as pleasant as the previous year had been. The Leafs team had a horrendous start to the season with just one win in the first 12 games (1-10-1). As the pressure mounted, Smith had to make a change: Doug Carpenter was fired just 14 games into his second season as Leafs coach.

This is when Smith would have quickly turned to Bryan Murray or Bob Gainey, had they been his American Hockey League coach. Though just a few weeks into his tenure, it was already evident that Frank Anzalone was nowhere near ready or qualified. Smith turned to the more experienced Tom Watt to take over the head coaching position from Carpenter.

Murray has continued as an NHL head coach and/or general manager in a number of stops, including his current position as general manager with the Ottawa Senators. Gainey added the position of general manager as well as coach with the North Stars when Bob Clarke left the Stars front office to return to the Philadelphia Flyers in 1992. Gainey later gave up the coaching and focused on being general manager. His Dallas Stars team won the Stanley Cup in 1999. Bob Clarke remains a senior member of Flyers' management, while Bob Gainey surprised the hockey world when he resigned as the Canadiens' GM in 2010.

The Leafs finished the season well out of the playoffs with a 23-46-11 record; with Tom Watt as head coach they were

22-34-10. Watt coached the next full season in 1991–92 and the team improved with a 30-43-7 record. They improved considerably in the second half of the season after acquiring Doug Gilmour and others from Calgary and just missed qualifying for the playoffs.

Though Cliff Fletcher kept Watt as a member of Leafs management when he hired Pat Burns in May 1992, Watt wasn't among those in management who were excited about the addition of an NHL coach of Burns's stature. In fact, Watt was quite disappointed that he didn't get a chance to stay on as coach.

The 1990–91 season continued to be unkind and unsuccessful for Floyd Smith and his Toronto Maple Leafs. They improved from their horrific start, but really, they couldn't go anywhere but up. Whereas Carpenter lost his job as coach early in the season, Smith lasted the season but was replaced as general manager by Cliff Fletcher in the off-season. Fletcher kept Smith on as an advisor and scout.

With Anzalone in Newmarket already out of the picture, Fletcher went ahead and hired the quality coaches for his American Hockey League team that Smith wished he had had a year earlier. Marc Crawford was named the head coach and Joel Quenneville the assistant coach. This gave the Leafs' AHL team a strong coaching nucleus for their first year in St. John's, Newfoundland.

Crawford and Quenneville remain today two excellent NHL head coaches, and both sport Stanley Cup rings, though obviously not with the Leafs. Crawford won with the Colorado Avalanche in 1996 and Quenneville with the Chicago Blackhawks in 2010.

Crawford badly wanted the open Leafs coaching position in 2005, but John Ferguson hired Paul Maurice. When Brian Burke joined the Leafs organization in November 2008, the incumbent coach was his friend and college teammate Ron Wilson. If Burke had been hired six months earlier by the Leafs when the coaching vacancy remained, his first choice as Leafs coach would have been Joel Quenneville.

Since that disappointment in 1995 of not being hired by the Leafs, Crawford has had two stops as an NHL head coach, in Los Angeles and in Dallas, where he was fired in April 2011.

Oh my God . . . have we traded away Eric Lindros?

Although Leafs management may never admit to uttering that thought, it was undoubtedly on the tips of their tongues as the Leafs' 1990–91 season went horribly awry. Leafs fans certainly were vocal about it.

When Floyd Smith made a deal with the New Jersey Devils in 1990 to bolster his blue-line corps, the terrible start to the 1990–91 season was obviously not anticipated as part of the equation. The Leafs had significantly improved the previous season and easily made the playoffs. Smith made a couple of additions that bolstered the Leafs defence, acquiring Dave Ellett from Winnipeg and Bob Rouse from Washington. Right at the start of the successful 1989–90 season, he had made a trade for a third veteran defenceman, acquiring Tom Kurvers from the New Jersey Devils for the Leafs' first-round selection in the 1991 Entry Draft.

The 1991 Entry Draft saw the introduction of a player with the potential to have the same impact as Mario Lemieux had had in 1984. Such was the unquestioned dominance of Eric Lindros that the NHL had altered the draft order. The San Jose Sharks would begin play in the NHL in the 1991–92 season. The often divisive NHL board of governors had no problem agreeing that there was no way they were going to award Eric Lindros to San Jose. The Sharks would get the second overall pick in the draft, while the team with the lowest points in the NHL regular season would get the right to draft Eric Lindros.

Based on the rather successful previous season, it looked like the Devils would be selecting somewhere in the middle of the first round with the pick acquired from the Maple Leafs. However, as the 1990–91 regular season continued and the Leafs' horrible start evolved into a horrible middle, with a horrible end looming, the unthinkable began to be discussed: that the Leafs might finish dead last and their first overall draft selection would be made by the New Jersey Devils. Had Floyd Smith traded Eric Lindros for Tom Kurvers months earlier, talk of that outcome would have been met with chuckles and a shaking of heads in the Leafs front office. Now it was being met with nervous laughter. To help alleviate the pressure, Smith made another, quieter trade, one that was really not in the best interests of the future of the Leafs organization but would, it was hoped, take the pressure off the growing Kurvers-for-Lindros speculation.

On November 17, 1990, former first-round pick Scott Pearson and two second-round selections were traded to the Quebec Nordiques for veterans Michel Petit, Aaron Broten, and Lucien DeBlois. It was a trade that didn't make a whole lot of sense for the Toronto Maple Leafs and was made strictly to make them a bit stronger on the ice and the Nordiques weaker. Though logical in an unfortunate way, it costs the Leafs' valuable future draft picks.

The Nordiques gained a little breathing space to ensure they would remain dead last in the NHL standings, especially with three veteran players off their roster. With the addition of those three players, the Leafs felt more confident that they wouldn't battle the Nordiques for last place and possibly have Lindros land in New Jersey via the Leafs' draft pick.

The ultimate value of the Lindros selection would be accentuated the year after the Nordiques made him the first overall pick and were able to trade him to the Philadelphia Flyers for $15 million and six players in return, including Peter Forsberg and Mike Ricci. Eric Lindros wasn't the final piece of the Quebec Nordiques winning the Stanley Cup in 1996, but the fruits of his trade were. Unfortunately for Quebec Nordiques fans that Cup was won by the Colorado Avalanche that first season after they had moved from Quebec City.

Any type of relief the Leafs may have felt for preventing Eric Lindros going to New Jersey was short-lived. After the San Jose Sharks selected Pat Falloon with the second overall pick, the Devils used the Leafs pick to draft future Hall of Famer Scott Niedermayer.

There was certainly a wonderful energy to all that surrounded the memorable playoff run by the Toronto Maple Leafs in the spring of 1993. The Fan had launched as Canada's first all-sports radio station in September 1992, just in time for the

Blue Jays' first World Series title, and gave insatiable Toronto sports fans 24-7 coverage during that mythic playoff run.

Just one month after The Fan launched, it was providing Toronto sports fans with around-the-clock coverage of the first-ever World Series victory by a Canadian-based baseball team as the Jays downed the Atlanta Braves.

The Fan then caught the wave of what evolved into a special Leafs regular season and that memorable playoff run in the spring of 1993. The fortunate timing of The Fan launch repeated itself with another Blue Jays World Series win in 1993 and another trip by the Maple Leafs to the Conference Final in the spring of 1994.

A major league baseball strike and NHL Lockout in 1994 would end that two-year glorious ride for Toronto sports fans with a thunderous and abrupt thud. Those two years remain a treasured memory. The Fan was a new and novel experiment that was embraced by the public, the players, and the teams. We could call players who were on the road in their hotel rooms and they would usually agree to come on with a moment's notice. That all began to change as they tired of the extensive coverage. Many now check in under an alias and many teams also insist that all interviews be set up through proper public relations channels.

Those first two years, The Fan benefited from arguably the most successful two-year run by professional sports teams in Toronto's history. I loved hearing the stories of how when Joe Bowen and I were calling the Leafs games on the radio, that car horns would start loudly honking when they heard us deliver the news of a Leafs playoff overtime goal and victory.

As part of the coverage of the first round against the Detroit Red Wings in 1993, The Fan reporter Howard Berger not only covered the series but also moderated a fun, informative, and entertaining roundtable over the seven games.

Before each game of the series, Berger moderated a discussion between the two respective assistant general managers. For Toronto, it was high-profile Bill Watters, who had been a respected and well-known player agent before joining Leafs management. He had great experience in the media as well and never met a microphone he didn't like. The Red Wings assistant general manager, Doug MacLean, was not as well known. He had been an assistant coach to Jacques Martin with the St. Louis Blues before joining Bryan Murray's staff first in Washington and then Detroit.

It added an entertaining flavour to the coverage over the two weeks. It helped MacLean's public and media profile in the Toronto area, where fans weren't all that familiar with him. After being deposed in Detroit a year later along with Bryan Murray, MacLean would enjoy successful runs as a coach with the Florida Panthers and later as the president and general manager of the Columbus Blue Jackets. Through all those years, one of his strengths was in the way he dealt with the media.

When he found himself out of work after the Columbus experience ended in 2007, the media opportunities came a calling. MacLean landed as a hockey analyst with Rogers' Sportsnet. One of his colleagues was none other than Bill Watters—and so the listening public got to enjoy their banter once again.

After two successful seasons to start his NHL career in 1985, Wendel Clark struggled with a chronic back problem the next two years. He played in just 28 games in the 1987–88 season

and just 15 games in 1988–89. It took over two years of rehabilitation under the guidance of then new Leafs trainer and
athletic therapist Chris Broadhurst.

Along the way, anxious Leafs fans provided Clark with
no shortage of advice or suggestions on how to deal with his
plaguing back problem. One such fan, who also happened to
be the wealthiest Leafs fan in Canada, took action.

Clark was surprised to receive the call from Lord Thomson
of Fleet. At the time, Ken Thomson was Canada's wealthiest
individual, with assets placing him in the exclusive billionaire's
club. Motivated by a desire to help the player heal his back
problems, Thomson made the arrangements and took care of
the tab for a *Lifestyles of the Rich and Famous*–type trip for Clark.

Thomson knew a back specialist in London, England, who
he felt was the best in the world at dealing with problems like
Clark's. The Leaf spent almost three weeks in London, courtesy
of the Canadian billionaire. Thomson provided Clark with a
luxury flat to stay in, a cook to prepare meals, and a chauffeur
to drive him wherever he pleased. Quite a change for the kid
from a farm in Kelvington, Saskatchewan! Clark's chauffeured
journeys took him not only to the back specialist but also to
the Maple Leaf Pub, where Canadian ex-pats congregated and
Clark could enjoy a different type of medicine.

The back treatment didn't prove to be a miracle cure for
Clark, but he sure appreciated the whole experience.

Granted, Cliff Fletcher's quick success in turning around the
fortunes of the Toronto Maple Leafs in the early 1990s would
be more difficult to duplicate nowadays in the salary-cap

era, but he continues to earn well-deserved credit for a masterful job.

He landed Grant Fuhr and Glenn Anderson from Edmonton for a package of players that included Vincent Damphousse and Luke Richardson. He made the famous 10-player trade with the Calgary Flames that brought Doug Gilmour and Jamie Macoun. Sylvain Lefebvre was acquired from Montreal for a third-round draft choice. Bill Berg was claimed on waivers from the New York Islanders. Fuhr was traded to Buffalo for Dave Andreychuk and a first-round pick. This formed the nucleus of the two teams that made wonderful playoff runs in 1993 and 1994.

His Midas touch seemed to make an abrupt U-turn after that second consecutive trip to the Conference Finals in the spring of 1994, however. It wasn't with the (at the time) unpopular trade of Wendel Clark to the Quebec Nordiques in June 1994. The best player in that trade, Mats Sundin, came to the Leafs along with Garth Butcher and Todd Warriner in exchange for Clark, Sylvain Lefebvre, and Landon Wilson. This would be the last of the string of deals where Fletcher ended up with the better end of the deal.

About a month after the blockbuster trade with Quebec, the Leafs had their eyes set on Mike Craig as the piece of the puzzle that could take them to a higher level. Boy, were they ever wrong. At the time, Craig was a 23-year-old who had just finished his fourth NHL season with the Dallas Stars organization. He had averaged a rather ordinary 15 goals per season, but the Leafs felt he was ready to blossom as a player. As a restricted free agent, the Leafs made the risky move of signing Craig to an offer sheet. This left the matter of compensation in the hands of an independent arbitrator.

That risk became even riskier when the Dallas Stars asked for top prospect Kenny Jonsson as compensation for Mike Craig, while the Leafs countered with an offer of Peter Zezel and Grant Marshall. The arbitrator's ruling in favour of the Leafs would be the only positive the Leafs would enjoy from the brief Leafs career of Mike Craig.

A supposed top-six forward, Craig scored just five goals in the lockout-abbreviated 1994–95 season, followed by totals of eight and seven the next two full seasons. His lack of production on the ice was matched by the lack of chemistry off the ice, as Craig just never fit in with a team comprised of strong characters and unselfish players.

The more significant loss in the Quebec deal was Lefebvre on defence. In addition, Bob Rouse had left as a free agent to sign with the Detroit Red Wings. Those were two significant and underrated losses from which the Leafs' blue line never recovered. With Zezel gone to Dallas and Mark Osborne allowed to sign with the New York Rangers, the Leafs lost two-thirds of their checking line and two more pieces of off-ice character.

Kerry Fraser has acknowledged it as the biggest officiating gaffe of his long and distinguished career as an NHL referee. At a Leafs luncheon several years ago honouring long-time front office employee Mary Speck, I was seated near Sally Stavro, the wife of then Leafs head Steve Stavro, with whom I shared pleasantries and small talk. But what struck me the most that afternoon was the sum of her hockey talk: the injustice of that call by Kerry Fraser years earlier.

After his retirement from the NHL, while promoting his book about his time as an NHL referee, Fraser reiterated his *mea culpa* about the most unfortunate event in his distinguished career. That did little to soothe the average Leafs fan, who describes that spring as a fabulous playoff run . . . "until the Leafs got screwed by Kerry Fraser." Wayne Gretzky should have been in the penalty box for high-sticking Doug Gilmour in overtime rather than still on the ice and scoring the game-winning goal. It's that simple. And it makes it easy to assign blame and leave the beloved Leafs team of that spring the heroes.

It's an easy grudge to hold. It also makes it easier for Toronto Maple Leafs fans to forget that there were factors other than Kerry Fraser's missed call in that bitter loss at the hands of the Los Angeles Kings in the Conference Finals in 1993. A win in the sixth or seventh game would have meant that dream Leafs final against the Montreal Canadiens. With both teams now in the same Conference, this isn't even a possibility under the current National Hockey League arrangement. And that seemed to be where the Leafs were heading on that Thursday, May 27, at the Great Western Forum in Los Angeles . . . until, Kerry Fraser single-handedly wrecked it all. Wayne Gretzky scored the game-winning goal in overtime when he should have been in the penalty box!

Leafs fans quickly moved on from their disappointment after a Game 7 loss two days later at Maple Leaf Gardens and gave their team a rousing civic reception, one befitting a Stanley Cup champion, though in this case, it was a team defeated in what really was the NHL semifinals. It was the Toronto equivalent of the celebration in downtown Manhattan the next year when the New York Rangers won their first Stanley Cup since 1940. So starved are Toronto Maple Leafs fans for playoff success that most were still able to celebrate that afternoon at Toronto City Hall their unofficial Stanley Cup, the win that unravelled because of one unforgivable call.

Like the ball going through Bill Buckner's legs at first base to allow the New York Mets to score their winning run in Game 6 of the 1986 World Series, Leafs fans conveniently choose to forget that there even was a Game 7, much as Red Sox fans did for years after that seven-game series loss to the Mets. The Red Sox had a chance to atone for Buckner's sixth-game error, much as the Leafs had another opportunity, on home ice, after Fraser's travesty of justice.

I had a great vantage point for that memorable sixth game at the Los Angeles Forum. I was doing the radio colour commentary with the play-by-play voice of the Maple Leafs, Joe Bowen, on the Leafs' radio network across Canada. It had been an incredibly exciting run by the Leafs team that spring. It ended up being 21 playoff games over 42 days. Game, off day, then right back at it—no extra days off for broadcasting reasons. This consistent rhythm was part of what made it so special and memorable. There were never lags in the schedule or even an opportunity for Leafs fans to catch their breath. Joe Bowen was struggling with keeping his voice during such an intense playoff run.

But there would be a few days off if the Leafs were able to wrap up the series in the sixth game in Los Angeles, as they held the 3–2 lead in the first five games. With the Leafs leading after 40 minutes of play, it seemed like that would be the case. Playing his best playoff game ever, Wendel Clark was the Leafs' offensive star with three goals.

The word came through to the press box that if the Leafs hung on to their lead, travel plans would be altered and our team charter would travel back to Toronto right after the game, landing in the early hours of the morning. We were scheduled to head back the next morning, the off day, because Cliff Fletcher was an advocate of not flying long distances directly after a game. He maintained that this strategy helped him with the Stanley Cup win in 1989. After the sixth game in Calgary, the Montreal Canadiens had flown back to Montreal directly after the game; Fletcher's Flames flew the next morning. The Flames remain the only visiting team in NHL history to hoist the Stanley Cup on Montreal ice after winning Game 7 there.

That informal travel update was when it all hit me. "Wow, this is really happening," I thought. "The Leafs are going all the way to the Stanley Cup Final, and it will be a dream match-up against the Montreal Canadiens . . . the unthinkable and the unbelievable is becoming the thinkable and the believable!" The next 20 minutes of action reinforced the unbelievable-ness of it. The momentum the Leafs had after the first 40 minutes turned in favour of the Los Angeles Kings. Glenn Anderson inexplicably took an ill-advised, unnecessary, selfish penalty late in the third period that gave the Kings a power play to begin overtime. He had won five Stanley Cups with the Edmonton Oilers and would win one more with the New York Rangers the next year, but that moment remains a play that in no way resonates as one from a Stanley Cup champion.

Then came overtime. We weren't feeling quite as confident as we had been in the second intermission, but who knew? Anything can happen in overtime, and the Leafs had more often than not been the victors in overtime sessions that fabulous spring run. Would we be flying home that night or heading back to the hotel for a flight the next morning, to prepare for a seventh and deciding game? It didn't take us that long to find out. Glenn Anderson wouldn't even be out of the penalty box yet when the game ended. But before the Wayne Gretzky overtime winner on a power play came the Gretzky overtime high stick.

Even watching the game closely from a good vantage point, it was unclear at first what had happened. Gilmour was obviously agitated, but it was unclear why. When it became apparent that Gilmour had been cut, the controversy heated up. Kerry Fraser hadn't seen the play—watching him closely, that was obvious. He looked to his linesmen for help—maybe they had seen what caused the Gilmour cut. If one of them had—and I do think one had—he was reluctant to make that kind of call against that kind of player (Gretzky) in that kind of scenario: a Leafs power play goal on a Gretzky-less King team trying to kill a five-minute major would have eliminated them from the playoffs. If anyone was to be taken to task, it should have been the linesmen who, I have to believe, must have seen enough of the play.

Later, as I watched the television replay back at home, it was apparent that the *Hockey Night in Canada* broadcast wasn't making that big a deal of it. Neither Bob Cole nor Harry Neale was sure of what they had seen. The replays were telling more of the story after the fact. It wasn't a dirty play by Wayne Gretzky, but it was a play that warranted a five-minute major or at least a double minor for being careless with his stick. If one of the linesmen had seen the play, he couldn't make a call for a minor or a double minor. He could only make the call for a high-sticking major penalty to Wayne Gretzky and have him kicked out of the game. That would have been a huge call for a linesman to make.

When Wayne Gretzky, who shouldn't have been on the ice in the first place, scored the overtime marker a few minutes later, it only added to what would be a nightmare for Kerry Fraser. Who scored and when he scored added to the injustice against the Toronto Maple Leafs.

I do know after many conversations with Leafs fans who stayed awake through the early morning hours back in Toronto that they were incensed by the missed call but were willing to put it on the backburner in the hopes that it would become incidental once the Leafs won Game 7 on May 29 at Maple Leaf Gardens. Though Kerry Fraser isn't supposed to cheer for any particular NHL team, you have to think that he is quite aware how different his legacy would be if the Leafs had won that next playoff game.

Two nights later, at Maple Leaf Gardens, Wayne Gretzky was the story again. Although this time there was no controversy, there was one question when the game began: Would this be the best game Wayne Gretzky ever played at Maple Leaf Gardens? Gretzky quickly confirmed that it was. He had played many memorable games in every NHL venue, many at Maple Leaf Gardens, and he picked the most important playoff game he ever played there to play his absolute best.

So there were many factors contributing to how that series played out, from the disbelief over how good things were during the second intermission in Game 6 to the defeated Leafs shaking hands with the victorious Kings after Game 7. It was a one-referee system, and Kerry Fraser didn't screw up, he just didn't see the infraction—Wayne Gretzky has always said that he was motivated for that seventh game by a bellman at the hotel where the Kings were staying. As he was leaving for the arena late that Saturday afternoon, the bellman remarked on the massive drubbing the Kings were about to take at the hands of his beloved Leafs. Gretzky actually had had, for him, a rather ordinary series over the past six games. He was the story in the seventh game.

So maybe Leafs fans should lay some of the blame on Fraser's fellow officials—and on the bellman at a downtown Toronto hotel, with his ill-advised comments.

4 GOOD TRADES AND BAD TRADES

Just as with the Leafs and their trades, other teams have had their
share of ups and downs. Sometimes trades that seem a good idea at
the time inadvertently give your opponents an edge. Here are some
that I remember—they may be ones some coaches and scouts prefer
to forget . . . and a few that didn't happen!

The one, and really the only, benefit of coming at or near the
bottom of the NHL overall regular-season standings is the
opportunity to select in the first and second rounds of draft
choices players who are the budding stars for the NHL, and
quite possibly superstars. The loss of that opportunity is what
has made missing the playoffs in 2009–10 and 2010–11, along
with the Leafs' first-round pick in 2010 and 2011 being traded
to the Boston Bruins in exchange for Phil Kessel, for Toronto
Maple Leafs fans an even more bitter bill to swallow.

Look at the quality names that have been selected with
one of the top two choices this past decade: Rick DiPietro,

Dany Heatley, Ilya Kovalchuk, Jason Spezza, Rick Nash, Kari Lehtonen, Marc-Andre Fleury, Eric Staal, Alex Ovechkin, Evgeni Malkin, Sidney Crosby, Bobby Ryan, Erik Johnson, Jordan Staal, Patrick Kane, James van Riemsdyk, Steve Stamkos, Drew Doughty, John Tavares, Victor Hedman, Taylor Hall, and Tyler Seguin.

The 1983 NHL Entry Draft provided just such an opportunity for the Minnesota North Stars and the Hartford Whalers, the teams making the first two selections that year. For the North Stars, who finished seventh out of 21 teams in the regular season, it would be a case of adding to the depth of their talent—they had moved up in the draft by trading with the Pittsburgh Penguins their first-round picks for the North Stars' 15th overall choice. These types of short-sighted trades helped to explain why a year later the Penguins would be on the verge of having to relocate (the rumour at the time was to Hamilton, Ontario). Fortunately, though having made some questionable trades, they didn't trade their first-round pick for the 1984 Entry Draft and were ultimately blessed with a true superstar, Mario Lemieux.

After the North Stars made their first choice, the Hartford Whalers selected second overall based on merit. They had accumulated just 45 points in the 80-game season, the same as the Penguins, but with 18 wins to the Whalers' 19 wins, the Penguins went first.

After a 96-point regular season, the North Stars looked to add to their youthful squad and selected Brian Lawton from Mount St. Charles Academy, the first high school player to be chosen first overall in the NHL.

The Hartford Whalers looked to add firepower as well, and selected Sylvain Turgeon from the Hull Olympiques, of the

Quebec Major Junior Hockey League, who had recorded 54 goals and 163 points in his final junior season.

With the benefit of 20/20 hindsight, it is now apparent that Lawton had only a modest NHL career, whereas Turgeon proved to be a decent NHL player. Lawton actually made more of an imprint on the National Hockey League off the ice as a player agent and later as the general manager of the Tampa Bay Lightning. His Mt. St. Charles high school team had played a 26-game schedule, and the rigours of the direct jump to an 80-game schedule in the NHL were too significant for the player. His top scoring season in his nine-year NHL career was 21 goals and 44 points.

Turgeon, on the other hand, continued his scoring prowess and enjoyed his best three years in the NHL in his first three seasons with the Whalers, scoring 40, 31, and 46 goals those years. His play tapered off and he struggled with injuries, and he had more of a journeyman career for his final nine NHL seasons.

The real story of the 1983 draft lies with the next two selections. What if the North Stars and the Whalers had selected one of the third- and fourth-overall choices made that year? The third spot went to the New York Islanders, who drafted Pat LaFontaine from Verdun, in the Quebec Major Junior Hockey League. The Detroit Red Wings followed, selecting Steve Yzerman from Peterborough, of the Ontario Hockey League. LaFontaine and Yzerman both went on to have illustrious Hall of Fame careers. How might the destinies of the North Stars and the Whalers have been different if they had chosen LaFontaine and Yzerman respectively? Would Minnesota have had to move to Dallas in 1993, and would Hartford have shifted to Carolina in 1997?

One star player doesn't necessarily save a franchise. However, if he leads to more wins on the ice, that can generate more support off the ice and possibly eliminate the need to move. Look what Mario Lemieux did for Pittsburgh when he was selected first overall in 1984. Wayne Gretzky rejuvenated the Los Angeles Kings in 1988, and Alexander Ovechkin has turned Washington from an average hockey city into a passionate hockey city.

Mario Lemieux, though, remains the most prominent case in point. Without his presence, there is no question that there would have been no future for the Penguins in Pittsburgh. Pat LaFontaine in Minnesota and Steve Yzerman in Hartford changing the course of history for the North Stars and Whalers? One can only speculate.

As mentioned, it was a good thing that Pittsburgh didn't trade away their first-round draft choice in 1984. But one of the reasons they were so firmly entrenched at the bottom of the NHL standings was because of bad trades.

Even though they ultimately missed when they took Lawton first overall in 1983, how did the Minnesota North Stars have the first overall pick, one that originally belonged to the Pittsburgh Penguins? What kind of trade had been made to give the North Stars that kind of windfall?

Unbelievably, the Penguins made a trade with the North Stars at the start of the 1982–83 season whereby they sent George Ferguson and that first-round pick (which ended up being first overall) to Minnesota in exchange for Ron Meighan and Anders Hakansson.

Hakansson would record just 21 points (9 goals, 12 assists) in 62 games in one, and only one, season with the Penguins. Meighan would play one season as an underage player with the Penguins on their blue line. He spent the following season in the American Hockey League and then the next year he was out of hockey altogether, at the age of 21.

The history lesson for NHL general managers begins just after the NHL expanded from 6 to 12 teams in 1967. Montreal Canadiens general manager Sam Pollock was an excellent evaluator of talent, and shrewd and successful at making trades to help Montreal. Through his trades and pursuit of first-round selections, his Montreal Canadiens team had 23 first-round picks over a nine-year period in the 1970s, including four first-round selections in the 1974 draft.

This first lesson, that of being leery to trade your own first-round pick, came when Pollock took advantage of the lack of experience of the new California Seals management group and acquired its first-round pick in the 1971 Amateur Draft, parlaying that first overall pick into Guy Lafleur. Looking a year ahead on May 22, 1970, to the 1971 draft, and projecting his best chance to land a potential superstar like Lafleur, Pollock traded career minor leaguer Ernie Hicke and the Canadiens' first-round pick in 1970 (California selected Chris Oddleifson) to California for that 1971 first-round pick.

Patience and great foresight played into Sam Pollock's hands and Lafleur and the Canadiens soon won four consecutive Stanley Cups. Later Pollock switched professional sports with the same success. He headed the Board of Directors for the Toronto Blue Jays when they won their two World Series in 1992 and 1993.

Give the Pittsburgh Penguins credit for another trade that ultimately salvaged somewhat the trade away of their first pick in 1983. After less than one complete season in Pittsburgh, Anders Hakansson was traded to the Los Angeles Kings in September 1983. In return, the Penguins received a young player from Boston College who the Kings had just selected in the sixth round of the draft two months earlier. Obviously, a Penguins scout had a good gut feeling about this prospect and encouraged Pittsburgh management to pursue him.

The player in question was Kevin Stevens. And even though he continued to play at Boston College and wouldn't play for the Penguins until four years later, he more than made up for the trade of the first-round pick: in his first five full seasons with the Penguins, Stevens averaged 43 goals and 96 points per season.

More importantly, Stevens provided important depth and scoring balance beyond Mario Lemieux that helped take the Penguins to consecutive Stanley Cup victories in 1991 and 1992. In 1991, he was the leading playoff goal scorer, with 17 goals in 21 playoff games.

The Islanders selected third overall because of a trade they made almost two years earlier. Bill MacMillan, the general manager of the Colorado Rockies, hoped his team would no longer be near the NHL standings basement two years down the road when he sent his first-round 1983 Entry Draft selection to the New York Islanders in exchange for centre Dave Cameron and defenceman Bob Lorimer.

Two years later, not only was MacMillan's vision inaccurate but his Rockies were now the New Jersey Devils and he had been replaced by Max McNab. Thus, the Islanders landed superstar Pat LaFontaine for two very journeyman players. LaFontaine's NHL career lasted 15 seasons, and he felt he still had more to accomplish when he was forced to retire in 1998 at the age of 33 thanks to the effects of a few serious concussions he had suffered. He had made the milestone of 1,000 career NHL points with 1,013 (468 goals, 545 assists) in 865 career regular-season games. He had two seasons where he scored 50 or more goals and an additional five seasons where he scored 40 or more goals. He was inducted into the Hockey Hall of Fame in 2003.

Years later, Dave Cameron achieved more success off the ice coaching the St. Michael's Majors in the Ontario Hockey League than he did playing in the NHL. He was the head coach of Team Canada at the 2011 World Juniors in Buffalo when they, unfortunately, suffered a third-period collapse in the gold medal game against Russia. He is now back in the NHL as an assistant coach for the Ottawa Senators.

Even though they had traded their own first-round pick, the third overall selection, Bill MacMillan and the New Jersey Devils had another first-round pick in the 1983 Entry Draft, which they had acquired through another trade. At the draft in June 1982, MacMillan had traded defenceman Rob Ramage to the St. Louis Blues for their first-round selections in 1982 and 1983. They had used that pick in 1982 to select Rocky Trottier from Nanaimo. They had the sixth overall selection in 1983 with the Blues' pick.

After watching the Islanders use the Devils' pick to draft Pat LaFontaine, the Devils made out pretty well themselves three picks later with their selection acquired from St. Louis: John MacLean from the Oshawa Generals. MacLean would become a New Jersey Devil for the majority of his playing career and beyond: as an excellent player on the ice for 15 seasons as a Devil, a significant cog in their Stanley Cup championships, and, later, part of their excellent player-development system off the ice. He was replaced as the head coach of the Devils by the return of Jacques Lemaire in December 2010.

The Ramage trade is part of one of the long-held myths about the St. Louis Blues and the 1983 Entry Draft. This was the summer that the Blues' owner, Ralston Purina, was in a hotly contested backroom battle with the NHL League office and the board of governors. Though hard to believe nowadays, the pet food corporate giant was looking to sell the St. Louis Blues but finding no takers.

The most interest generated was from the legendary Western Hockey League owner and operator "Wild Bill" Hunter. He spearheaded a much-publicized attempt to purchase the St. Louis Blues and move them to Saskatoon. Whether he did or didn't have the financial backing became a moot point when the National Hockey League powers put a stop to the notion of any such move.

In a game of corporate brinkmanship, Ralston Purina, the owner in limbo, used the 1983 Entry Draft to make its own public statement, announcing it would not be participating in the draft and would forego making any draft selections whatsoever. The NHL head office tried to figure out what was the appropriate course to take. One idea was to have the NHL Central Scouting Bureau make the selection based on who they had rated the top player when it was the Blues' turn to pick.

Ultimately, the league opted to just let the Blues' owner's plan run its course. An empty St. Louis Blues table was a stark contrast to the energy and buzz at the 20 other draft tables. The Blues' full-time scouts Ted Hampson and Jack Evans sat among the general public in the stands at the Montreal Forum, a low day in their professional lives. Each time the Blues were to make a selection and no team representative answered the call, Brian O'Neill would just say that they forfeited their pick.

The Toronto Maple Leafs' draft table was beside the empty St. Louis Blues' table. It was a strange sight, never seen before or since at an NHL Draft—like a neighbourhood of prime real estate in downtown Toronto or New York City with that one mysteriously empty lot. And, like squatters taking possession of an abandoned house, low-level front office staff were opportunists, ready to "loot" that lonely, abandoned table.

It has always been considered quite an opportunity for those on the periphery of an NHL front office to be one of the chosen few to sit at a draft table. At that time, each NHL team was assigned a set number of chairs, and it was up to the team to decide how to use them. That didn't present much of a problem to the Leafs, since Ballard had kept our organization pretty lean; however, I knew of teams where noses would be out of joint at not being able to sit at the draft table. Now, some of those front office personnel had found a way to get themselves to the draft table—the 20 or so chairs that were at the Blues' table were quickly snatched up and squeezed in at various team tables.

Later that summer, entrepreneur Harry Ornest purchased the Blues hockey team and their arena in St. Louis for the bargain-basement price of $6 million. With a new general manager in Ron Caron and new coach in Jacques Demers, the Blues made great strides on the ice. Ornest would ultimately cash in millions of dollars off the ice when he sold the Blues to Michael Shanahan in 1986 for $38 million. This kind of scenario helps explain why NHL commissioner Gary Bettman remains supportive of poor hockey markets like Phoenix and Atlanta, while cities like Winnipeg and Quebec City were long denied an NHL team. Winnipeg finally landed an NHL team for the second time in 2011 with the Atlanta Thrashers moving to Winnipeg.

It was often pointed out how much the Blues had improved even without the benefit of draft picks from that 1983 draft. What is both overlooked and significant is that the Blues had already traded away their first-round and second round selections anyway, the two most valuable picks in any draft.

The first-round pick that New Jersey used to select John MacLean had landed the Blues Rob Ramage. As well, they had traded their 1983 second-round pick to the Montreal Canadiens in exchange for Guy Lapointe, who played a little over a year on the Blues' blue line. Montreal used that selection to draft Sergio Momesso.

So while it is true that the Blues forfeited the opportunity to add further players via the draft from the third round onward, it's important to remember that they did get value for their selections from the first two rounds.

The NHL Drafts remain a special memory from my time working for the Toronto Maple Leafs and New York Rangers. Years later, we all reflect on the draft selections who made it to the NHL and those who didn't. It seems that cut and dried.

The actual day is like one giant hockey party. The previous season is in the rear-view mirror and the future seems bright for each team as they add prospect after prospect. Often the ownership group loves being able to briefly play the role of a hockey executive as they get to sit in on something that is priceless in the world of sports fantasies. Everyone wants feel and be perceived as a "somebody" when it comes to how a professional sports team is operated.

It is the greatest day to date for the young players who are drafted and one of the greatest days for their families. I really enjoyed and remember fondly meeting the parents of the young men who are selected. It is the culmination of so many hopes and dreams.

It is the only time of the year that all hockey executives are in one venue. Catching up with friends and acquaintances on other teams is valuable personal and professional time spent well. There is a vibe and an energy in the entire building as the spectators share being on the front line with their particular favourite NHL teams as they hopefully add another star player or two and make significant progress on their Stanley Cup journey.

If a trade is made during the draft, a loud gasp and murmer immediately permeates through the crowd as soon as NHL Commissioner Gary Bettman utters those four words from the central podium, "We have a trade." All of the other 28 NHL Draft tables momentarily stop what they are discussing to hear the details. The crowd reacts vocally, the NHL executives all offer immediate assessments to each other, there is no shortage of head shaking or nodding!

As great as that energy and feeling is . . . it begins to fade in a large way as the draft enters the later rounds. After the first three rounds, many of the young players aren't in attendance and the crowd is down to about half capacity and another thousand or so will leave after each round. It has the feeling more of a political convention waiting for votes to be tabulated.

Those first few rounds remain a favourite memory. It is not just about those who are drafted. It is all about people . . . the drafted players, their families, the NHL family, and the thousands of fans who love NHL hockey.

When you're hot, you're hot! Seems to happen in all walks of life and certainly in the world of hockey, both on and off the ice.

In Cliff Fletcher's first two years as Leafs general manager, from 1992 to 1994, he seemingly could do no wrong. Whatever trades or roster moves he made, he batted 1,000 in those first two seasons. The jewel of all his trades was, of course, swung with his old team, the Calgary Flames: Doug Gilmour, Jamie Macoun, Rick Wamsley, Ric Nattress, and Kent Manderville to Toronto in exchange for Gary Leeman, Craig Berube, Alexander Godynyuk, Jeff Reese, and Michel Petit.

It was a trade that started small and grew in many directions. Cliff Fletcher in Toronto and Doug Risebrough in Calgary were like two master chefs adding and subtracting ingredients as they created their crowning dish. The initial talks had fewer players involved than the final number of 10 who switched franchises. Not only were names added and subtracted between Toronto and Calgary but the Hartford Whalers came close to completing a trade with Calgary that would have landed Doug Gilmour in Hartford.

The final trade certainly worked overwhelmingly in favour of Fletcher and the Toronto Maple Leafs. Even the one last-minute modification made at the request of his trading partners worked in his favour: Bob Rouse was to have been included in the Leafs package of five players heading to Calgary. At the eleventh hour, however, the Flames requested that Michel Petit be included rather than Rouse.

Rouse played a significant role on the Leafs defence those next few seasons, far beyond what it is likely Petit would have contributed. Petit wasn't a bust in Calgary, but Rouse was a far better fit on the Leafs' blue line. When you're hot, you're hot.

My first trade deadline day was in March 1981. Up until a year earlier, it had not been that big a deal, but things had changed with the first significant trade deadline deal that had had a tangible result in the Stanley Cup playoffs.

The New York Islanders had traded former first overall pick Billy Harris and defenceman Dave Lewis to the Los Angeles Kings in exchange for centre Butch Goring. The Islanders had experienced too many playoff heartaches the previous few years, including being eliminated by the Toronto Maple Leafs in 1978. They hoped that Goring would provide the necessary ingredient to their team.

They hit the jackpot, as Goring proved a significant upgrade to their second line behind the powerhouse first line of Mike Bossy, Bryan Trottier, and Clark Gillies. He immediately added to the Islanders offence at a pace of about a point a game, with 11 points (6 goals, 5 assists) in the remaining 12 regular-season games and 19 points (7 goals, 12 assists) in 21 playoff games as the Islanders won the first of their four consecutive Stanley Cups. Goring was a part of all four Stanley Cup teams, and his second playoff as an Islander was even a smidge better offensively, with 20 points (10 goals, 10 assists) in 18 playoff games. He also won the Conn Smythe Trophy as the Most Valuable Player in the playoffs.

It wasn't just with his scoring and offensive abilities that Goring upgraded the Islanders team. With the addition of Butch Goring, Islanders coach Al Arbour began the practice of using two centres to take many of their faceoffs that weren't in the neutral zone. This meant Bryan Trottier could be more aggressive in attempting to win the draw. If the linesman ruled him too aggressive and threw him out of the faceoff circle, he was replaced by another natural centre and excellent faceoff player in Goring. This was an advantage for the Islanders that became even more important in the playoffs.

The year 1981 for all intents and purposes seemed to be the beginning of the modern-day trade deadline, which has become a media frenzy. The immediate impact of the addition of Goring to the Islanders a year earlier had team executives and fans more interested in trying to make a comparable last-second upgrade. But in 1981, there still existed a quirky deadline rule, one not standardized until a few years later. For the past two decades, the trade deadline has been 3 p.m. Eastern Standard Time for all NHL teams, but back in the early 1980s, it was still noon in whatever time zone the particular team was located. This meant that teams could continue to make trades past noon EST as long as it was still before noon in the time zone of one of the trading partners.

We at the Leafs finalized a trade we had been discussing with the Montreal Canadiens well before noon Toronto time. Robert Picard was traded for goaltender Michel "Bunny" Larocque and a draft choice. The clock struck 12 p.m. and we seemed done. There had been nothing else brewing for the Leafs on the trade front, and we sat tight to see what calls might come in.

About a half hour later, Lou Nanne, the general manager of the Minnesota North Stars, called. He wanted to know if the Leafs had any interest in forward Ron Zanussi. He was very aware that Zanussi was represented by the Leafs' general manager's son, Brent Imlach. I don't know how much the blood-lines were a factor, but after a short discussion we traded a second-round pick to Minnesota for Ron Zanussi. For us, the time was 12:40 p.m. EST, but it was only 11:40 a.m. Central Time, the zone in which Nanne and the North Stars operated.

As the clock struck 1 p.m. in the east, it struck noon in the Central Time zone, meaning Nanne and his colleagues in Chicago and St. Louis had hit their deadline. The next hour saw many discussions with the Calgary Flames and Edmonton Oilers, as they were in their final hour. At 2 p.m. in the east, it was noon in Alberta—so they too were now out of the picture. Only the Vancouver Canucks and Los Angeles Kings remained open for business.

After having added a goaltender in Michel Larocque, Punch Imlach was anxious to try to move one of his existing goaltenders. At 2:40 EST, the Los Angeles Kings called Imlach back to acquire one of our surplus goaltenders. Goaltender Jim Rutherford (later the long-time president and general manager of the Carolina Hurricanes) was traded by the Leafs to the Los Angeles Kings, 20 minutes before the final deadline.

The non-standardized trade deadline made for some very unusual dynamics, and we in Toronto had made the most of them that year. The standardized deadline we have today makes much more sense, but I do have to say it was more fun with the chaos and variables, at least for me during my first real trade deadline experience.

Nowadays, player agents are an integral part of the business side of the game. Back in the 1980s, however, they were tolerated as a necessity but were told to keep their noses out of team business.

That's why I have to give the late Norm Caplan credit for helping to increase their influence. In the early 1980s, he and Bill Watters were the player agents for most of the Toronto Maple Leafs players. Despite being the two most influential agents to Leafs players at the time, Caplan and Watters were anything but a partnership and were actually fierce competitors in a very tough and at times unsavoury business.

As part of an agent's duties, he would occasionally contact a general manager to air any grievances or problems his player might have. Norm Caplan called Leafs general manager Gerry McNamara late in the morning of January 11, 1983. His client, Bunny Larocque, was unhappy that he hadn't evolved into the first-string goaltender in Toronto as had been assumed when they had traded for him on March 10, 1981.

Caplan's grievances on behalf of his client gave McNamara, a former goaltender himself, a chance to vent his displeasure at how Larocque's skill in playing backup to Ken Dryden in Montreal had not transformed into him being a legitimate number one goaltender. It was a classic plight of a losing team: Larocque blamed the Leafs for the way he had been handled, while the Leafs felt Larocque's abilities were far less than they had envisioned.

Rather than engage McNamara in an argument, Caplan listened. McNamara expected their argument to escalate. Instead, Caplan offered his services as a problem solver. He asked McNamara if it would be okay for him to shop Larocque with other NHL general managers, since it wasn't working out for him in Toronto. McNamara was a bit taken aback by Caplan's surprising but constructive proposal, but agreed, figuring he had nothing to lose.

An hour later, Caplan called back. Would McNamara trade Bunny Larocque to Philadelphia in exchange for goaltender Rick St. Croix? McNamara said he would. "Then call Keith Allen in Philadelphia; he's expecting your call," Caplan told the Leafs general manager. And so Caplan took care of two of his unhappy clients while also helping two NHL general managers move forward in situations that weren't working out.

Although the Leafs "won" this particular deal, it is somewhat hollow, as neither goaltender thrived in their new environment. St. Croix played in 47 games over parts of the next three seasons for the Leafs, with a goals-against-average around a very high 5.00. Bunny Larocque played in only two games for the Philadelphia Flyers and, later, in five games for the St. Louis Blues, with a goals-against-average near 6.00 in those seven appearances. Both were soon sent to the minor leagues. Larocque retired from hockey in 1985, and St. Croix followed him a year later, in 1986.

The role of the player agent has evolved with the big money and big business that the National Hockey League has grown into. They interact much more often with team management. But in 1983, Caplan, well on the road to establishing himself as the top player agent in professional hockey, was something of an innovator.

I can still remember vividly that late August day in 1984. Sandy McPhie, the Leafs administrative assistant, came into my office, her face ashen. "Norm Caplan just dropped dead of a heart attack while he was vacationing in Paris with his family" was her shocking announcement. He was only 41 years old.

Caplan was finding time for a family vacation after another successful summer negotiating contracts for his existing clients and recruiting some of the top junior players. That included Wendel Clark of the Saskatoon Blades, who would be the first overall pick that following June. Clark had been a client of Caplan's for only a few weeks when he found himself needing a new agent. Newcomers like Don Meehan, who Clark ended up hiring, and established agents like Bill Watters and Rick Curran, all grew their client list because of Caplan's untimely death.

Not only had Caplan been successful in recruiting new players, he had also been successful in luring NHL players to his stable of clients and away from other agents. Although this poaching is understood to be part of the business, it was still viewed as distasteful. Most agents at that time feared that a client would be poached by Caplan. As one player agent told me a few years later with questionable humour but the utmost respect, "Whenever I went to Montreal [Norm Caplan's hometown] for a few years after he died, I checked to make sure his tombstone was still there."

Anyone ever associated with Norm Caplan had no doubt he would have been as big a player as there is in the agent business if it weren't for his unexpected death.

The passing of the torch is important to a team maintaining its excellence on the ice. Bill Torrey will acknowledge he grew too sentimental about the veteran corps that won his four consecutive Stanley Cup championships in the early 1980s. Rather than get something of value for the likes of Denis Potvin, Bryan Trottier, Clark Gillies, Mike Bossy, and company when they were still close to their prime, the Islanders had plummeted to the bottom of the NHL standings by the end of the decade. In the end they got next to nothing in return for Trottier, and had others like Bossy end their careers early because of injuries.

Nobody was as popular or held in as high regard as Kent Nilsson was during his six-year run with the Calgary Flames (the first year was in Atlanta before the team moved to Calgary), after two successful seasons with the Winnipeg Jets in the World Hockey Association. After averaging 38 goals and 94 points over his six seasons with the Flames, Nilsson was traded to the Minnesota North Stars in 1985. The Flames were an emerging power in the NHL and Nilsson was facing more competition at centre. His scoring had dropped dramatically in the playoffs, with just 4 goals in 33 career playoff games with the Flames. Cliff Fletcher was able to secure two second-round draft choices from the North Stars in return for Nilsson.

The first of these second-round picks was used to draft Joe Nieuwendyk from Cornell University in 1985. Nieuwendyk would provide a youthful version of what Nilsson had provided, but with more playoff success. In seven full seasons with the Flames, Nieuwendyk averaged 41 goals and 94 points. In the playoffs he averaged nearly a point per game—60 points (32 goals, 28 assists) in 66 games—and was a key cog in the Flames' Stanley Cup victory in 1989.

When, as with Nilsson in 1985, Nieuwendyk's scoring dropped significantly in the 1995 playoffs, the Flames were again able to get full value in return. Nieuwendyk was traded to the Dallas Stars for a young player named Jarome Iginla whom they had selected as their first-round pick from the Kamloops Blazers six months earlier.

With his excellent play and strong character, Iginla quickly became the face of the Calgary Flames franchise both on and off the ice. All of Canada cheered as he aggressively made the key play in the U.S. offensive zone in overtime in the gold medal game at the 2010 Winter Olympics. He gained control of the puck and passed it to Sidney Crosby for the golden goal that secured a gold medal for Team Canada and ended the Olympics on an incredible high note for the host country.

The Dallas Stars received quality back in 1995, but they paid a steep price for it in the years that followed. Joe Nieuwendyk won his second Stanley Cup as a key player for the Stars when they won their first and only Stanley Cup to date, in 1999. Nieuwendyk is now the general manager of the Dallas Stars. Jarome Iginla joined the exclusive 1,000 regular-season NHL points club with Calgary in 2011. The thread and connection, through trades of Kent Nilsson to Joe Nieuwendyk to Jarome Iginla has stood for a star player in the Calgary Flames' line-up for over three decades.

5 THE GREATS OF THE GAME

Everyone has their heroes in the sport. Let me tell you about those whom I admired most over my career. It is the people who make the game great!

The NHL was finally back underway in August 2005 after a much-anticipated lockout resulted in the National Hockey League earning the dubious distinction of being the first North American professional sports league to shut down for an entire season due to a player-owner conflict.

The NHL Entry Draft being held in Ottawa was the first tangible sign that we were getting back to business as usual. It was a splendid environment in which to catch up with all those in the hockey world after a year of idleness, slashed salaries, sacrifice, and bitter feelings—things not normally associated with the game. And it was refreshing to not have labour issues top of mind when discussing the state of the game, as had been the case for a number of years previously.

It was a few days to enjoy reconnecting with friends in hockey and looking forward, rather than dwelling on the recent past. An hour or so before the draft began, I ran into Colin Campbell, the senior vice-president of operations for the National Hockey League. We chatted for a bit about hockey and the people in the game, and then our talk turned to that of one of the all-time greats. As we reminisced about our mutual friend, Roger Neilson, Campbell pulled his personal phone directory out of his pocket. "I update my directory every year," he said, "but I still can't erase Roger's name." Neilson had passed away more than two years earlier.

Campbell had played junior hockey with the Peterborough Petes, with Neilson as his coach. Neilson remained one of Campbell's closest friends, even though they rarely worked together after their junior hockey connection.

I was fortunate to have worked with Roger Neilson on two occasions: during his two years as head coach of the Toronto Maple Leafs, and with the New York Rangers in August 1989. When he assumed the Leafs job in 1977, Neilson was considered a bit of a coaching revolutionary. Nicknamed "Captain Video," he implemented modern technology at a franchise that was as old school as they came in the NHL. His methods and style were never embraced by Harold Ballard, but that didn't dissuade Neilson from doing things his way. Working with him at the Leafs taught me to be true to what you believe in.

What Ballard did like was that Neilson brought instant success in the NHL standings that first year of his with the Leafs. He was a one-man show. After each game, Neilson replayed the video and had a statistical report and analysis of the game completed, photocopied, and at each player's stall by the time they reported for practice the next morning. For most of the road games, Neilson would begin the task in the wee hours of the morning after returning to Toronto. The few longer trips to the West Coast, the team would return the next day. When I chatted with him a number of years later, he smiled as he recalled the antiquated video equipment of the time.

No pro scouts employed by the Toronto Maple Leafs? No problem for Neilson; he simply quietly added that task to his professional portfolio. On occasion, he would be out of town on a Friday night to scout the Leafs' opponent of the next evening. That team would fly charter to Toronto after their game, while Neilson flew home on a regular commercial flight the next morning. On one occasion when he encountered weather problems trying to get back, Leafs assistant general manager Johnny McLellan just grinned and shook his head, and kidded about Neilson missing a game because of his scouting ambitions and his focus on being prepared.

After his Leafs experience, Neilson was a coach with the Buffalo Sabres, Vancouver Canucks, and Los Angeles Kings. Each stop brought some degree of success for Neilson, particularly leading the underdog Vancouver Canucks to the Stanley Cup Final in 1982. After being let go by the Los Angeles Kings in 1984, his head coaching career took a five-year break.

He spent those years as an analyst for TSN and working as a pro scout with the Chicago Blackhawks, assisting their coaching staff from time to time. One of my vivid memories of working for the Maple Leafs was the year I was general manager. We got clobbered in Detroit by the Red Wings, 8–1. Neilson's final line on TSN that night was, "Playing the Leafs is like eating Chinese food . . . two hours later you want to play them again." Though I could have done without the humour, I had to smile, as I knew Neilson had not an ounce of malice or any hidden agenda.

Those years, Roger Neilson was a frequent visitor to the Leafs press box in downtown Toronto and to our American Hockey League games in Newmarket, about a 45-minute drive north of Toronto. Neilson drove to all our Gardens games in his pickup truck with his dog, Mike. Mike looked like a German shepherd, but I know he was more of a mutt. The passenger window was left open so that Mike was free to come and go as he pleased, wandering downtown Toronto or the less congested Newmarket while Neilson took in the game. The odd time Mike hadn't returned when Neilson returned to his truck, Neilson would simply wait, catching up on some notes or reading. Mike always did return not long after.

When we worked together in New York, I once got a ride with Neilson to our practice facility in Rye. En route, Neilson kept pointing things out to me—"Look at those trees," he would say, or "Look at that deer at the side of the road." Finally, I asked him what he was doing. He told me that he was so used to travelling with and talking to his faithful companion, Mike, that he instinctively pointed out these things even when it was a human being in the car with him.

Neilson loved his summers in the Peterborough area, and he was a lifelong big kid. He never lost his love and enthusiasm for summer hockey camps, summer activities, and the enjoyable life for those treasured few months off. He told me that it always took him a week or so to adjust to the adult world when he returned to the rigours and reality of an NHL training camp.

In the summer of 1989, I was struggling during what ended up being my last few weeks as general manager in Toronto—struggling with my ailing owner and me not being on the same page about how to upgrade the organization, as well as with a new head coach. I would have loved the opportunity to bring a couple of top talent evaluators into the fold. Neilson would have been perfect for the job, but I knew that he was a non-starter as far as the Leafs owner was concerned.

One August morning I received a phone call in my office. It was Neilson, who had read about one of Ballard's tirades in the local papers and was calling to offer his support and encouragement—he had been on the receiving end of very public Ballard rebukes on many occasions. It was wonderful to hear from my good friend. I was unaware that when he called, Neilson had been on his way to meet with the New York Rangers brass about a vacant coaching position. He was hired for that position, and two days later I left the Leafs to join Neil Smith as his assistant general manager of the New York Rangers.

Neilson landing the job was another example of his persistence and belief in his own abilities. Scotty Bowman and Herb Brooks had both publicly turned down offers from Neil Smith to be head coach. And although Neilson had not been on the initial shortlist for the position, he persevered: he had no problem that some might perceive the Rangers as having settled for someone other than their first choice.

Neilson was probably the ideal choice for that particular Rangers team, and he would do what he was best at in his first year there: implement a system and a structure that resulted in a vast improvement in the standings. The Rangers finished first in the Patrick Division, their first first-place finish since 1942.

While I really enjoyed the experience and working with a few top-notch people like Neilson, my working relationship with Neil Smith wasn't ideal and I was fired at the end of the season. Neilson's supportive phone call included his line, "Look, I've been fired three times in one year; you've got a long way to go to catch up to me." He had been fired by Vancouver in the early part of the 1983–84 season, then coached the Los Angeles Kings for the rest of the regular season, was fired again, and then played a low-profile role with the Edmonton Oilers in the playoffs. His sole purpose was to analyze the opposing New York Islanders for an Oilers team that had been eliminated handily by the Islanders the previous year. As always, Neilson did his job well, and the Oilers won their first of five Stanley Cups that spring of Neilson's part-time assignment.

Neilson left the Leafs in 1979, and the next year I was pleasantly surprised to receive my first Roger Neilson Christmas card, a Buffalo Sabres team card, reflecting his new employer. From then on, I was one of thousands who received his annual Christmas wishes. As Neilson changed jobs—his coaching career ranged across a variety of NHL teams—his cards reflected that. He always included a handwritten note: that year with the Rangers, I witnessed first-hand how every spare moment in November and early December Neilson was busy writing personal notes on thousands of Christmas cards. In the mid-1980s, card recipients noticed a change in the tone of his cards as Neilson embraced Christianity and included a verse from the Bible.

I continued receiving the annual Christmas card even after being fired from the Rangers. Until one year, a number of years later, I didn't receive a card. Months later, when I saw Neilson, I kidded him that I must have dropped to his B list or even his C list, since I hadn't received a card.

That next December, the distinctive handwriting brought another Neilson classic. "You are definitely an A-list friend," read his note. Neilson had thousands of A-list friends. He never changed at all as the game evolved to be more corporate focused and less about people. Like his first year with the Leafs under Harold Ballard, he remained true to what he was and what he believed in.

I miss the Christmas card. I miss him. Hockey will always miss him.

Steve Yzerman is a person who I'm sorry to say I don't know personally. The only occasion that I worked with him was when I was hosting Hockey Hall of Fame Induction events. Yzerman was part of a remarkable group in November 2009 being inducted into the Hall. Brian Leetch, Luc Robitaille, Brett Hull, and Lou Lamoriello rounded out as impressive a fivesome that could be in one Induction "class."

Hull and Robitaille were easily the most outgoing and out-wardly fun-loving of the group. Although Leetch appears to have a serious demeanour and Lamoriello is perceived as being all business, they both were relaxed and enjoying the weekend. If Steve Yzerman was, he didn't really show it. It was a weekend to celebrate, but it was also a time of the other big challenge in Yzerman's career: he was the general manager of the Canadian Olympic men's hockey team headed to Vancouver in 2010.

Yzerman was taking his position and duties very seriously. Team Canada was looking to avenge finishing out of the medals in 2006 and felt even more pressure given that these Olympics were to be held on home soil. When Team Canada won their previous gold medal in 2002 in Salt Lake City, Yzerman played despite an injury that ultimately meant missing the rest of his NHL regular season with Detroit. Talk about true Olympic spirit. We all now realize that he selected a team that was able to win gold in Vancouver in 2010.

I am always struck by how young and youthful Yzerman looks, far younger than his 46 years. He looks the same as he did when I saw him at the Memorial Cup in Portland in 1983. His agent at the time, Gus Badali, took him there to enjoy the experience. We joked about Badali's and the 18-year-old Yzerman's "excellent adventure" as they played racquetball and did various other recreational activities throughout the week while enjoying the hockey experience.

Getting to know him from afar, I am even more impressed with the Hall of Fame person he is. For me, his first words when interviewed on the ice by *Hockey Night in Canada* in 1998 after Detroit won the Stanley Cup epitomize what makes Yzerman a great of the game. "We sure miss Grapes being here," he said— a touching tribute to Don Cherry, who had to miss much of that playoff because of the death of his beloved wife, Rose.

Although Yzerman missed much of the regular season after playing on Team Canada's gold medal squad in 2002, he was back in fine form for the playoffs and a big contributor to another Red Wings Stanley Cup. My wife, Lisa, was involved in a hockey instruction video shoot in late June, barely a week after the Stanley Cup win. Yzerman had agreed to participate in it. The money was ordinary for someone of his stature, but he was being loyal to the person who had found him some commercial opportunities years earlier—sports marketer Keith McIntyre. Yzerman wasn't now going to just turn his back on him.

The shoot was taking place in an arena in Mississauga, west of Toronto. As the day of the shoot dawned, the air was electric with excitement. Steve Yzerman was then the hottest NHL player, fresh from his Olympic gold and Stanley Cup victory. He could have easily cancelled the shoot and nobody would have dared argue with him. He had struggled with injuries and was scheduled of have off-season surgery.

A large car with Michigan plates pulled into the arena parking lot on schedule. Out stepped Steve Yzerman. No handlers or public relations people, no fuss. Just an unassuming-looking NHL superstar. For all any non–hockey fan would know, he was a parent coming to pick up his kid. Yzerman did an excellent job on-ice for the video, then took time to sign autographs and chat with the hundreds of fans who had shown up after hearing of his arrival. Job completed, he climbed back into his car and drove himself back to Detroit.

A good friend and colleague of mine, Christine Simpson, tells this story about the 2003 playoffs when the Detroit Red Wings were eliminated in the first round in a stunning upset by the Anaheim Ducks. She received a call from a friend in her hometown of London, Ontario. A young boy there was terminally ill; he was a big Red Wings fan, and Steve Yzerman was his absolute idol.

The Red Wings public relations staff arranged for the boy and his father to sit in a private box for the Red Wings' first game against Anaheim, giving them the VIP treatment, complete with souvenirs. Christine had asked whether the boy might meet Yzerman after the game. The staff said they would try to arrange it but naturally couldn't make any promises.

It was a difficult overtime loss at home for the Red Wings, and the players were exhausted and, of course, upset about the result. Christine, reporting for ESPN/ABC TV, was down in the dressing room area after the game. The boy and his father thanked her for her help and wanted to know if there was any chance of the boy meeting his idol. Christine told them that, given the circumstances, she thought it unlikely.

Just as the two visitors were leaving, Yzerman came strolling out of the dressing room and headed straight to his young admirer. He took his time chatting with the young boy, and signed the boy's Red Wings sweater—and got his teammates to do the same. Though the playoff game had been an important loss, Yzerman quickly put it in perspective, recognizing what was truly important.

When the young boy died, Christine Simpson received a call from his father, who explained how much that night had meant to the two of them and how it had brought some joy to their final months together.

"He'll never see the snow." I heard Pat Burns say this a number of times with a look of satisfaction, defiance, and redemption on his face during his first few years coaching the Toronto Maple Leafs. It was his go-to one-liner, meant to show that he never forgot how tenuous coaching a professional sports team could be. It was also part of his gospel in proving all those "bastards" wrong, whoever those bastards might be.

And what of the bastard who wrote the headline "He'll never see the snow" when Burns's Canadiens team got off to a slow start in his rookie season in 1988? Burns quickly proved that headline writer wrong and lived to see all seasons, all types of weather, and much success in his NHL coaching career.

Pat Burns and I followed similar career paths for a brief time in the late 1980s. When I was named general manager of the Newmarket Saints, our American Hockey League team in 1987, Burns was named the head coach of the Canadiens' AHL team in Sherbrooke around the same time. Andre Boudrias, the assistant general manager of the Canadiens, introduced me to Burns at a general AHL meeting that summer in Utica, New York.

Our careers accelerated rapidly after just one year in the AHL, when I was promoted to general manager of the Leafs, while Burns was tabbed as the head coach of the Canadiens. My Leafs team got off to a great start that season. Burns's team, however, struggled. That included a 6–2 win by "my" Leafs over "his" Montreal Canadiens right in the Forum on October 17, 1988. But his team soon got back on track, whereas the Leafs team fell off. From that point onward, our careers took divergent routes.

It was a stunning morning in June 1992 when Pat Burns appeared at a press conference in Montreal to announce he was stepping down as coach of the Montreal Canadiens. That afternoon he appeared at a press conference in Toronto to be announced as the new head coach of the Toronto Maple Leafs. Given today's strict sanctions for tampering with NHL employees of other teams, this wouldn't have been possible now, but back then, agent Don Meehan represented Burns in working out this arrangement with Serge Savard in Montreal and Cliff Fletcher in Toronto, both of whom had excellent working relationships with Meehan.

Almost immediately, Burns became the first larger-than-life personality for a Leafs coach since George "Punch" Imlach in the 1960s. He appeared an intriguing, gruff, and complicated person. He worked hard at that public persona, which he wanted to present to the hockey world and to the public at large.

In fact, he wasn't complicated and actually lived life quite simply. He wasn't intriguing as much as street-smart from his years as a police officer in Gatineau, Quebec. He appeared extremely confident, yet he could be insecure. His veneer as a tough guy was really used to test those in his world. If you backed down, Burns owned you. He appreciated if you stood up to him, and detested suck-ups but would use them to his benefit.

Revisionist history has us all remembering that Burns and his 1992–93 Leafs team were instant winners, that his coaching presence meant an immediate change in the Leafs team's fortunes on the ice. But the Leafs actually struggled for the better part of the first half of the season. Their record was an underwhelming 13-16-5 as they hit the new year in 1993, but 1993 remains their most successful calendar year in decades, possibly in team history. They had a record of 31-13-6 for the remainder of the 1992–93 season, had that memorable and successful run through three rounds in the 1993 playoffs, and opened the next season, 1993–94, with 10 straight victories, which set an NHL record for most wins beginning a regular season.

The players, Pat Burns, and Cliff Fletcher all deserve their share of credit for the turnaround. Fletcher did his best work in player trades in his first two years as Leafs general manager and made a number of moves, the most significant landing Dave Andreychuk in a trade from the Buffalo Sabres on February 2. The Leafs acquired Andreychuk, goaltender Daren Puppa, and a first-round pick (which was used to draft Kenny Jonsson) in exchange for Grant Fuhr and a fifth-round draft choice—a move bordering on grand larceny.

A less notable but underrated earlier move was Fletcher claiming Bill Berg on waivers from the New York Islanders on December 2. Though Burns would soon use Berg as part of an effective third line with Peter Zezel and Mark Osborne, his initial reaction was memorable. When asked on the day it occurred what he thought of claiming Berg, Burns replied, "I wouldn't know Bill Berg if I ran over him in my car." This reaction was significant in that it showed the extent to which Burns's personality was that of a larger-than-life coach. He wouldn't have said this about choices made by Serge Savard, his previous boss in Montreal, or, in later stops, with Harry Sinden in Boston or Lou Lamoriello in New Jersey—Burns understood and appreciated that they were the boss. Toronto remains that one stop where he could enjoy being larger than life! And, he enjoyed and relished every second of it.

That Burns said this doesn't reflect any weakness on Fletcher's part but that Burns saw the opportunity to let his personality with the public supersede that of his boss. That is why I think this was Burns's greatest coaching job and this Leafs team grew to assume the personality of their head coach. Toronto was the one stop where Burns could flex his muscles to be "the guy."

In a St. Louis sports bar the day before a game against the Blues, we were watching NFL football and a mid-game feature on Dallas Cowboys' head coach Jimmy Johnson. Burns turned to me and said, "That's exactly like me; that's who I am." I don't know if this was entirely accurate, but Toronto was the stop that seemed to allow Pat Burns to be as Jimmy Johnson was in Dallas. His TV car commercials in which he was dressed in a tux and conducting an orchestra were accurate depictions of Burns's role: he was the conductor of the Toronto Maple Leafs symphony.

One of his coaching challenges was to work out a resolution with defenceman Jamie Macoun, with whom he had battled the first half of the season, even making him a healthy scratch for a game in Detroit on December 22, 1992. When Burns realized that Macoun was the type of player who wasn't going to back down, he figured out more effective ways to use him. Soon, Macoun and Sylvain Lefebvre became the top defensive duo on the Leafs' blue line, always on the ice against the opposition's best scoring threat.

Burns made a point of embracing and getting the most out of his best players, Doug Gilmour in Toronto and later Ray Bourque in Boston. Often a coach who hasn't played NHL hockey himself tries to show NHL elite players how to do it his way. Burns allowed them to get the most out of *their* way. The two key overtime goals in the first round of the 1993 playoffs against Detroit were by Mike Foligno and Nikolai Borschevsky. Neither was a regular player on the top three lines, but Burns had the knack of having the right players on the ice at the right time.

His public confidence and ease with the media grew in comparison to what they had been in Montreal. During his first couple of seasons with the Leafs, Burns was truly bothered that legendary Montreal writer Red Fisher was angry and refused to talk to him. Fisher felt that he and Burns had an understanding and was holding a grudge because Burns exited from Montreal to Toronto in June 1992 without any advance notice. Despite many overtures from Burns, Fisher held his grudge for many years. I found it fascinating that this bothered Burns for such a long time, yet at the Leafs, he felt no pressure from or connection to the media. Instead, he was media savvy, best at promoting Pat Burns and using the media for the best interests of himself and his team.

Burns was fired in March 1996, midway through his fourth season with the Leafs. Actually, it was not so much a firing as a mutual parting of ways. Burns was anything but stupid. He could see the cash crisis that had enveloped the Leafs front office as Steve Stavro struggled to maintain control. The combination of Stavro feeling the cash crunch and Fletcher struggling to maintain his budget was hurting the hockey team—Pat Burns's hockey team. Burns had been a winner and he excelled in situations that gave him an opportunity to be a winner. Now, he could see that opportunity slipping away. He was fired while on the road with the Leafs in Denver, on March 3, 1996. He returned to Toronto with the team, keeping quiet about his new status. He collected his belongings in the early morning hours in the solitude of the Leafs dressing room. He wrote a note to the players on the dressing room chalkboard, wishing them good luck, and then he was gone, slipping out of town in the darkness of night.

As we all well know, he was anything but gone from the National Hockey League. Two more successful stops in Boston and New Jersey earned him another Coach of the Year award, in 1998 with Boston, to go with his awards from 1993 in Toronto and 1989 in Montreal, and ultimately the greatest of all rewards, the Stanley Cup victory with the New Jersey Devils in 2003. The beat cop from Gatineau had accomplished it all. He was truly one of the greatest coaches in NHL history.

And so "He'll never see the snow" turned out to be less an indictment of Burns's professional fate than a challenge that he never forgot and never backed down from. Even all those "bastards" came to respect what he had accomplished.

I sensed a set of piercing eyes watching me as I waited my turn to talk to the members of the assembled group of the Boston media who were covering the Boston Bruins' game-day morning skate at Maple Leaf Gardens. It was February 1978, and my role as a part-time employee with the Leafs had expanded about a month earlier. I was now in charge of compiling and publishing the press notes and statistics for all Leafs home games. This meant getting an early start in the Leafs office on the day of the game.

It also meant keeping up-to-date with the individual player statistics in an era of technology vastly inferior to what we have today. Individual player statistics were published by the NHL head office in Montreal just once a week, on Monday mornings. That meant I had to keep track of the Leafs individual player statistics and those of any visiting teams in Toronto that week via the Toronto newspaper summaries throughout the week. The Bruins had played the Friday night before against the Buffalo Sabres. The papers supplied all the information I needed from that game except one. The Bruins had changed goaltenders during the game and the papers didn't state when that had happened. Obviously, that was important for me to know in order to figure out the up-to-date individual statistics for the two Bruins goaltenders, Gerry Cheevers and Gilles Gilbert.

Realizing that the Bruins were having their morning skate, I headed down to the ice to get the information from a familiar face, perhaps the personable Nate Greenberg from the Bruins front office or beat writers Fran Rosa from the *Boston Globe* or Joe Giuliotti from the *Boston Herald-American*. They were all part of the small audience with the Bruins coach. I waited my turn, standing a few yards behind the small group but directly in the line of vision of Don Cherry.

Having got to know Don Cherry quite well—both his public side and his personal side—in the decades since then, I can understand how much he was enjoying that Saturday morning. He was the head coach of the Boston Bruins, on the ice overseeing their game-day skate, standing near the Bruins bench, holding court with the media at Maple Leaf Gardens. One can only imagine that this was the perfect environment for Cherry: he was living the perfect hockey dream, and nobody enjoyed it as much as he.

I've also come to learn that Cherry isn't a person who likes crowds, or feeling cornered or watched. His initial reaction can be one of suspicion and annoyance when someone he doesn't know invades his personal space. Long ago, he decreed that the set of *Coach's Corner* on CBC's *Hockey Night in Canada* be open to only a bare minimum of production personnel. If he feels the pressures of a large crowd, he finds an escape. At a morning skate, he and Ron MacLean will sit in the highest seat in a near-empty arena, away from everyone else. After a game, he doesn't go out with the boys; rather, he and MacLean retire to one of their rooms to order room service and watch and talk more hockey.

He is comfortable professionally with few people. His syndicated radio show, *Grapeline*, remains a success because of his relationship with co-host Brian Williams. Their producer, Prior Smith, a respected, long-time radio guy, is the engine behind the show, as he understands best how to use Cherry's skills and how to provide him with a comfortable working environment. Ron MacLean provides that as well with *Hockey Night in Canada*. Behind the scenes, there are production people like Kathy Broderick, Sherali Najak, and Brian Spear, who have earned his hard-won trust.

So I was an interloper that February morning. Cherry continued to hold court with the media but his piercing eyes remained fixed on me as I lingered just behind the group. Here he was having a nice conversation with a few people he was comfortable with and then I appeared, poking my nose where it wasn't welcome. My intrusion had taken him out of his comfort zone.

As the group dispersed, I didn't get a chance to ask anyone my question about the Bruins' game the night before. "What do you want? What are you hanging around for?" a gruff and displeased Cherry said to me. Though unnerved, I was able to muster a reply. "Mr. Cherry, my name is Gord Stellick and I just started working with the Leafs and I'm doing the press notes for tonight's game and I have one question I just want to ask one of the Boston writers about your game last night in Buffalo." His demeanour changed immediately as he realized I was not an enemy. "Well, why don't you ask me; I'm the coach of the team," the now friendly Cherry said, suddenly comfortable with me. I know that Cherry is a quick read and I would like to think a good judge of character. I think he quickly saw me as a non-threatening kid and not some kind of troublemaker.

I explained that I just needed to know when the Bruins had changed goaltenders the night before in Buffalo. Rather than a quick answer, Cherry was expansive. "Christ, I took

Gilly out after that third goal. I wasn't sure whether I should do it, but that was just a brutal goal and I wanted to give him some rest to use him tonight. So, that's what I did. Lot a good that did, as we got creamed by the Sabres anyway." I thanked him, we shook hands, and I turned to walk away. "Anything else, kid?" He was ready to be accommodating with any further questions I had. "No, that's all I need, thanks again." "Okay," he said with a smile, those piercing eyes now friendly and warm.

Don Cherry doesn't remember this story, but he has heard me tell it a few times and always enjoys it. That morning was a big thrill for me. What it showed about Cherry was his ability to make me feel like a somebody in the Leafs front office when, really, I was the lowest in the hierarchy. This is how Cherry connects with everyone on *Coach's Corner* and with the common hockey fan—it's his ability to make the little guy feel like the big guy, his sticking up for and supporting the little guy when he needs that support the most.

He has been a national presence on *Coach's Corner* for over 30 years, defying all the odds in sports broadcasting. I look at someone like Howard Cosell, who reached enormous heights of popularity in North America in the 1970s, but Cosell's act ran its course and his popularity waned in the 1980s. Don Cherry and *Coach's Corner* are still a must-watch on Saturday evenings during the first intermission of *Hockey Night in Canada*.

Cherry is predictable in much of what he has to say. He doesn't break any scoops nor does he pretend to. He is continuously and aggressively self-promoting. Incredibly, it all still works. That's because he retains that quality that resonated so strongly with me in our first meeting, the ability to connect to the ordinary person and the ordinary hockey fan.

Years later, in the spring of 1989, I was watching the play-offs as Leafs general manager. My struggles with the team's owner, Harold Ballard, were growing. My biggest problem was trying to convince Ballard that George Armstrong was no longer interested in coaching and that we had to hire a new coach. But Ballard was supportive of Armstrong and treated me like a young guy who was trying to squeeze out the old guy—Armstrong—when in fact that was anything but the truth. Compounding matters was that with each overture I attempted, I found myself slipping more and more out of favour with him, while Armstrong became more and more entrenched as the owner's coach.

Ballard made headlines decreeing that Armstrong was now the "head bottle washer" in the Leafs hierarchy and had sup-planted me. It was not a good day. It would be a tough few weeks and months before I finally left. For the playoff game between Montreal and Philadelphia, I was looking forward to just relaxing and spending a quiet night alone watching it. The television coverage began with the usual opening of Don Cherry and Ron MacLean going over what was going on in the hockey world. Cherry commented, "Gordie Stellick was get-ting a bit too big for his britches in trying to squeeze George Armstrong out as the coach of the Leafs . . . and now not only is George still the coach of the Leafs but he's Gordie's boss as well." That one hurt at a time when I had been striving not to take negative comments personally. Just as he had made me feel so important years earlier, he really cut me down to size with that remark. I've come to understand that I was now the "big guy" in Cherry's world and Armstrong, the admired for-mer Leafs captain, was the "little guy." Don Cherry was, once again, sticking up for the little guy.

But Cherry doesn't like hurting people. I found that out getting to know him as a broadcaster and on the few occasions that he was my co-host of the *Morning Show* at The Fan 590 radio. He is protective of his name, his shows, and his brand and will take issue with anyone who criticizes him. He's always up for a fight when he feels he is being attacked, yet it also bothers him to think he has said something that hurts someone.

That surprised me when we talked about it. He mentioned a few instances where he felt badly about what he had said about someone. One such person was Hardy Astrom, whom Cherry had made famous with his stories about his ineptness as a goaltender while Cherry was in Colorado. Cherry told me what a great person Astrom was and how he felt badly that Astrom had been depicted over the years, in large part because of Cherry's stories, as an inept goaltender. When I told him about his hurtful remark about me that he had made back in 1989, I was surprised how much it bothered him. During one or two of the show's breaks afterward, he said, "Geez, I feel terrible about that."

I would get the odd phone call from him when he took issue with something I had said or if he felt *Grapeline* wasn't being promoted enough on our show. I appreciated that he wouldn't speak about you behind your back but would tell you what he thought to your face. He was another guy who would respect you if you went back at him in an argument, as long as you respected what he had to say.

Then there was the call on my voice mail a few days after I had been fired from the *Morning Show* on The Fan in June 2010. "Gordie Stellick, what can I say . . . what can I say . . . what can I say . . . I know you are tired of hearing me say what can I say . . . you are a good man . . . I can't believe what happened . . . what can I say!"

Thanks, Grapes. That 10-second voice mail encompassed all that I find great about Don Cherry.

I feel fortunate to be in the hockey business and to have got to know some really fine people over the past three decades. One of the greats is Peter Mahovlich, nicknamed the "Little M" (his older brother, Frank, is, of course, the "Big M.") Peter's nickname often brings a smile to one's face, as he is tall and muscular, bigger than his older brother. What I often talk about when I am introducing or interviewing Peter at a charity event or for a media interview is how, in my opinion, he scored the most outstanding goal by a home team player, ever, at Maple Leaf Gardens.

My saying this makes little sense to those who know that Peter Mahovlich played for the Detroit Red Wings and Montreal Canadiens but never the hometown Toronto Maple Leafs. Could it possibly be his older brother Frank who I'm confusing him with?

Actually, I'm sure Frank did score many great goals at Maple Leaf Gardens in a Leafs uniform, but I was from the era that saw him score more as an opponent, with Detroit and Montreal. I have the right Mahovlich when I'm talking about the most memorable Maple Leaf Gardens goal.

Peter Mahovlich played in 884 regular-season games with Detroit, Montreal, and Pittsburgh. He moved with his family in his youth as they followed Frank's path from Timmins,

Ontario, to Toronto to join the Leafs organization. Their father, Peter Sr., was the skate sharpener for many years at Leaside Arena, in north Toronto. Among the many youngsters who considered it a thrill to have the Mahovlich father sharpen their skates was a very young John Candy.

The more memorable Leafs goals in past decades have often been scored in the Stanley Cup Playoffs and on the road, whether it was by Bob Baun on a broken leg in Detroit in 1964, Lanny McDonald on Long Island in 1978, or Nikolai Borschevsky in Detroit in 1993.

Bob Pulford scored in the second overtime period for a win over Montreal in the 1967 final, and Doug Gilmour did the same against St. Louis in the second round of the playoffs in 1993. In both instances I remember exhaling a sigh of relief in a game that had gone longer than Leafs fans anticipated. In the case of Gilmour's memorable goal, it was more relief that St. Louis goaltender Curtis Joseph proved to be somewhat human after being on the verge of being the sole reason behind a Blues second straight game win in Toronto—if they had won, that is.

For Peter Mahovlich, I have to go back to Labour Day 1972. The opener of the much-anticipated Summit Series had been two nights earlier at the Montreal Forum. Many Canadians thought that Canada would win all eight games against the Soviet Union and wondered how the Summit Series would sustain interest if the Canadian Team opened with a couple of lopsided victories. When Canada had a quick 2–0 lead in the first game, there was little to dispel that notion. Unfortunately, as Canadian hockey fans remember all too well, the game ended with a dominant 7–3 win by the Soviet Union.

The next 48 hours was a mini-crisis for all of Canada. Now many wondered if "we" would win even one game given how the first game had played out. To have another similar result that September evening at Maple Leaf Gardens was distressing just to think about. Hockey is *our* game, and we were being embarrassed by a country that, up until 48 hours earlier, we believed we were far superior to.

While Paul Henderson would score three game-winning goals weeks later in the Soviet Union, this was the one victory Team Canada needed on home soil. It ended up being a vintage effort by the Canadian team as they rallied for a 4–1 victory over the now respected Soviet Union team. Peter Mahovlich's solo effort, short-handed, was the memorable clincher. Eschewing all usual penalty-killing protocol, Mahovlich created an end-to-end rush where he powered through the entire Soviet team straight to the Russian goal crease and stuffed the puck behind Vladislav Tretiak.

A second later, millions of Canadians exhaled for the first time in 48 hours.

It was one of the greatest days in my life, yet I was facing an unexpected dilemma. Having worked for Harold Ballard for the previous 11 years, I had learned the art of thinking on my feet. Don't BS him, tell him the truth, and don't tap dance. But also be creative in solving problems—which has been one of my strengths over the years.

That strength was one of the reasons I landed the position of general manager. I had been fortunate to be at Leafs training camps for many years, but on the first day of training camp in September 1988, as I sat in the stands of the Newmarket arena, it was my first as GM of the Toronto Maple Leafs.

What had happened the previous day had made the start of camp all that much sweeter. The one difficult contract negotiation, with Wendel Clark, had come to a successful conclusion after a protracted negotiation that summer. As I watched the first day of scrimmages, I could tell that Harold Ballard had arrived because I heard a clicking sound and saw that the heaters directly overhead had been turned on. A keen eye among the arena staff had spotted Ballard's car pulling into the parking lot. And sure enough, about 10 minutes later, the 85-year-old Leafs owner sauntered over to our now warm area in the stands.

Wendel Clark had been the first overall pick in the 1985 Entry Draft. Reflecting what a different time it was then, Clark's contract looks like chump change nowadays: he received a signing bonus of $175,000; his salaries were $100,000 the first year, $110,000 the second year, and $120,000 the third and final year. The clincher had been that we had paid around $3,000 for a television satellite dish to be installed at his parents' home in Kelvington, Saskatchewan, so they could watch their son's NHL games.

During his first two seasons, Clark had taken the Toronto hockey world and the NHL by storm. His third year, he played only 28 games, and we all felt that he was going to need more time off at the start of the next season. Ballard liked Clark, but he hated spending money. And he wasn't completely sold on Clark's mysterious back ailment, worried that he was damaged goods.

His skepticism about the extent of Clark's injury showed when we were going over the player salaries, I pointed at Clark's $120,000 salary and said that he was due a new contract. "He's not looking for a raise, is he?" Ballard shot back. I didn't have the heart to tell him that Clark's agent, Don Meehan, had asked for a salary of $400,000 per season to begin negotiations.

"What we've got here is a failure to communicate," goes the famous line from the movie *Cool Hand Luke*. I, on the other hand, actually had both sides communicating to me rather well what they felt a fair salary was. Over the next few weeks, I was involved in a process of negotiation with Don Meehan, while warming Ballard to the idea that Clark deserved a raise for his contributions to the Leafs.

It did get a little heated during the hot days of early August when Meehan used the media to voice his disapproval about the way negotiations were going. I used the media the next day to present my point of view, constructively I hoped, and make sure I kept the lines of communication open so that Clark understood he was a valued member of our team. Meehan wasn't happy about my sharing my views with the media. "Gordie, I don't want to get into a pissing contest" was his greeting to me later that afternoon when he phoned. "Well, Donny, don't piss then," was my comeback.

And there it basically stood for the next month. We kept it out of the public forum and exchanged phone calls, but made little significant progress. The day before the medicals, held the day before the team hit the ice for the start of training camp, Meehan called my office. I could tell he was intent on making a deal. It was clear that Clark would be missing a significant chunk of the upcoming season, though missing 65 of the 80 regular-season games was far more than I expected that late summer day.

We had a long, productive conversation and settled on a new two-year contract with a salary of $255,000 the first year and $265,000 the second. When Meehan called me back after confirming the details with Clark, he told me, "Wendel's thrilled to get this done. We'll sign it tomorrow in Newmarket and Wendel will take us out to lunch." Which is exactly what we did the next day, and I think we stuck Clark for a grand total of $16 for lunch at a Kelsey's restaurant!

At the end of the day, I included Clark's signed contracts in a package of documents that I was sending to the NHL Central Registry in Montreal. The next morning, Ballard asked me if Wendel was happy with his contract. I answered affirmatively. Ballard then said, "Go get me his contract, I want to sign it."

In the past, the only contract Ballard had wanted to sign on behalf of the Maple Leafs hockey team was Borje Salming's, who Ballard always felt a special bond with. Otherwise, the general manager (as Gerry McNamara, Punch Imlach, and Jim Gregory had done before me) had signed players' contracts. And wasn't I being the efficient administrator by getting the signed copy out to the proper NHL office as soon as possible?

Sitting two seats over from the Leafs owner, I knew that this wasn't a story he wanted to hear. He wanted to officially give Clark the personal touch. Despite his initial dismay at the prospect of Clark getting a salary raise of any kind, he genuinely liked the young man from Saskatchewan and had befriended Wendel's parents, Les and Alma Clark. Despite my comfortable seat at the Newmarket arena, I felt as though I were between a rock and a hard place. This was going to be a tough one—either I had to quickly come clean to Ballard about the negotiation or come up with a foolproof alternative. This was when I earned my master's degree in thinking on my feet—even if sitting down.

I told Ballard that I would be right back. I quickly went to our makeshift office to make sure we had NHL contracts on hand. Check. I walked back to the rink and could see that Clark's group was on the ice. I called Clark over and explained my dilemma—that Mr. Ballard was so pleased to have him back in the fold that he wanted to personally sign the contract but that I had already sent it to Central Registry.

I took a shot with my quickly devised plan. I showed Wendel the new "contract" that I had "drawn up." A standard NHL player's contract is folded in three parts. I had filled in the bottom part, typing in the date and the names of the signing parties. I asked Wendel if we could stage the signing and then I would tear up the pages.

Without a moment's hesitation Clark agreed. He came off the ice, dulling his skates on the concrete pavement as he made his way to a small room in the bowels of the arena where I had asked Ballard to wait. Wendel shook hands with Ballard and they exchanged pleasantries. He took off his glove but left his helmet on as he signed the three copies of the new contract, sweat dripping onto the documents. I made sure to arrange the three copies so that only the bottom third of each page was visible. That done, they shook hands again and Ballard said, "It's great to have you back."

Clark hustled back to his group on the ice. Ballard slowly made his way out of the office and to the stands. I took a deep breath, tore up the contract, and went back to my (once again) comfortable seat in the stands.

Though he missed many games that season, the good news was that Clark was able to resume almost a full slate of regular-season games the following season. In his rookie season he had almost single-handedly brought respect to a Leafs team that was sorely lacking it and that had been dead last in the standings the previous season.

Not only did Clark score 34 goals his rookie year, in 1985–86, he physically took on all comers, fighting NHL heavyweights like John Kordic, Rick Tocchet, and Behn Wilson. The late John McCauley, the NHL director of offici- ating (and whose son Wes is considered a top referee in the NHL today), had an excellent observation one game as I sat beside him in the press box. Clark had won yet another fight and was skating off the ice in the direction of the Leafs dress- ing room, as it was near the end of the period. "Look at that," McCauley marvelled. "He just beats one of their guys and then he skates right by the visiting team bench and nobody says a word to him. That's an incredible sign of respect for a 19-year-old kid."

After coming back from his two injury-plagued seasons, his fights were fewer in number, though he did have a rare playoff beauty after Marty McSorley decked Doug Gilmour near the end of the second game of that fateful series against the Los Angeles Kings in 1993. More importantly, Clark had 20 points (10 goals, 10 assists) in 21 playoff games that spring. That was the prelude to his best regular season ever in 1993–94, with 76 points (46 goals, 30 assists) in 64 games, a pace that would have led to well more than 50 goals had he been able to play in more games.

The next season was fractured by the first NHL lockout. When a reduced schedule began the following January, teams played only against other teams from their NHL conference. Wendel Clark was now a member of the Quebec Nordiques. Had the season started as scheduled, the Leafs' fifth home game early that season would have been against Quebec. All Leafs fans lost the opportunity for what I believe would have been an unparalleled event. We have seen many ex-Leafs play- ers come back to rousing ovations, polite applause, or, in some cases, wholehearted booing. Wendel Clark's popularity among

Leafs fans had never been greater, and I believe we would never have heard a louder crowd reaction at a Leafs game.

Nowadays, Wendel Clark fits the bill perfectly as an ambassador with the Leafs front office. He has successfully and naturally merged the endearing qualities of a farm kid from small-town Saskatchewan with those of a big city kid thriving in the hockey hotbed of Toronto. He remains one of the great people of the game.

6 YES, THAT IS WHAT IT WAS LIKE WORKING FOR HAROLD BALLARD

I worked for Harold Ballard from 1975 to 1989. People loved to hate him, and there is no doubt he was not an easy man to work with. Still, he was a great character of the game. I learned how to think on my feet!

Talk about instantly being thrown into the fire. Because I was so young and not so intimately involved, I was fortunate to merely observe the fire burning from a ringside seat. I guess I shouldn't have been so surprised at anything unusual with a Harold Ballard–owned hockey team given the unusual way I was able to become a part of it.

I was lucky to have a few unexpected breaks. I lived in North York, just north of Toronto, in a middle-class neighbourhood. A friend of mine, Ken McMurtrie, lived across the street from Stan Obodiac, who was then the publicity director for the Leafs and Maple Leaf Gardens. I envied my friend when he was hired to work game nights as a press box assistant for Leafs home games. That was while we were both in Grade 12 at Georges Vanier Secondary School. A year later, in 1975, Obodiac needed another assistant for game nights and asked Ken if he had any friends who might be interested. I am always incredibly appreciative that Ken offered me that unbelievable opportunity.

A little over a year later, just before we rang in 1977, Howie Starkman, who had been working for the Leafs in public relations and administration, left in the middle of the season to take a job as the first-ever public relations director of the Toronto Blue Jays. They had to find someone urgently, to write, tabulate, and publish the game night press notes and statistics, which had been among Starkman's many duties.

Over the course of my occasional work there, I developed close relationships with several people in the Leafs office, including General Manager Jim Gregory and Assistant General Manager John McLellan. I remember someone had asked me whether I was a good typist. I was, largely because of my poor handwriting. I could type 70 words per minute in an era when typing wasn't as much of a necessity as it is now. Importantly, I was a *male* who could type 70 words per minute in an era when the front office was still a men-only domain.

Gregory knew I was attending the University of Toronto, where I was majoring in commerce and economics. Out of the blue one night, when I delivered a copy of the final game statistics to his office, he asked me if I thought I could find time from my courses to do more work in the Leafs office. My quick "yes" answer was a no-brainer. Then he showed me a collection of press notes and statistics from other NHL venues. Most were about five pages in length. Could I do something similar like this for each Leafs game? Piece of cake. I was now a part-timer in the Leafs front office.

The morning of the next Leafs home game, I made my way for the first time to the small and anything but flashy Leafs executive offices. But for me, seeing the Toronto Maple Leafs logo on everything from the walls to the memo pads more than made up for whatever it might have lacked in looks. The two receptionists sat in the modest waiting area. A Plexiglas door adorned with a Leafs logo separated them from the back offices. A doorbell-type buzzer had to be pushed to open that door.

It was the first time that I felt as if I had been welcomed to the inner sanctum. I was given a vacant desk to work at and noticed a few pads of memo papers that said "From the desk of Red Kelly" beside a Leafs logo. Kelly had been fired months earlier, very little went to waste in the Leafs front office.

After being very personable and welcoming, getting me situated in the office, and going over what he expected again, Gregory closed with a stern warning: "Now, you get this all done yourself. Don't go bugging the secretaries for help, they have enough work to do as it is." Meaning, figure it out yourself. So I taught myself to type on stencil paper (mistakes were covered by bright pink correction fluid, to be typed over when dry), which I then wrapped around the drum of a Gestetner duplicating machine, cranking out copies the old-fashioned way.

I learned later that Gregory had to go to Harold Ballard to get his approval for this new part-time kid in the office. I didn't know Ballard at all, had never even spoken to him, and he could have ended my front-office career in a matter of minutes.

I appreciated my great fortune over the next two years to be working the Leafs games and a very small part of the front office. Until the day I left the Leafs more than a decade later, I just loved going into work, and I got to work in a hockey shrine, rather than a regular office. Later as a full-time employee, I felt energized as I made the final trek south on Church Street toward the building.

But back in 1977, if I was particularly busy at school the day before a game, I would go into the office that night to prepare the statistics and notes for the next evening. Sometimes someone else was in the office, other times I was alone. But one was never totally alone—not as long as that office at the back doubled as Harold Ballard's residence.

I learned this first-hand one evening. I heard a noise and then the very large Leafs owner walked briskly through the office, wearing nothing but his boxer shorts. He seemed unaware that I was sitting at a desk in the back corner. I could hear him out in the reception area, looking for something on his secretary's desk. As he walked back to his office/apartment, he stopped to read whatever paper he had picked up. He was in full view of me but was still unaware of my presence.

I cleared my throat loudly, worried how this embarrassing moment was going to end—badly, I feared. As it turned out, it would be an appropriate beginning to learning about life working with Harold Ballard: expect the unexpected. Often what you feared might not fly with him did, and what you thought would, didn't. Ballard looked up and gave me a warm greeting, not annoyed at all. And rather than making a quick return to his office/apartment, he squeezed himself into the chair at the desk in front of me, turned around, and stared up a conversation with me.

I found it difficult to ignore the rolls of flesh—the result of living the good life—hanging down from his nearly 80-year-old body, almost covering his boxer shorts. It was our first in-depth conversation. He was incredibly friendly and engaging and he asked me all about my school work, family, and background. After about 10 minutes, he said, "You're doing a helluva job, Gordie," stood up, and was gone.

A little over a year later, on another late night for me at the office, he stopped by as I worked at my desk, sat down (a little more clothing on this time), and offered me a full-time position with the Toronto Maple Leafs. I agreed on the spot, asking only for the few months I needed to finish up my year at the University of Toronto. It was that simple. I still had another full year at university left to do, and in the split second before I answered I wisely made a mental note to adapt my original post-secondary education plans and finish my degree part-time, which I did a few years later.

Once my school year ended and I had a few weeks' break before exams, Ballard let me accompany the team on a charter flight to Minneapolis on April 7, 1980, for their first-round playoff series against the Minnesota North Stars. It was the end of the first full regular season during Punch Imlach's second term as Leafs general manager, and the division between management and players had grown to an unfortunate level of acrimony. The trading of Lanny McDonald to Colorado a few months earlier had taken the hostilities to a new height and they had continued to escalate in the ensuing weeks.

I was certainly aware of what had been going on, but I hadn't yet been as involved in the Leafs inner sanctum as I would soon become. The level of the organizational acrimony was vividly demonstrated when we arrived at the airport in Bloomington, Minnesota, just a few miles outside Minneapolis. We were booked at the Bloomington Marriott, just across the street from the Met Center and a five-minute drive from the airport.

As part of its excellent service, the Bloomington Marriott provided two shuttle buses for transfer to the hotel. Having already cleared U.S. Immigration and Customs in Toronto, we conveniently walked right off the plane and onto the hotel shuttle. We had 23 players and 8 staff on the flight, and each shuttle bus could comfortably accommodate about 15 people.

Since management sat at the front of the plane, we got off ahead of the players, boarding the first shuttle bus. Our entourage included President Harold Ballard, Vice-President King Clancy, General Manager Punch Imlach, Coach Joe Crozier, Assistant Coach Dick Duff, scout Floyd Smith, broadcaster Peter Maher (Maher was the Leafs radio broadcaster for two seasons before leaving for Calgary, where he has been the voice of the Flames for over 30 years) and me, the new "executive"— really, the wide-eyed new kid and junior member of the team.

The eight of us waited for our shuttle to fill up, assuming that the first players off the plane would come on our bus. Well, that wasn't to be. All 23 players walked right by the shuttle bus, preferring to be squashed like sardines on the second one rather than interact with management. One or two of the players even made as if to board our bus, much to the amusement of their teammates, before heading to the second bus. I found it all very surreal.

While the players were clearly amused, Punch Imlach was clearly unamused. "Look at those bastards," he could be heard muttering a few times as the steady herd of Leafs players walked by.

I guess that none of us should be surprised that this statement by the players was a precursor to the Leafs losing both games in Minnesota, 6–3 and 7–2. A 4–3 overtime win by the North Stars at Maple Leaf Gardens gave them a three-game sweep. Al MacAdam, later a coach of the St. John's Maple Leafs, scored the overtime winner for Minnesota.

Harold Ballard loved the limelight and publicity of any kind. "Just make sure they spell my name correctly—that's 'Ballard' with two *l*'s," he loved to chortle. Although he loved the limelight, he loathed spending money—he was reluctant to spend money when it was necessary, so one can imagine his disdain for spending money when it wasn't necessary. Which is why, when faced with a $10,000 fine, he obeyed an NHL edict—but reluctantly, very reluctantly.

And that was where things stood on February 26, 1978. A few years earlier, the board of governors had passed a bylaw that all NHL team sweaters bear the player's name on the back, along with his number. This practice had been gaining popularity during the 1970s, but there wasn't an actual rule about it until 1977.

Ballard, thinking old school, believed that having the players' names on the backs of the uniforms would adversely affect the sale of programs. This was the same kind of thinking that had Bill Wirtz blackout Chicago Blackhawks home games for decades in the belief that televising the games would affect ticket sales.

Faced with the possibility of a $10,000 fine, Ballard relented at the eleventh hour. Only a select few knew that Ballard would pull what turned out to be one of his best publicity stunts. As many remember, the Leafs did in fact play the game in Chicago in late February 1978 with their names on their sweaters for the first time. The only problem was that the names were applied in the same dark blue as their road jerseys.

Ballard's antics were the talk of the hockey world for the next few days. He was excited by the media attention and also pleased that the Leafs had won, 5–3, in Chicago and wearing his innovative jerseys to boot. Even John Ziegler, the president of the National Hockey League, saw the humour in Ballard's stunt. The next day he sent Ballard a message over the teletypewriter reminding Ballard of the NHL bylaw and emphasizing that the names were to be in contrasting colours, with a heavy emphasis on the word "contrasting." It was a firm but friendly notice.

It has often been reported that Ballard paid the $10,000 fine. Actually, Ziegler didn't enforce the fine but gave Ballard another chance to comply with the regulation. The next Leafs game was also on the road, at Long Island, and again players skated without their names showing clearly on the back of their jerseys as that would have to wait until they returned home.

Ziegler's extension of the deadline ended at the Leafs next home game, which was a day later, on March 1, 1978, against the Philadelphia Flyers. Ballard was ready to play out the second act in his (so far) successful sweater charade. In fact, Ballard did have a set of Leafs jerseys ready for the next home game and the names were indeed in contrasting colours—but they were the players' first names. *Borje passes to Ian, over to Tiger, back to* . . . well, you get the picture.

Ballard was ready to play his game one more time in order to keep the media spotlight. But Bob Sedgewick, the respected Leafs legal counsel, advised Ballard that it would likely result in a fine that could be as high as $25,000, as Ziegler likely would no longer see the humour of Ballard's antics—this second act could be expensive. Ballard took Sedgewick's advice and decided against paying cash to play the joke. Me, I would have loved to have seen the reactions to those jerseys at the Leafs home game.

Harold Ballard certainly occupied a disproportionate amount of John Ziegler's time as NHL president. Ballard had almost revered the former president, Clarence Campbell. For Ziegler, however, Ballard showed little respect. He was an American and, to Ballard, an outsider. He would often deride Ziegler's stature and refer to him as "that little squirt" or "that little runt."

Ballard prided himself on not being, as an owner, a "team player" with the NHL office, located in New York. The NHL having moved most of its operations from Montreal to New York was one of his bones of contention. When the NHL began hosting an annual Hockey Hall of Fame dinner, the member teams were expected to show their support by purchasing tickets for at least one table. Even though the dinner was held in Toronto, Ballard took a pass. The board of governors went to the extraordinary—and annoying—length of adding a bylaw to the effect that all member teams would be billed for one table for the annual Hockey Hall of Fame dinner even if they didn't attend. All because of Ballard.

Ballard had a quirky and unpredictable side. The board of governors was meeting to discuss extending a new contract to Ziegler, in June 1983. It was reported to me that the meeting had been somewhat contentious, as Ziegler had his fair share of opponents. Apparently, Ballard changed the flow of discussion by his comments. "Look," he said, "nobody causes more trouble for Ziegler than I do. He makes his share of screw-ups, but I don't think anyone else could do this job any better under the circumstances, and I move we should offer him a new contract."

I told Jim Gregory what I had heard. "No way, that can't be true" was his reply—he was more than aware of Ballard's publicized comments about Ziegler. I told him that I had it from a good source and he reiterated that he seriously doubted it. A few hours later, I was chatting with some people in the lobby of a Montreal hotel. Gregory saw me and came over. "That story you told me is 100 per cent true," he said, shaking his head and letting out one of his infectious chuckles. "Hard to figure out the old bastard," he said, smiling as he walked away. Yes, hard to figure out the old bastard is right.

The former NHL president John Ziegler confirmed the story to me in a radio interview in 2011.

Harold Ballard had an obsession about giving away as few tickets as possible as comps. A ticket sales and turnstile report was slid under Ballard's office door by a member of the box office staff at the conclusion of any event at Maple Leaf Gardens. For Leafs games, Ballard simply eyed the bulk of the report and honed in on the number of comps issued and the number of standing-room tickets sold.

If we were carrying extra players, he was most concerned about the two extra comps that were required, as that was what each player was entitled to under the collective bargaining agreement. Even though the player's NHL salary was in those days an average of $700 per day, the cost of those $45 complementary tickets for home games was his ongoing obsession.

A few times I had to resist the urge to tip off a player, to say to him, "Look, if you just take a pass on your comp tickets for home games, you'll fly under the radar and have a much better chance at staying up here in Toronto longer." This was because, from time to time, Ballard would make the pointed observation, "We've got too many people up here, time to move some bodies down to the minors."

One Wednesday, the day of a home game, Normand Aubin was just that player. After the morning skate at the Gardens, Aubin was being returned to St. Catharines. With our American Hockey League team just an hour's drive west of Toronto, in St. Catharines, the logistics of sending players there were relatively easy—certainly much easier than sending them down to Cincinnati or Moncton, our previous minor league affiliates, or to a future affiliate like St. John's. The box office had already checked with me about roster changes and knew about Aubin.

But an internal mix-up meant that Aubin hadn't been advised by the coaches that he was returning to St. Catharines. After practice, Aubin bounded up the steps to the special ticket office to collect his comps. The person at the box office handling the player tickets that day was Al Rennick, a wonderful, sweet, methodical senior who handled his job with pride and extreme competence. He was stunned to see Aubin at the ticket window and could only mutter, "Aren't you supposed to be in St. Catharines?" A distraught Aubin then made his way to the Leafs executive offices, where the matter was smoothed over to a degree. He wasn't surprised at being returned to the

American Hockey League, just taken aback at they way he found out about it.

Al Rennick always felt badly, having seen how devastated Aubin had been by the news he had delivered. For years afterward, friends of Al's in the box office would kiddingly ask if we required the services of Al Rennick to assign any of our players to the minors.

Much like his obsessing over handing out as few complementary tickets as possible, Ballard was also conscious of extra players resulting in extra travel costs, especially the per diem each player received for meal expenses. We could usually cover travel costs, since there was no incremental cost for an additional player on a charter flight. With the players doubling up in hotel rooms, we could sell Ballard on the idea that the additional player created an even number and incurred no additional hotel cost. However, the per diem, which at that time was about $30 per day, was a different story, and, again, it seemed to matter more to Ballard than the average $700 per day salary that an additional player earned.

We had a young, naive rookie who was basically decent but a little rough around the edges. He was strictly an enforcer and had been used with mixed results. The coaches liked his toughness, but Ballard wasn't sold on him. He was also sitting out more games than he was dressed for. He was that "extra" player. And around Ballard, it was best to work at being invisible if you were an extra.

This particular player, however, was quite unaware of this. On a few trips he took the seat beside Ballard at the front of the bus, an unusual move. Usually management sat there, or the odd time a veteran player would take that seat and engage Ballard in conversation.

I could sense that the rookie, not realizing he was a player the Leafs owner wasn't big on, was unwittingly digging himself a deeper hole. A focus of the rookie's conversation was how he was saving most of his per diem on the road trips. He took extra food from the team meal back to his room and, being an extra player, he also enjoyed the pre-game fare that was served in the press box. He thought Ballard was enjoying these stories, and I could see by Ballard's good-natured participation why he would think that. Ballard was always great in person with the players, acting the kindly uncle, with no bark or bite—he saved that for behind closed doors. I don't ever remember him having an angry exchange with a player, contrary to what people might think.

I knew my gut instinct was correct when we left the bus one morning upon arriving at an arena for a pre-game skate. Ballard quickly sought me out. "How much per denim [he always mispronounced it as "per denim"] is [that player] getting on this trip?" I told him the amount and he nodded.

About a week later, we had a brief two-game, four-day trip. Ballard wanted to know from the coaches if the rookie was going to play. They said they doubted it but emphasized that he was a valued member of the team, and that there was a possibility he could be used depending on circumstances. Ballard again asked for a flat-out yes or no: Did they plan to use him? "No," was the answer. The rookie didn't go on the trip. He stayed back in Toronto collecting his NHL salary over those five days, but Ballard had successfully saved the organization five days' per diem . . . or per denim.

Harold Ballard was always frugal when it came to approving the front office's operating expenses. It was well known that he certainly did whatever he could on the cheap. There was also an assistant in treasurer Don Crump's office who didn't do the hockey office any favours either—as part of her job, she took the basket of cheques in to Ballard to sign; while he was doing so, she would offer her opinion on where money was being wasted. We needed her like a hole in the head, but for a number of years in the 1970s and early 1980s, her unofficial power was an unwelcome reality.

Directly in front of Ballard's office/apartment was a larger office area that housed four large desks. Chief scout Gerry McNamara sat at one, scout Johnny Bower at another, and the other two were idle, as they had belonged to George Armstrong, who had left the organization, and Al Dunford, a statistician who had been hired by Roger Neilson and who was fired along with Neilson.

They were now "at large" desks, which I used early on in my tenure when I was there as a part-time employee and which other members of the organization who were passing through town used. I don't know whether it was Ballard's own idea or if the seed for it was planted by the office busybody, but it was decided to have just one phone for the four desks. The other three phones were to be removed.

Gerry McNamara's phone was the one to survive. Two other phones were removed. Johnny Bower, goaltender for four Leafs Stanley Cup championship teams and a Hall of Famer, hid his in his desk drawer. When it rang or if he had to place a call, he took the phone out of the drawer, returning it there when he was finished, the slim phone line jutting out of the drawer and across the desk.

After about a week of this, his phone rang when he wasn't at his desk. Ballard, though, happened to be walking by. And once Ballard had in his mind something to do with cutting expenses, he wouldn't let it go. Bower's phone was removed that afternoon. The next morning, Bower arrived to find a note on his desk that read, "Your drawer rang." It marked the beginning of his no-phone era.

This ridiculous and demeaning cost-cutting measure ended about a month later when Johnny's phone was reconnected.

"Look at what he did," said an annoyed and somewhat beleaguered Dan Maloney as he showed me a Maple Leaf Gardens cheque. "How do I give it to them like this?"

It was in the mid-1980s and Dan Maloney was the head coach of the Leafs. He had pushed hard to have a weight room installed in a smallish room across the hall from the Leafs dressing room. As well, he had struck a deal with a local fitness consultant to implement and oversee an upgraded and more intensive approach to team fitness. Though Ballard agreed to the expenditure, he remained supportive of neither.

He definitely had an outlook from a different era. Once in a while, usually when we were on the team bus going somewhere, when he saw someone jogging, he would say, "Ask that guy to do an honest day's work." As if there was any connection between the two, but he obviously believed there was.

Unfortunately for Dan Maloney, it was a tough year for the Leafs hockey team. On the upside, plenty of young talent was starting to show through, but it was also a last-place finish to end the 1984–85 season. That didn't help to enamour Ballard to the new fitness equipment and consultant who would be on-site.

A final payment was due to the fitness consultant and I don't know whether it was Ballard's doing or not, but it was not forthcoming. Maloney felt responsible for getting the people, whose work he was very satisfied with, the money they were owed. After it was well overdue, he finally got the cheque himself from the accounting department.

Maloney walked down the one flight of stairs from the accounting offices to the Leafs executive offices and headed straight to the back, to Ballard in his office. To Maloney's relief, Ballard signed the cheque without comment. He then did what he did on the odd occasion. With his fountain pen he wrote a message on the face of the cheque. In this case it was "Thanks for nothing."

I had seen Ballard do this a few times. Earlier, Ballard had felt that a player named Laurie Boschman had lost his feisty hockey makeup when he became a born-again Christian after his rookie season. Ballard stated this publicly, which caused a great deal of controversy. When Boschman was traded to the Winnipeg Jets about a year later, his last Leafs payroll cheque contained the note, "God bless you my son" on its face. Player agent Bill Watters was the recipient of a cheque from Ballard with the inscription, "You're a crook Bill"—and this to an individual he truly liked!

Part of Ballard's enthusiasm for the phone caper might have been prompted by the previous two occupants of the "at large" desks. As I mentioned, one had been George Armstrong, who had been both a Leafs scout and the coach of the Toronto Marlboros, and had left not under the best of terms. The other had been occupied by Al Dunford.

Who was Al Dunford? A low-key, witty, and bright individual. He was as nice a guy as you could ever meet, who unfortunately and unfairly drew the ire of the Leafs owner. After Roger Neilson's successful first year as Leafs coach in 1977–78, he asked Leafs general manager Jim Gregory to hire his friend and former student Dunford to the Leafs front office. Neilson was an innovator in using NHL video and team statistics as coaching tools.

His first year, Neilson had done it all himself. He later kidded that with our cutting-edge video equipment, he had to push three buttons simultaneously to operate certain functions. He would use a finger from each hand for two of the buttons, and then stick a pencil in his mouth to push the third. He requested a video of every Leafs game at a time when about one-third of the games on the road weren't televised in any market. For these, Neilson hired a local kid to take video of the game. Not surprisingly, the quality of the final product was at the mercy of the skills of whichever audio visual student he had hired. For one particular road game, Neilson missed the first minute or so of play, as he was busy instructing his hire on how to operate the video camera. He then had to rush through the stands to get behind the Leafs bench.

While Ballard viewed Neilson's work ethic as more a curiousity, Jim Gregory appreciated and admired the hard work Neilson put into his job and the new level of organization and preparation he brought to the profession. He was receptive to adding Dunford to the staff. His challenge, though, was to sell it to Ballard, who had to approve all hirings. Despite Neilson's successful first year, Ballard wasn't sold on his style and ingenuity. He was never enthused about adding another salary and didn't understand the need for videos and statistical information.

He reluctantly agreed to add Dunford to the Leafs staff and to allow him to travel with the team. Dunford started with two strikes against him and quickly became known as not being Ballard's "type." I don't know what Ballard's type was, really, but he was always quick to deride anyone whom he classed as a "schoolboy." Neilson fit that bill and so did Dunford. I was appreciative that I never got painted with that brush by Ballard, even though I was more of a schoolboy type than either Neilson or Dunford.

In Neilson's second year, the Leafs did not enjoy the same success as the previous year. The success of that year had raised expectations—especially those of the Leafs owner. Unfortunately, Al Dunford's position made him the ideal scapegoat for anything wrong with the Leafs team—he became Ballard's whipping boy. Ballard didn't hide his personal and professional disdain for Dunford, who everyone else in the organization enjoyed having around and appreciated. Just a few months into the season, Dunford began trying to stay out of Ballard's way as much as possible.

This was also the spring of the legendary firing and rehiring of Roger Neilson. The Leafs lost their fourth consecutive game on Wednesday, February 28, 1979, 6–4 to the Atlanta Flames at Maple Leaf Gardens. They immediately took a chartered plane to Montreal for a game at the forum the next night.

Against one of the all-time great Montreal Canadiens teams—eventually Stanley Cup champions—the Leafs played their hearts out in a narrow 2–1 loss. Paul Harrison was outstanding in the Leafs goal that night, but the five-game losing streak was too much for the impatient Ballard. The game was broadcast locally on CHCH-TV in the Toronto and Hamilton area; long-time Toronto media personality Dick Beddoes was part of those broadcasts.

With just a few minutes left in the game, the cameras caught Beddoes chasing down Harold Ballard and King Clancy in the Montreal Forum concourse, about to leave the building. Apparently, they had seen enough, even though it was a tight one-goal game. It was then and there that Ballard told Beddoes that he was firing Roger Neilson as coach of the Toronto Maple Leafs. I really wondered if Ballard truly planned to take such action or if his sense of theatrics got the better of whatever common sense he had—that, being caught on camera, he wanted to show viewers that he was able to take instantaneous and decisive action with *his* hockey team.

It made for an unusual flight home from Montreal after the game. Ballard and Clancy were on the flight, as was Neilson. The post-game media talk was dominated by Neilson's firing. A stunned Dunford offered his support to Neilson. "I'm sorry you got fired," he sincerely told his long-time friend. "Well, you're gone too," Neilson wryly commented. Dunford hadn't thought of that part of the equation.

When, two days later, Neilson was rehired by the Leafs owner, nobody in management asked about Dunford's status. As the saying goes, don't ask if you don't want to hear the answer. Upon Neilson's return, Dunford went from maintaining a low profile to maintaining a ridiculously low profile. He basically hid in the bowels of Maple Leaf Gardens, doing his work for Neilson in places that the Leafs owner was sure not to find him. He never set foot in the Leafs executive offices again.

Nobody asked Ballard the question of whether they could rehire Dunford along with Neilson as the answer was predictable. An unspoken arrangement continued that Dunford just stayed out of Ballard's way as much as possible and went back to his duties with Neilson.

About two months later, after losing in the second round of the playoffs to that top-notch Montreal Canadiens team, Neilson was fired for the second and final time, and the charade of Al Dunford's position came to an end as well.

Al Dunford returned to teaching and has been a much-respected hockey coach at St. Andrew's College in Aurora, Ontario, for a great many years—a "schoolboy" done well.

As one can imagine, if Harold Ballard wasn't particularly fond of you, he made it pretty obvious. If he felt you had somehow crossed him along the way, he made that even more obvious.

Soon after his arrival at the Leafs, the infamous Czech defector Miroslav Ihnacak became one such individual. It wasn't an anti-European bias on Ballard's part, as Ballard remained a booster of Ihnacak's older brother, Peter, who had a decent career on the Leafs teams in the 1980s. Ballard had also been genuinely pleased to assist Ihnacak and his fiancée flee from a Communist regime (Ihnacak's companion was also issued a special minister's permit by the Canadian government to defect from Czechoslovakia). That was part of Ballard's ongoing public political persona, and he basked with pride in the attention he received for being a "good" guy in helping the two escape from behind the Iron Curtain.

That Miroslav Ihnacak would prove unable to play at the NHL level was disappointing. He would eventually find success in the American Hockey League. But that wasn't what caused Ballard to change his view of Ihnacak, from expecting the second coming of Borje Salming to an attitude of disdain. I believe that Ballard would still have taken pride in having helped two people escape from behind the Iron Curtain and wouldn't have taken Ihnacak's disappointing NHL career personally.

It was the almighty dollar that he took personally and it was with this that he felt Ihnacak had crossed him. Shortly after defecting from Czechoslovakia and arriving in Toronto, Ihnacak had second thoughts about the NHL contract he had agreed to. The renegotiations didn't result in a substantive increase. Instead, some never-achieved performance bonuses were tweaked, but Ballard viewed Ihnacak's request as an act of disloyalty, showing a lack of appreciation for what the Leafs organization had done for him. If Ihnacak thought the Communist government an unforgiving regime, he was to discover that Ballard wasn't much better once you were in his doghouse.

In the spring of 1987, the Leafs won their first playoff round for a second consecutive season and were battling the

Detroit Red Wings in the second round. New coach Jacques Demers enjoyed a successful rookie season behind the Wings bench taking over from Brad Park.

Miroslav Ihnacak's first full season with the Leafs had gone much the way his first partial season had the previous year after his defection: not that well. A very marginal player at the NHL level, he finished the season as an average player with the Leafs' American Hockey League team in Newmarket. For the playoffs, he joined a group of Leafs players that formed the Black Aces—extra players to be used only in cases of emergency. That emergency had transpired.

The Leafs assembled for their flight to Windsor the afternoon before Game 7 against the Red Wings. Each making their own way to the airport, they arrived either individually or in small groups. It was a quiet team that boarded the plane, as they faced a game that at one point in the series didn't seem as if it would be required. When Mike Allison scored in overtime in Game 4 to give the Leafs a three game to one lead, it seemed that a series-clinching win in Game 5 or 6 was academic. That proved to not be the case. Outstanding goaltending from Glen Hanlon and Demers's strategy of playing Joey Kocur directly against his cousin, Wendel Clark, were two components that had turned the momentum toward the Red Wings. They won Game 5, 3–0, in Detroit, and then won on Gardens ice, 4–2, in Game 6. The scores flattered the Leafs, as the Red Wings were the dominant team in both games and could have won by larger margins. And now, injuries were an additional factor for the Leafs team, to the extent that Miroslav Ihnacak would see his first NHL playoff action in that deciding game.

We have seen how a Game 7 in any best-of-seven playoff series can truly go either way. But that wasn't the feeling on the Leafs plane that day. The team's spirit lacked life and confidence. They needed a spark. And Ballard was about to prove his lack of interest in providing that spark. Ballard had been one of the first to board the plane and was sitting in a seat at the front. I had a clear view as a nervous Ihnacak boarded. I could see his anxiety rise as he spotted Ballard, then took a few measured steps down the aisle. But trust Ballard to diffuse a tense situation. "Hi, Miroslav, how are you doing?" he bellowed in a loud, friendly voice. A surprised and visibly less tense Miroslav uttered, "Very good, Mr. Ballard, thank you," as he continued toward his seat.

With all we were to face the next night, I was pleased that encounter had gone well. Well, I was pleased for all of two seconds. As Miroslav passed Ballard's seat, the Leafs owner turned his head back slightly and bellowed to no one in particular, "We're really scraping the bottom of the frickin' barrel on this one." That certainly did nothing to create the much-needed spark.

Harold Ballard was right, Game 7 was a bottom-of-the-barrel game; the exuberance of Allison's overtime winner a week earlier had long dissipated. Hanlon and the Red Wings shut out the Leafs again, 3–0, to win the series. Miroslav Ihnacak never played another NHL game again in a Leafs jersey.

Harold Ballard's propensity for avoiding people and often also avoiding delivering tough news in person was evident at the end of the second reign of George "Punch" Imlach as the Toronto Maple Leafs general manager. Whereas Imlach's first successful run (as the GM and coach of four Stanley Cup championship teams in the 1960s) had ended when then Leafs president Stafford Smythe told him to his face that he was fired, a few minutes after the Leafs were eliminated from the playoffs in a four-game sweep by Boston in 1969, Imlach would be hard-pressed to get a face-to-face meeting with Ballard (who was the vice-president to Stafford Smythe in 1969) a little over 12 years later.

Training camp for 1981, Imlach's third season, began in St. Catharines, about an hour's drive from Toronto. On the eve of the first day of camp, Imlach suffered a heart attack and was admitted to hospital in St. Catharines. He was scheduled to be transferred the next day to the cardiac unit at Toronto General Hospital.

We discussed it within management that first morning, and the overriding concern was unwanted press coverage. The strategy was one of absolute secrecy. From those who had spoken on the phone to Ballard, who was back in Toronto, it became apparent that this plan was supported by the Leafs owner. When I talked to Ballard on the phone, we went over some administrative details and then he confirmed that we all had to keep quiet about what had happened to Imlach. But I could almost hear Ballard's mind racing as he repeated the mantra of secrecy.

The following morning, the front-page picture of the *Toronto Star* showed Imlach connected to an oxygen tank, being wheeled into Toronto General Hospital on a stretcher. It was obvious that Ballard had tipped off his close friend Milt Dunnell at the *Star*, giving him the scoop. So much for team secrecy.

It also gave Ballard a master plan to rid himself of Imlach without meeting the problem, or the Leafs general manager, head-on. In the ensuing weeks of training camp and the start of the regular season, Ballard instructed us to not talk to Imlach ("for the good of his health") and told us that Gerry McNamara and Mike Nykoluk were in charge. I was to get another life lesson about working for Harold Ballard over those next few weeks.

Imlach soon underwent quadruple bypass heart surgery, so it wasn't difficult to "ignore" him, as he was obviously unable to handle the day-to-day operations of the team. When the regular season started, however, and Imlach experienced a very positive recovery, it became more problematic. I found myself in the middle of it all, the only person talking to everyone involved. Gerry McNamara as interim general manager and coach Mike Nykoluk operated in a cone of silence, shielding themselves from their supposed boss.

Imlach appreciated the awkward position that I was in and certainly could sense the silent treatment he was getting from his front-office colleagues and the Leafs owner. As the regular season moved into late October, Imlach felt a need to take a stand with the Leafs owner and so sent Ballard and the Leafs front office word that he would be returning to his office on the morning of October 26. If Imlach had any doubts where he stood with Ballard, they were soon put to rest upon his arrival at Maple Leaf Gardens. Imlach pulled his car into his reserved parking spot on Wood Street, adjacent to the north side of the building. The only problem was that it wasn't his spot any-more. Ballard had instructed that the "Reserved for G. Imlach" sign be taken down.

Parking in what had been his spot, Imlach made his way to his office. When he tried to make his first phone call, he found he had a problem: his phone had been disconnected. So much for subtlety on the part of the Leafs owner. Ballard had ducked talking to Imlach for almost two months, but the revelations to Imlach in his first 10 minutes back at the Gardens confirmed what the owner felt.

Imlach finally cornered the Leafs owner in his office. Ballard proclaimed innocence about any looming firing—he just wanted Imlach to take a reduced role for the sake of his health. "I don't want to be responsible for putting Punch in a wood box," was Ballard's refrain. "Why don't you quit and just blame it on me, say that I'm a bastard to work for," was Ballard's suggestion. I always wondered whether Ballard's professional advice on these occasions was sincerely about one's welfare or if he was just hoping to get out of the remainder of a contract by having an employee quit.

Imlach didn't take Ballard's bait. He left Ballard's office and Maple Leaf Gardens for the final time a little more than an hour later. His final words to Ballard were "Give me a call when you want a real manager." For the rest of the season, every second week, on pay day, my phone would ring: Punch Imlach was outside on Church Street, at the north end of the building, with his car engine running. I would hurry down with his cheque and visit with him for a few minutes in what was still a company automobile. It was always a very pleasant conversation, and Imlach would leave with his money from the Maple Leaf Gardens' vault.

And his parking spot? That summer a new sign went up that read "Reserved for G. Stellick." I had made the big time: a reserved parking spot. Though Punch Imlach's second term as Leafs general manager has few fans among players, management, or media, I always appreciated how well he treated me. So I did feel a sense of sentiment in assuming his old parking spot. Certainly, not having to pay for parking anymore was appreciated as well.

Though the Leafs never won a Stanley Cup, nor even played in the Stanley Cup Finals, in the Harold Ballard era, the Leafs owner was responsible for a huge victory off the ice in an area where he had little active involvement: helping a group of rock concert promoters evolve into corporate giants. His son, Bill Ballard, along with promoter Michael Cohl, operated a company called Concert Productions International (CPI). Ballard father and son had a comfortable arrangement whereby Bill Ballard enjoyed exclusive access to the Maple Leaf Gardens venue, while Harold made an easy profit for his company Maple Leaf Gardens Ltd. each time his venue was used. The usual arrangement was for Harold and Maple Leaf Gardens Ltd. to be paid a flat fee or 25 per cent of the gate, whichever was greater. He pretty well always earned the 25 per cent.

The "rock concerts," as Ballard always called them, though I doubt that soft rock entertainers like John Denver, Billy Joel, Carole King, and Barry Manilow put on concerts quite like Genesis, The Who, and Queen did. But Ballard lumped them all together in his critical analysis, and he loved that they all meant easy money for the coffers of Maple Leaf Gardens Ltd., for which he was about 80 per cent owner.

Working in the office on those nights, a constant loud beat of the music reverberated around the building. Ballard spent most of those nights sequestered in his apartment or out of the building. The odd event, such as Luciano Pavorotti singing opera, interested him, but he seldom cared to watch any of the other acts that came to his building.

For those of us who worked full-time in the building, a bonus was being able to watch the sound check, usually around the lunch hour on the day of a concert. Back then, the star attraction would often do a dry run to make sure the sound system and all else was up to snuff. One of my early favourite memories was watching Bruce Springsteen in 1981 run through a few songs like "Hungry Heart" while about a hundred or so of us sat scattered in the Maple Leaf Gardens seats, a VIP audience of sorts.

One act that Harold watched a few times was evangelist Jimmy Swaggart, who booked Maple Leaf Gardens for his concert/service for about three days. I think Ballard saw a lot of Swaggart in himself. What an operator and promoter he was of religion, just like Ballard aspired to be in the sports and entertainment world. He did make a point of sending a Gardens accounting representative to double check that we were getting our appropriate share of the cut for any bibles that were sold by Swaggart's people.

The week of the year I loathed the most was when the circus came to town. The stench in the building was unbelievable (it's true what they say about panther piss) and made working conditions a little more difficult. Fortunately, we usually had some road games so wouldn't be at the Gardens the full week. One morning I pulled into my parking lot after a brief road trip, only to find that the circus people had taken advantage of my vacant parking spot to make it the temporary outhouse for the elephants. Not a pretty sight at all.

In 1980, CPI was on the brink of financial extinction, having to pay high interest rates on a considerable debt load and with no additional line of credit available. The company had been relatively successful and Bill Ballard and Michael Cohl felt they were on the verge of much larger success. Enter Bill's father as the friendly banker. Friendly because he was going to get a 20 per cent rate of return for the $5 million that he loaned to Cohl and his son—he loved to talk about that easy $1 million he made in just one year for helping CPI get through a rough spot.

While Ballard talked of his easy million, CPI soon made millions and millions. The loan kept it solvent at a most critical time. The company was called in to rescue the Michael Jackson North American Victory Tour after another promoter was fired, and from that time, CPI never looked back as it booked acts like the Rolling Stones, Bruce Springsteen, and other big entertainment names across North America. Cohl and Ballard sold a 45 per cent interest in CPI to Labatt Breweries in 1986 for $5 million. They had also just signed an exclusive marketing rights contract to Molson Breweries for another $5 million for a number of years. Neither brewery knew of the other's involvement at the time of the sale.

Bill Ballard could be a wily operator just like his old man.

By the 1980s, Harold Ballard was letting his son deal with the rock promotion business, but in the 1960s he was a member of the Maple Leaf Gardens executive that turned Conn Smythe's hockey shrine into much more than that and promoted an endless stream of non-hockey events at the Gardens.

One of the most exciting was the Beatles' first visit to Toronto, in 1964. With thousands of excited fans lined up around the Gardens in the hopes of purchasing tickets, Ballard seized the opportunity to sell tickets to a second show without first getting approval from the Beatles and their manager, Brian Epstein. This proved not to be a problem, as Epstein agreed to a second show, on September 9, 1964, sparing Ballard any embarrassment.

Rumours spread that Ballard had seized upon the Beatles' appearance in 1964 to feed his insatiable appetite for money. Stories that Ballard ordered the air conditioning turned off on that hot day, that the concession stands were instructed to sell just large-size drinks, and that he ordered the drinking fountains shut off were among those that made the rounds.

In fact, Maple Leaf Gardens never had air conditioning, it sold only one size of drink at the concession stands, and even I wouldn't know where a drinking fountain was located at the Gardens! An interesting thing about Ballard is that he loved these stories, even though they weren't true. He loved the notion that they helped perpetuate his standing as a big-time promoter who would find every conceivable way to squeeze out a few more cents from some such act.

The stories about how much more difficult it was to get our team picture taken once Harold Ballard had decided it had gone to the dogs are true, however.

The Harold-Yolanda sideshow made for great amusement for Leafs followers, yet much of it was not amusing to team employees nor good for the ultimate result on the ice. Yolanda MacMillan suposedly forced her way into Harold Ballard's life like a bull in a china shop and soon was a part of the lives of all working at Maple Leaf Gardens.

I first wondered who this mystery woman was who would hang around the offices for hours on end to see the Leafs boss. As it continued and persisted, I began to realize that she was making inroads. I feel that Ballard as an 80-year-old widower was not the least bit oblivious to her motivation and methods, but he started to enjoy her company and it filled a void in his life.

She was attractive for her age and at least twenty years younger than the Leafs owner. She could take Ballard's verbal abuse and she could give it back. He actually liked that part of her makeup and that she was persistent. I thought she had the ability to speak gutter talk with a group of unsavoury characters in the morning and then dine with royalty in the evening.

In trying to win the favour of the Leafs owner and later her life partner, Yolanda MacMillan (who later legally changed her last name to Ballard) made an astute move by adding a beautiful Bouvier des Flandres dog to their family. The dog was named TC Puck: "TC" for Ballard's football team the Hamilton Tiger Cats, and "Puck" for the obvious hockey connection. TC Puck became the child they never had.

TC Puck soon had the run of the Leafs executive offices, and a member of the maintenance staff's defining role became taking TC Puck out for long walks in downtown Toronto. How attached the Leafs owner was becoming to his adorable dog, who an ecstatic Yolanda termed "our child," was evident months later.

Team picture day was always a big event early in the season. The bleachers were set up on the ice for the picture, then moved for the team practice. Much thought went into the positioning of the players, with the more "important" players seated in the front row or standing directly behind in the first row, closer to the middle. Players would be placed according to height as well, so that the photo would be aesthetically pleasing, with some symmetry created by the tallest players being in the middle, the row gradually getting shorter as it worked its way to the sides.

On this particular day, there was a notable surprise addition to the photo. Typically, once the team was in place and the photographer had taken a few practice pictures, Ballard would be summoned from the Leafs dressing room. He always made a grand entrance, knowing he was the last person to take his place. He would be dressed in his finest suit and quickly skirted across the ice to take his spot. He wanted to project an aura of youth to the many media on hand. The only problem was that on a couple of occasions he slipped and had to be steadied so that he didn't end up with a bloodied head.

This day he was walking slowly and he wasn't alone. "You've got to be frickin' kidding," was surely the silent reaction of all. TC Puck was going to be in the photo. Ballard held TC Puck by a leash while he took his position seated at the centre of the front row. Fine, get TC Puck to sit and let's move on with the shoot. Now, TC Puck wasn't a stupid dog. When TC Puck sat, as instructed, his butt was on the cold Maple Leaf Gardens ice—never a good idea for a human and certainly not for a dog. Ballard would get TC Puck to sit but it was only a few seconds before TC Puck would stand back up. It was like a family taking a picture with a newborn, the final Leafs team picture contingent on TC Puck sitting appropriately.

Several years later, Yolanda solved this dilemma by placing a white towel under TC Puck. For the next few Leafs team pictures, that proved to be a workable solution.

In telling stories about working for Harold Ballard, like anyone, he had many different sides. The best of Harold Ballard was when he was outside the building. When he was in the building, it was important that everyone know he was the boss. It was his building, his hockey team, his concession, his everything.

Outside the building he was like a favourite uncle. He loved being on road trips where he was just one of the guys. He never wanted a suite at whatever hotel we stayed in—the general manager or coach could take that. He loved to sit up front and talk to the bus drivers in the various cities we visited. Many of them grew to look forward to driving the Leafs team around because of the personable "old guy" who was the owner.

It was on these road trips that my relationship with Ballard really grew over the years. When I think back, I can still hear the phone in my hotel room ringing far too early in the morning for my liking. I knew who would be on the other end bellowing, "Get that broad out of bed and come down and join me for breakfast." Having no "broad" to get out of bed, I quickly dressed and joined the Leafs owner in the hotel coffee shop.

The first words out of a friend's or relative's mouth after I had introduced him or her to Harold Ballard and we were once again alone was "I can't believe how nice he is." It was a side to him that many thought didn't exist. I was having breakfast in a hotel coffee shop in Edmonton with my great-aunt Gina. She lived just outside Edmonton and had come into town to see me. She didn't follow hockey and so wasn't up on the great Edmonton Oilers team. She certainly didn't know any of the Toronto Maple Leafs, many of whom were eating breakfast at tables near ours.

But she did recognize one person. "Is that Harold Ballard?" she whispered to me. Ballard was sitting with other members of team management a few tables over. When Ballard was leaving a few minutes later, I introduced the two as he stopped to chat with me. "Mr. Ballard, this is my grandmother's sister, Gina." "Grandmother's sister? Christ, you look like a chorus girl!" was his retort, spoken with an engaging smile, his eyes friendly. "Oh, Mr. Ballard, I've been a pensioner for 15 years," my great-aunt Gina said, surprised by his remark. "Well, you look great," was his final line. He made her feel appreciated, and I appreciated him for that, and for taking the time. That was the side of him I really enjoyed.

7 TALL TALES AND SMALL TALES
MORE STORIES FROM THE FIELD

Can't get away from drafts and trades—they define so much of the game and are an integral part of a manager's job.

The greatest moment in the Leafs' history since their last Stanley Cup victory in 1967 remains forever etched in fans' memories. Bob Rouse takes a shot from inside the blue line and Nikolai Borschevsky somehow puts it in. Then bedlam. A shot of the Leafs bench as Pat Burns pumps his first into the air; equipment manager Brian Papineau sprays a water bottle as if it is foaming champagne. A quick shot to the Joe Louis Arena press box, where General Manager Cliff Fletcher and assistant coaches Mike Murphy and Rick Wamsley embrace in a jubilant yet awkward manner. As Burns walks onto the ice, he looks up and directs another celebratory fist pump to the three Leafs executives.

At that moment, neither Pat Burns, nor anyone else in hockey, had an inkling that as the perpetrators of this devastating playoff loss for the Detroit Red Wings, he and his Toronto Maple Leafs team had laid the first brick in a foundation that a few weeks later would see the annual salary of NHL coaches crack the million-dollar barrier. Indeed, that was nowhere in Burns's mind as he continued to soak up the aftermath of a huge upset victory. A small contingent of about two thousand Toronto Maple Leafs fans cheered lustily as about sixteen thousand Red Wings fans sat in stunned silence. My future wife, Lisa, and other friends were among that Leafs minority. For a minute or so, I was a little worried that Red Wings fans wouldn't tolerate the Leafs fans' celebration.

I was relieved to see that I was wrong. The Detroit fans showed no reaction—there was just silence. They seemed to be collectively numb. Losing in the first round to the Leafs had been unthinkable to them, and they had seen this early Red Wings playoff demise a few too many times. Rather than boo or shout slurs, they simply left the building, still in disbelief and now angry.

And that was exactly the mood in the owner's box: a smouldering anger at yet another playoff disappointment for Mike Ilitch as he bore the indignity of seeing the Red Wings faithful exit the building, once again greatly disappointed. He was the one person who could try to do something about it, and he intended to take swift action. He turned to the first manager hired when he purchased the team in 1981. He asked his advisor and former general manager Jim Devellano who he felt would be the appropriate coach to take the Red Wings to playoff success.

"I told him two names," said Devellano later. "Scotty Bowman and Al Arbour."

"Then get one of them no matter what it costs," Ilitch ordered. After being somewhat kicked upstairs in the Red

Wings management structure, with Bryan Murray assuming his old job as general manager, Devellano was energized by the challenge.

Devellano focused on Scotty Bowman, who was in the midst of coaching the Pittsburgh Penguins further into the playoffs, after they had won consecutive Stanley Cups in 1991 and 1992. Bob Johnson had coached the Penguins to their first Stanley Cup, while Bowman had to quickly take the reins the following season when Johnson was forced to step down for health reasons.

Whether the Red Wings were guilty of borderline tampering remains unclear. Bowman's Penguins in 1993 reached the second round, where they would be upset by the New York Islanders. Direct contact or not, Bowman was certainly aware of the Red Wings' interest. It was also clear that an established and successful coach like Bowman would relish a new challenge like coaching the Red Wings. And ultimately, money talks, and Ilitch gave Bowman a million reasons to make the move to Detroit.

The playoff success was not immediate. Bowman would be the coach for the 1994 playoffs where, again, the Red Wings suffered a first-round upset, this time at the hands of the San Jose Sharks. Bryan Murray and Doug MacLean paid the price and were fired as general manager and assistant general manager respectively. Bowman, though, continued to have the confidence and support of the owner.

In 1995, Bowman's Red Wings still failed to win the Cup, but made it to the Stanley Cup Final, and a year later the Conference Final. Although the Stanley Cup eluded the Red Wings, the fans and, more importantly, the owner were satisfied with the improved playoff success. When many least expected it, the Red Wings won the Stanley Cup in 1997 and again in 1998. Bowman left in a blaze of glory as he carried the Stanley Cup around the Joe Louis Arena ice with his third and final Red Wings Cup win in 2002. Mike Ilitch's million-dollar investment had paid off handsomely.

Now, back to Scotty Bowman's arrival in Detroit for his first year there. Training camp 1993. Bowman is still four years away from his first Cup victory in Motown, and his million-dollar contract is the talk of the coaching world. On the Toronto side, Leafs fever has never been at a stronger pitch since the Leafs' last Stanley Cup in 1967. Pat Burns is happy with what he has accomplished. But Pat Burns is also unhappy. A little over a year earlier, Burns had left the Montreal Canadiens and enthusiastically agreed to a four-year contract to coach the Toronto Maple Leafs at $350,000 per season, a significant increase from what he had been making in Montreal.

Now the team his Leafs had eliminated that previous spring had brought in a new coach at about triple Burns's salary. It didn't take long to see that the passion Burns brought to his coaching position was the same when it came to money. "I'm going to need your help," he said to me one day early at training camp. I was just into my third year working on the media side after being a colleague on the management side. I was not the only media "insider" he spoke to on the subject. He made it clear that he was anxious and being proactive to have his contract renegotiated for the final three years.

So a day later, when I had him as a guest on my radio show on The Fan, I asked him about all the talk that was going around about the Leafs and Burns renegotiating his deal. "I don't know anything about that," Burns quickly said. "I've left that with my representative [Don Meehan] and I don't worry about that stuff. I just concentrate on coaching." This process showed me Burns's acumen for reading people and circumstances and being unafraid to push hard for whatever was in his best interests. While espousing the party line, his contract negotiations were first and foremost in his mind. That was part of what made him an excellent coach.

He, of course, soon got the new contract and a salary increase to $450,000. A year later, the Leafs had another successful season at the helm—they won their first two playoff series and made it to the Conference Finals, losing to Vancouver in five games. A few months later, at the 1994 training camp, Pat Burns gave another somewhat predictable overture: "I'm going to need your help." And, for a third season, he had his contract renegotiated upward to somewhat close the gap the million dollar coach he and his team had helped to create.

In the 1980–81 season, I witnessed an unusual eve-of-playoffs event that had a predictable on-ice result.

What a difference a year makes. For the Toronto Maple Leafs team, a number of things had changed in just a year. Harold Ballard had overruled Imlach's choice of coach. He had forced Imlach to fire Joe Crozier at the midway point of the season and choose Mike Nykoluk as the new head coach. Imlach was no fan of Nykoluk and vice versa, but they both understood that, in this case, the owner was calling the shots.

Nykoluk was a player's coach and the complete opposite in style to Imlach during his almost two-year stint as the Leafs general manager. Once Nykoluk took the position of coach, a very different atmosphere surrounded the team. Instead of being filled with bickering and constant criticism, the atmosphere became fun, relaxed, and positive.

The Leafs needed to win their last game of the season against the Quebec Nordiques in Quebec City on April 5, 1981. And they did just that with a surprising 4–2 win at Le Colisée with the colourful and personable Ron Sedlbauer the offensive star with two goals. This gave the Leafs the 16th and final playoff position on the last day of the regular season. Sedlbauer, a former first-round pick of the Vancouver Canucks, would have no idea that it would be his last regular-season NHL game of his career, a career plagued by inconsistent play and defensive shortcomings. That inconsistency showed with his scoring 40 goals in one season in Vancouver (1978–79) but never scoring more than 23 in his other six NHL seasons with Vancouver, Chicago, and Toronto.

Sedlbauer played the next season with the Leafs' minor league team in Cincinnati and then retired in 1982 at the age of 27. With a solid business acumen to go with his engaging personality, he entered the well-established family business of Cougar Shoes, based out of Burlington, Ontario. He enjoyed and celebrated his last moment of NHL glory on the Leafs charter flight home from Quebec City on that April 5, 1981, night.

The 1980–81 season marked the final year of a playoff format based on overall standings before the change to playoffs based on divisions. The following season, teams would have to play through their respective divisions (Norris, Adams, Smythe, and Patrick) in the first two rounds.

In 1981, it was a more basic format. Sixteen of the 21 teams qualified for the playoffs, and the matches were determined on overall standings. Number 1 played number 16, number

2 played number 15, number 3 played number 14, and so on. As team number 16, our first-round opponents were the defending Stanley Cup champions, the New York Islanders. That realization tempered the jubilation just a little bit on that flight home from Quebec City.

I will say it was a much happier and unified group that landed on Long Island the day before the first playoff game, unlike the divided group of a year earlier that I witnessed in Minneapolis. Mike Nykoluk wanted to keep up the camaraderie and high spirits—important if his underdog Leafs were to have any chance of upsetting Denis Potvin, Bryan Trottier, Mike Bossy, Clark Gilles, and company.

Nykoluk instructed me to find a restaurant a short walk from our Long Island hotel, and the team would have dinner and a night out on the team account (not a common practice back then). After getting advice from a few players, I made the reservation at a large Chinese food restaurant that was about a three-minute walk from our hotel. A few hours later, the players headed out early to start the evening.

I was the handler, or "bank," for the team's cash on the road. This included cash for player per diems, trainer expenses, transportation, game tickets, and other incidental items. When Harold Ballard was on the road with us, as he usually was, the incidental items tended to grow. Though I was pulling in a starting salary of about $12,000, I usually had thousands of dollars in Canadian or American currency in my possession when we were on the road. This was before credit cards were prevalent and debit cards had not yet been invented. Cash was king, the preferred method of payment for business transactions. For longer road trips, I typically carried the equivalent of my year's salary in cash.

A couple of thousand dollars from my bankroll was earmarked for the team dinner that night. When I arrived at the dinner a few hours later to settle the bill, it was apparent none of the players was ready to leave. Nykoluk's plan that the evening be a chance for the players to relax, bond, and enjoy themselves was certainly unfolding to perfection. That was why I had decided to let the players dine by themselves and I would arrive near the anticipated end. When the bill arrived, it was obvious that the players had followed instructions to enjoy themselves at the team's expense.

As often happens, it was a minority group that pushed the envelope. Having a beer or a glass of wine was not unexpected but the alcohol bill that evening went far beyond that. Throw in shooters and even cigarettes and it certainly didn't make for a breakfast of champions. Not ideal the evening before a playoff outing to face the defending Stanley Cup champions.

As some of the more responsible members got the team to disperse and head back to the hotel, I settled the bill in cash. I headed outside for a breath of the nice New York spring air before going back to the hotel. The always classy Dan Maloney was waiting for me. "You can't be walking around alone with that kind of cash, especially when people know you have it," he said as he accompanied me on the short walk back to the hotel.

Predictably, our series with the New York Islanders was comparable to that of the previous year. Even though it was a much-improved atmosphere, we still lost three straight, the first two games on Long Island by scores of 9–2 and 5–1 and then back in Toronto by a 6–1 score. We were outscored by a margin of 20–4.

While Mike Nykoluk's style of being a player's coach was welcomed by his players, that evening's dinner bill was a harbinger of things to come: a few years later, being a player's coach was no longer effective for Nykoluk. He put a great deal of trust in his players, and rather than set a curfew, he would have a 9 p.m. meeting in his room the night before a game, assuming that this strategy would keep the players in the hotel and they would head straight to bed afterward. Only years later did he learn that a (again) minority of players had hit the town on a regular basis after the meeting.

When Mike Nykoluk was fired in 1984, it was Dan Maloney who took over as the head coach.

Al Michaels's memorable call of "Do you believe in miracles?" remains an indelible moment and arguably the greatest hockey victory by the United States ever. It certainly gave hockey a greater public profile in that country and inspired many American kids to play a game that just a few years earlier had been foreign to them. Less remembered than Michaels's play-by-play is that future Leafs president and general manager Ken Dryden was the colour commentator beside Michaels for the Miracle on Ice game on ABC television.

A year after the gold medal victory at Lake Placid, there was a new American hockey story. He was a phenomenon, a high school kid who was expected to be drafted the highest any American ever had been in the 1981 Entry Draft. His name was Bobby Carpenter and he played for St. John's Prep School in Connecticut.

Carpenter was certainly popular and high-profile—he remains the first high school hockey player to be featured on the cover of *Sports Illustrated*—but NHL scouts remained very divided as to how good an American high school player could be and where he would fit in the draft. That debate appeared to be a moot point when the final draft order was established. The Hartford Whalers would select fourth overall. They made it clear that, no matter what others felt, Carpenter was going to be their pick. They were confident of his play on the ice, and equally cognizant of his value off the ice: he was the all-American kid who could help a franchise that struggled to sell tickets.

Draft day came and those at the Whalers' table waited the few minutes that it would take to make their much-publicized selection. Among the Whalers brass at the draft table was Bob Carpenter Sr., a Whalers' scout, who was about to realize a dream in welcoming his son to his NHL team.

The three teams drafting ahead of Hartford were Winnipeg, Los Angeles, and Colorado. While there were teams that seemed to have an active interest in Bobby Carpenter, Whalers scouts were confident those three teams weren't in the mix.

Winnipeg opened the draft by selecting Dale Hawerchuk of Cornwall, and Los Angeles followed by selecting Doug Smith from Ottawa. Now it was the Colorado Rockies' turn, who quickly called "time." This was a curious call to make when the third overall pick should be rather straightforward, but still there was no hint that the Whalers' plan was going awry and no cause for concern at their table.

That changed when the Colorado Rockies announced a trade rather than making their selection. The Washington Capitals were to select fifth overall, right after the Whalers. The Rockies and Capitals agreed to a trade that included the two teams switching their picks. Now Washington was selecting third overall, and they wasted little time in selecting the all-American kid, Bobby Carpenter.

An angry and emotional Whalers' entourage sat in stunned silence. Carpenter's father bolted from the table for a few minutes to regain his composure, aware that the once-in-a-lifetime father-son moment would not become a reality. For the Whalers' organization, the past few minutes had totally erased its on-ice and off-ice strategy and its team plans of the previous months.

As with the Boston Bruins two years earlier when they were bitterly disappointed about missing out on Keith Brown, the Whalers had to get back to business and figure out who they should select. Possibly they could get lucky with a Ray Bourque–type consolation prize, as had happened with Boston.

They decided to stick with drafting a centre like Carpenter, but there were no other high school all-American kids to be had. So they went with the solid Ontario Hockey League and selected Ron Francis from the Sault Ste. Marie Greyhounds. He is still affectionately referred to as "Mr. Whaler" by legions of Whalers fans. Lightning did strike twice in the New England area: again like the Bruins with Bourque, the Whalers had also drafted a future Hall of Famer.

In fact, Ron Francis became the heart and soul of that Whalers franchise. To most Whalers fans, the day the Whalers franchise actually died in Hartford was March 4, 1991, the day that Francis was traded to the Pittsburgh Penguins. Francis scored 1,798 points (549 goals, 1,249 assists) in 1,731 regular-season games over 23 seasons. He was inducted into the Hockey Hall of Fame in 2007.

That 1991 day the Whalers traded Francis marked a day of rebirth of NHL playoff hockey in Pittsburgh. Though Lemieux had become a true NHL superstar and made the Penguins a more respectable team, the Penguins had failed to qualify for the Stanley Cup playoffs in five of Lemieux's first six NHL seasons. Slowly but surely a stronger supporting cast was being assembled around him. In one fell swoop with the acquisition of Ron Francis, the Penguins were legitimate Stanley Cup contenders. And, much to the chagrin of Whalers fans, Francis would hoist the Stanley Cup the next two seasons (1991 and 1992) as a Pittsburgh Penguin.

The bigger lesson to all NHL teams was to not advertise who you are planning to select, a lesson that has been strictly followed in ensuing years, with possible draft selections guarded like state secrets. Though they won big in the long run, on that draft day in 1981, the Whalers wished they had kept their selection secret.

Ron Francis is back being "Mr. Whaler" as a member of the front office of the Carolina Hurricanes. The last time I met Bobby Carpenter was at the Hockey Hall of Fame Induction Gala in November 2010. Carpenter is currently a pro scout with the Toronto Maple Leafs.

Carpenter had a more successful NHL career than many fans give him credit for. He was an instant hit for the Washington Capitals. In his first five seasons, he recorded at least 27 goals and 56 points each season, highlighted by a total of 95 points (53 goals, 42 assists) in 1984–85.

He was used less as a front-line player in stops in New York (Rangers), Los Angeles, Boston, Washington (again), and New Jersey. He played a total of 1,122 regular-season NHL games, scoring 718 points (318 goals, 400 assists) over 17 seasons.

David McNab has been a respected NHL scout for decades and a significant reason that the Anaheim Ducks won their Stanley Cup in 2007. As their chief scout, he heads up a staff that drafted the likes of Corey Perry and Ryan Getzlaf. His father, Max, was a long-time NHL executive, and his brother, Peter, was an NHL player and broadcaster.

David McNab likes to tell a story about years earlier, when he was a scout with the Hartford Whalers. McNab was at their table for the 1985 Entry Draft in Toronto. In typical fashion, Harold Ballard refused to allow the NHL to use Maple Leaf Gardens as the venue for the draft, so proceedings were held in the smaller space at Metro Toronto Convention Centre. Most drafts the previous decade had been held in hockey environments, such as the Montreal Forum, but the more intimate surroundings made for a more vibrant atmosphere.

For one, all the noise we were making created a loud buzz, an excited energy, under the lower ceiling of the convention centre. Bleachers had been set up that were just a few yards from the temporary gates surrounding the draft floor. The spectators were pretty much right on top of the action, which lent a sense of intimacy to the proceedings. In Montreal, on the other hand, spectators would be much more distant observers. As well, fans could mingle with NHL executives once they left the draft floor for whatever reason. (In Montreal, there were refreshment and washroom areas for NHL team personnel only, which were cordoned off from the fans.)

The Hartford Whalers had an end table in the draft table mix, just a few yards from metal barricades, behind which interested fans gathered to get a really close view of the action.

As the draft progressed, McNab remembers that each Whalers selection had a constant teenage presence, which encouraged his team to select Randy Burridge. Later, in the common area outside the gated compound of NHL Draft tables, McNab bumped into the same kid who had earlier encouraged him to select Randy Burridge from the Peterborough Petes. Small in stature but with a big heart and big goal-scoring capabilities, Burridge remained available as the draft moved into the fourth, fifth, and sixth rounds. The young teen positioned himself near the Whalers' table once again and offered his unsolicited advice.

"This kid kept pestering me to take Burridge, and after every time we didn't, he told me what a mistake we made," McNab related. "Finally I had enough of this kid, he was getting to me and distracting me so I just turned and said, 'Randy Burridge won't be drafted, and he will never play in the NHL.' I certainly surprised the vocal kid with my reaction, and that seemed to quiet him down."

Burridge was taken in the eighth round by the Boston Bruins and ended up being one of the steals in the draft. He played most of that season with the Bruins as an underage player and scored 27 and 31 goals in his first two full NHL seasons. He was the best late-round pick in that year's draft and every NHL team would have done well to listen to that kid who was chirping at the Hartford table.

Not only did McNab watch Burridge enjoy instant success in the NHL, he had to watch him play for the Whalers' division archrival, the Boston Bruins, and often at the expense of his Whalers team. "And every time I saw Burridge play— and he always seemed to play especially well against us—all

I could think about was this kid, who turned out to be Burridge's brother, and my ill-advised comments."

Summer of 1988 and I'm surprised by an unexpected call from Randy Burridge of the Boston Bruins. He was looking for a try-out for his younger brother, Joel—that cheeky spectator in the 1985 Entry Draft who had been pushing McNab to pick Randy. We had very few spots for completely unproven walk-ons, but I respected Randy for making calls on behalf of his younger brother. "He's just like me," he said just before hanging up. That was the clincher, and I made Joel Burridge a late addition to our training camp roster. From the little bit I got to see of Joel, I thought that off the ice he was a character guy like his older brother. However, the tryout proved he wasn't quite the same on the ice. Very few were.

Many Toronto Maple Leafs fans remember the 1985 Entry Draft mostly for the first overall selection of Wendel Clark. That was another reason for the heightened energy, excitement, and buzz. A mostly pro-Leafs audience was bubbly and enthusiastic that their beloved team had the first overall selection. The moments after Clark was selected first overall was my 15 minutes of fame . . . or should I say 15 seconds of fame.

After the NHL-WHA merger, the NHL Draft moved to the larger location of the Montreal Forum for the first time in 1980. Prior to that, the draft had been held at a ballroom in a downtown Montreal hotel. The draft began at 9 a.m. on a weekday and was open to a few hundred spectators, who straggled in. I remember for a few years telling friends about this best-kept secret: just drop by the Montreal Forum on draft day and you can have a front-row seat to one of the biggest hockey events of the year. The NHL eventually caught on to this and began to use it as a marketing tool, particularly in Canada. The 1985 Entry Draft was moved to Toronto partially for that reason, to give other NHL hotbeds the opportunity to experience what had evolved to a spectator spectacle. It was also the first draft to be televised live by CBC and was moved to a Saturday afternoon—a better time for live spectators and television viewers.

The Toronto Maple Leafs had the first overall selection that year, having finished dead last in the 21-team NHL for the 1984–85 season. Like the New York Islanders did in 2009, we kept our first overall selection a secret until we actually made the pick. With the Islanders in 2009, it still seemed obvious to pretty well everyone that John Tavares would be their selection, but it wasn't obvious who we were focusing on that draft day in 1985.

Wendel Clark, Craig Simpson, and Dana Murzyn seemed the consensus for the top three selections, and they were who we debated about in our Leafs scouting meetings. We had sweaters printed up for all three players while the debate continued. But we seemed to always lean toward Wendel Clark as our pick, and at the final meeting the night before the draft that was confirmed.

The day before the draft, I was in a meeting with CBC representatives, who went over the protocol for their televising the draft. The late Don Wittman would meet the drafted player as he left the bleacher area and walked toward the team table that drafted him, conducting a walking interview with him for about 30 seconds or so.

Being the first overall pick, I wanted to make sure that we had it right. I believed I had an understanding with CBC that we would get that Leafs jersey to our number one overall pick and that he would wear it while being interviewed by Wittman.

On the morning of the draft, I wanted to give our player a heads-up. Don Meehan represented both Wendel Clark and Dana Murzyn. I told Clark and Murzyn that if one of them was our pick, we would get a Leafs sweater on him and then he would be interviewed by the CBC as he walked to the draft table. I then shook hands with both and headed back to the draft table.

Bill Torrey of the New York Islanders made a last-minute trip to our table to offer the New York Islanders' two first-round picks (6th and 13th overall) in exchange for our first overall selection. We talked about it for five minutes before getting back to Torrey to say we weren't interested.

Just as the draft was about to begin, I asked one of our staff, Dan Marr, for Clark's Leafs jersey. Just as I did, I was aware of a CBC camera rolling behind us, taking in all that was going on at our table. The jerseys for Clark, Simpson, and Murzyn were still under the table, and Marr had to be careful that the camera didn't film us picking up the wrong jersey or sorting through the three of them.

Having ducked that potential television blooper, I proceeded to just outside the draft area, holding the folded Clark jersey. I wanted to make sure I got to Clark as soon as the pick was announced. I felt I had the jump on what was about to unfold and was positioned perfectly, with Clark seated about 20 yards directly in front of me. When Gerry McNamara made the announcement from the Leafs table, I made a beeline to Wendel and then waited for him to complete his congratulatory handshakes and walk the few steps down to the floor.

He was so close that I could almost touch him . . . and, then, *boom!* . . . a shoulder block from Don Wittman and the CBC crew as they got right on Clark and began the interview. So, really, my first 15 seconds of television fame is of me walking aimlessly behind Wendel Clark, looking like a fifth wheel at a dinner party.

As often happens in life, sometimes the unexpected can turn out better than the expected would have. Wittman finished interviewing Clark when we were about 15 yards from the Leafs table, in the middle of the draft floor. I held Clark back, helped him take off his jacket, and held it for him as he put on the Leafs jersey. The roar of the crowd was deafening, far louder than it would have been had I got the jersey on him a few seconds after the announcement. *That* was my 15 seconds of fame, and it all made for excellent theatre. Then he walked the final yards to meet the staff from the organization he still works for to this day.

I always liked Clark's line when asked by a writer, "Who was the first person to meet you from the Leafs organization?" "Some guy from the front office with a sweater" was his reply. I'm glad that our relationship has become closer than a "some guy" one since then.

Harold Ballard was in fine form that draft day as well. When asked by a reporter how long ago we decided on Clark as our pick, he said, "We decided weeks ago; we had his name put on our sweater back then." The reporter took Ballard at face value, unaware that we had done the same for Craig Simpson and Dana Murzyn.

It is interesting how actions by the Toronto Maple Leafs have caused change within the Detroit Red Wings organization, the upset in the 1993 playoffs being a classic example, when Scotty Bowman began his long, successful run as head coach.

What should have been a meaningless regular-season game at Maple Leaf Gardens on January 13, 1986, proved to be a turning point. Harry Neale began the season as the coach of the Red Wings and suffered a brutal losing streak that saw him jettisoned after 35 games. One of the final games in his short tenure as Red Wings coach was a 9–3 loss to the Leafs at Maple Leaf Gardens on November 23, 1985.

Mike and Marian Ilitch made the trip to Toronto and sat in the visiting team's premium seats, which were on the gold rails, right beside the Red Wings team bench. "With each of the nine goals scored against us, and with my job hanging by a thread, I had to see those steely angry eyes of Mike Ilitch right beside the bench," Neale remembers. "I told our staff after the game that I didn't know what I could do to improve the team, but next time I wanted Mike Ilitch seated elsewhere when we came to Toronto," he quipped.

Although Neale's firing was a loss to the coaching profession, it was a great gain for the broadcasting fraternity. Neale would immediately begin work with *Hockey Night in Canada* and a few years later would be the colour commentator on all Toronto Maple Leafs broadcasts and the colour voice on the top duo on *Hockey Night in Canada* alongside Bob Cole.

Neale had handled the adversity in Detroit with great character, and he continued to respect the Red Wings hierarchy and Jimmy Devellano as his general manager. The new hire, Brad Park, would be an "owner's guy." Ilitch was getting impatient with the long-term plan prescribed by Devellano and was enthusiastic with Park as a short-term fix.

With his Red Wings team at the time turning things around on the ice and aware of the support of the Detroit owner, Park had little use for any chain of power when he had a direct connection to the owner. After five seasons of following a long-term plan to turn the Red Wings franchise around, General Manager Jim Devellano found himself working in a vacuum as his power was usurped by the new ambitious coach.

I saw Devellano standing by the Gardens ticket office on the morning of a game day, January 13th, 1986, as I made my way around the building during the morning skates. He could make some humorous hockey analogies, and I especially loved one he had made a year earlier in assessing the Norris Division, which then was the weakest of the four NHL divisions. "Playing in the Norris Division is like puppy love," he said. "To understand it, you have to be in it." So our two teams, along with the Minnesota North Stars, St. Louis Blues, and Chicago Blackhawks, understood the NHL style of puppy love.

But he was far from being in a good-natured mood that January morning. I was aware that he had been unhappy with his situation in Detroit since Park had been hired six weeks earlier, but I was surprised by his acid tongue. Exchanging regards as I walked by, I kidded Devellano about the "battle of the heavyweights tonight"—the Leafs and Red Wings were the bottom two teams in the Norris Division. "Battle of the heavyweights," an unamused Devellano retorted. "Maybe in 10 fucking years . . . battle of the heavyweights, what a fucking joke." I kept walking so as to keep his expletive-laden rant short.

That seemingly meaningless game ended up being a memorable night for quite an unexpected reason. It was the last-ever good old-fashioned bench brawl for the Leafs. It would also be the night that Brad Park's almost two-month run as the apple of the owner's eye would begin to lose its lustre.

The NHL had instituted strict rules that called for a 10-game suspension for the first player off the bench, possible sanctions against that player's coach, as well as a liberal dispensing of game misconducts to other combatants. The NHL had turned a page, and it was no longer worth it to clear the benches. Evidently, on that night Brad Park felt differently.

I remember it as a very strange bench brawl in how it evolved. The Leafs were winning the game handily and it wasn't really overly physical or nasty. Wendel Clark was on the ice for the Leafs and Barry Melrose (Clark's cousin) for the Red Wings. There was some pushing and shoving behind the Detroit net and some gloves were dropped. Then, with no forewarning whatsoever, the Red Wings bench emptied to join the fray. The Leafs bench followed seconds behind.

I don't remember any great fights that night, which one seems to be able to recall readily with bench brawls from an earlier era, but I do remember a humorous one. It was one of the first games that Miroslav Ihnacak was in a Leafs uniform after defecting from Czechoslovakia, and he dutifully headed over the boards with his teammates. Then, *whack!* He had no idea what hit him. It was Red Wings backup goaltender, Ed Mio, picking the least formidable fighting opponent in Ihnacak. Their bout looked like the slapstick antics of the Three Stooges.

After the 7–4 Leafs victory, Devellano made the long drive back to Detroit with his two top assistants, Ken Holland and Neil Smith. Smith would later leave the Red Wings to become general manager of the New York Rangers. A few years after that, Holland would assume Devellano's role, after a few years of the Bryan Murray regime, and become the long-time successful general manager of the Red Wings, where he remains today.

The Stanley Cup rings they would all later earn were a long way off and seemed like a pipe dream as they drove back home. The three sat mostly in silence as they stewed about what they had witnessed that night. Finally, Smith broke out in a tirade. Like Devellano, he was a Toronto native. He spewed venom about the embarrassing performance by the team at Maple Leaf Gardens, but especially about Park's classless act of instigating the bench brawl by sending the Red Wings team over the bench first, and the fact that he and Devellano had to endure this in their hometown, with family and friends at the game.

"Would you say all that to Jim Lites?" an enthused Devellano asked. Lites was the son-in-law of Mike Ilitch and vice-president of the team. He was the top hockey guy to deal with when it came to channelling information to and from Mike Ilitch. Devellano felt that Lites had also put him in a decision-making vacuum for a number of months in favour of the flavour of the month Brad Park. Devellano was looking for allies and looking for them to speak up against Park.

Smith agreed and they pulled their car off Highway 401 and stopped at the first pay phone they saw. Devellano called Lites at his home and told him that Neil Smith had something he wanted to say. Smith repeated his tirade. It was soon apparent that it was not falling on deaf ears. That night, the Red Wings ownership took issue with Park's actions. The next day was his first with his loss in status as the prodigal son of the ownership group.

Devellano began to work his way back up the Red Wings hierarchy with the powers he had about a year earlier but felt them eroded while Park was the coach. Park's coaching career ended in a matter of months, at the end of the season. Like they would do later with Scotty Bowman, the Red Wings lured an active NHL coach, Jacques Demers, from the St. Louis Blues to become their head coach in 1987. Actually, the lure involved a level of tampering that at that time wasn't treated as seriously as it is today. The Red Wings paid a team fine and agreed to play two pre-season games in St. Louis as their punishment for talking to Demers when he was still under contract with the Blues.

I had a great laugh with Devellano recounting the events of that low evening in his NHL executive career as I conversed with him at a Fan Forum during the Hockey Hall of Fame Induction Weekend in November 2010. Jimmy D had made it to the Hockey Hall of Fame!

When the New York Rangers won the Stanley Cup in 1994, Mike Keenan was behind several trades that were made at the trade deadline, even though Neil Smith was the general manager. The most memorable was acquiring playoff asset Stephane Matteau from the Chicago Blackhawks in exchange for Tony Amonte. Keenan was also instrumental in adding Brian Noonan from Chicago and Craig MacTavish from Edmonton at the deadline.

The last of the New York Rangers deadline trades was initiated about a half hour before the 3 p.m. Eastern Standard Time deadline and completed with minutes to spare. Little did Mike Gartner realize at the time, but it would have been his best opportunity to be a part of a Stanley Cup winner. Gartner was inducted into the Hockey Hall of Fame in 2001 after a career with 1,335 points (708 goals, 627 assists) in 1,432 regular-season games over 19 NHL seasons. He is that rare breed of Hall of Famer who never tasted champagne out of the Stanley Cup.

For someone like Ray Bourque, a trade was arranged to the Colorado Avalanche from the Boston Bruins so that he would have a better opportunity to realize that dream. Gartner spent most of his career with a really good Washington Capitals team, but one that was never able to enjoy the same success in the playoffs. While Bourque was traded to a team with a better chance to win the Stanley Cup, Gartner was traded away just at the deadline from his best Stanley Cup opportunity.

Trade deadline day 1994. While the New York Rangers were active on the trade front, Leafs general manager Cliff Fletcher was waiting on a deal he felt was all but done. The Leafs and Nordiques had agreed in principle, at least Fletcher felt, for Mike Ricci to join the Leafs in exchange for defenceman Dave Ellett and prospect forward Landon Wilson.

As the minutes and then hours ticked away toward the deadline, Fletcher was bothered that he hadn't received a return call from Pierre Page, the Nordiques' general manager. Fletcher also had a larger-than-life coach in Pat Burns, who was unafraid to pressure Fletcher internally. Burns was extremely keen on the trade, believing that the addition of the skilled and gritty Mike Ricci would be the perfect second-line centre behind Doug Gilmour.

Fletcher was also irked because the lack of any kind of confirmation on the deal was holding him up in seeing what else he could to do with other teams. After another unreturned call to the Nordiques general manager and another visit to his office by an annoyed coach, Fletcher was getting less optimistic about the Nordiques deal—there was less than an hour to go to the trade deadline.

The coach decided to take action. Pat Burns went back to his office and did a bit of an end-run with regard to the chain of command with both the Leafs and Nordiques. He called Marcel Aubut, the president of the Nordiques, directly to find out what the story was about the prospective trade. Aubut gave Burns the quick and simple answer that Fletcher couldn't get from Page. The trade was a no-go according to the Nordiques owner.

Burns stormed back upstairs to Fletcher's office to report on his brief chat with Aubut. Fletcher was angry about the lack of a direct answer to him but tried to think of alternatives for the trade. The energy of the trade deadline day had enveloped the whole organization, which was anxious for some kind of a move. He had a coach, Burns, who was blunt that, to him, no news on the trade front was bad news.

A phone call came in from the New York Rangers with 20 minutes left before deadline. Mike Keenan had identified Glenn Anderson as the type of player he wished to bring to New York for the Rangers' upcoming playoff drive. Would the Leafs take Mike Gartner in return? Fletcher asked his front office staff and head coach and they all quickly answered in the affirmative. The trade was done in a matter of minutes.

Mike Gartner headed to Toronto from New York in exchange for Glenn Anderson, the rights to Scott Malone, and a fourth-round draft choice in the 1994 Entry Draft.

Three months later, Glenn Anderson sported his sixth Stanley Cup ring after having won five with the Edmonton Oilers. He was inducted into the Hockey Hall of Fame in 2008. Had Fletcher taken a pass on the last-minute trade proposal, Gartner likely would have gone into the Hall of Fame with at least one ring.

8 THE HOLY GRAIL

Leafs fans have a couple of things in common: patience and loyalty. It has been a long time since a Leafs player held the Stanley Cup aloft. There have been highs and lows from 1967 forward. Here's a look at the highs and lows that Leafs fans have endured over the years.

It seems like everyone, sports fans and non-sports fans alike, can answer without hesitation when the Leafs last won the Stanley Cup. The year 1967 is better remembered as that last Stanley Cup victory than even the celebration of Canada's centennial.

Current Leafs president and general manager Brian Burke has heard that year mentioned time and time again as Leafs fans' exasperation grows with each year added to the drought. "I can only take the blame for the past three years," Burke retorts. "You can't pin the first 41 on me."

What is the Leafs' team record for most consecutive losses and when was it set?

"Take your choice," would be the response of those Leafs fans who have endured the Leafs' losing streaks of the early 1970s, most of the 1980s, part of the 1990s, and much of the past decade. However, to put things into perspective, it is actually the last Leafs Stanley Cup championship team that holds that dubious record. That championship team, so beloved and revered, also rang in the New Year in 1967 with 10 consecutive losses. The ultimate high of winning the Stanley Cup dwarfs the low of this standing Leafs team record.

It was about two weeks into the new year when the team's record losing streak began with a 4–0 shutout loss to the Chicago Blackhawks, on January 15. The first game they didn't lose after the 10-game losing streak was actually a tie, 4–4, against Chicago on February 11, to make them winless in 11 straight games.

The next night, February 12, they finally posted that long-sought-after victory, the first in nearly a month, winning 2–1 against the Boston Bruins. To their credit, that Leafs team quickly rediscovered their winning ways and this game marked the first of seven consecutive victories for the Leafs, who used that stretch to build momentum leading to the playoffs.

Over the last 44 years, Leafs fans have cheered the likes of Willie Brossart, Joe Lundigran, Dave Dunn, Pierre Jarry, Serge Boisvert, Jiri Crha, Frank Nigro, Ted Fauss, Zdenek Nedved, Paul DiPietro, Dmitri Khristich, Aki Berg, Craig Wolanin, Jeff Finger, and many others who played on woeful Leafs teams that most felt surely must hold the team record for consecutive losses.

That proves not to be the case, however. Despite the many poor seasons over the past 44 years, the 10-game losing streak of the last Leafs Stanley Cup champions remains a team high. In the big picture, though, not a bad trade-off for a Stanley Cup!

We have all received rejection letters. They're a part of life, and most of us learn to not take them personally and to continue to believe in ourselves and pursue our goals and interests. Thank goodness that arguably the greatest defenceman in NHL history didn't take things personally. Yes, Bobby Orr received a rejection letter at a very young age—from the Toronto Maple Leafs.

In the pre–Entry Draft era, the Leafs had the advantage over the other five NHL teams in procuring talent from Ontario. Most Ontario kids dreamed of playing for the Leafs, and knowledgeable minor hockey insiders provided the Leafs with an endless supply of information on who were the top young players.

In March 1960, Anthony Gilchrist, a minor hockey organizer in Parry Sound, wrote to Leafs general manager Punch Imlach about a 12-year-old named Bobby Orr, whose father, Doug, and grandfather Robert were diehard Toronto Maple Leafs fans. Gilchrist suggested the Leafs take a serious look at the boy, "or I feel sure it will be too late." These were exactly the types of tips that gave the Leafs that decided advantage over their five NHL counterparts.

Imlach passed the note on to his chief scout, Bob Davidson. In a letter dated April 7, 1960, Davidson courteously thanked Gilchrist for the information but declined to follow up on Orr, writing, "The boy is a little too young to be put on any list for protection." Davidson continued, "I will keep his name on file and when he gets to be 14 or 15 we will contact him and, if he is good enough, I would recommend a hockey scholarship for him here in Toronto." Davidson ended the four-paragraph letter with a haunting remark. "I hope that some day Bob Orr will be playing for the Maple Leafs."

So, while the 12-year-old Orr was spared the harsh reality of his first real-world rejection letter, the note to Gilchrist was basically that. Though the Leafs would soon win three straight Stanley Cups, beginning in 1962, perhaps this letter marked the beginning of the end, with the Leafs no longer taking strong action to protect the advantage they held in Ontario.

While the Leafs' attitude was "let's wait and see," it took only one look by the Boston Bruins scouts and management to be smitten. Bruins executive Wren Blair leaped at the opportunity of this diamond in the rough and pretty well lived in Parry Sound for the next two years. This paid huge dividends, as two years later, the 14-year-old Orr signed with the Bruins and began his OHA Junior A career with the Oshawa Generals.

The Leafs' hands-off policy meant that Leafs fans got to watch the dominant player of the 1970s on Maple Leaf Gardens ice only when he came to town with the visiting Boston Bruins.

When Bobby Orr did finally sign his first NHL contract, in September 1966, it was the first time in many years that the Boston Bruins dominated overall sports coverage. They had missed the playoffs for the previous seven consecutive seasons, twice finishing in fifth place and on the other five occasions finishing sixth and dead last in the six-team National Hockey League.

Orr's first contract also made news for being the most lucrative contract ever signed by an NHL rookie. Although that apparently is true, the actual numbers aren't as staggering as some of the inflated rumours would have us believe. Bobby Orr signed a two-year contract for a total of $35,000. In his rookie year, 1966–67, he earned a salary of $10,000 and an additional bonus of $5,000 for playing in 40 NHL games that season. The second year of the contract, he played for a salary of $15,000, again with a bonus of $5,000 for playing in 40 NHL games that season.

The Leafs' last Stanley Cup win in 1967 would also prove to be a pivotal moment in the balance of power among the original six NHL teams. Specifically, Chicago suffered a loss of player talent, balanced by a commensurate gain on the part of the Boston Bruins.

The loss to the Leafs in the first round of the 1967 playoffs was an especially bitter pill for the Blackhawks organization to swallow. The Blackhawks had dominated the NHL regular season with a record of 41 wins, 17 losses, and 12 ties in 70 games, for 94 points. That was 17 points more than second-place Montreal Canadiens, a significant gap. To put these numbers into perspective, the 94 regular-season points attained by the Blackhawks was the second-highest point total over the previous nine seasons of all the teams in the NHL—only Montreal's

98 points in the 1961–62 season beat that mark. Interestingly enough, after that outstanding regular season by Montreal, the Leafs were the Stanley Cup champions that year as well.

During that last Leafs Stanley Cup season of 1966–67, the Bruins were an emerging team, with Orr having had an exceptional rookie year, giving the hockey world a taste of his greatness to come. Another key strength for the Bruins was the solid goaltending of Gerry Cheevers, who had been a "gift" courtesy of the Leafs in 1965. As the top young goaltender in the Leafs system, Imlach was expected in 1965 to protect the young Cheevers, along with veteran Johnny Bower, for the purposes of the old Intra-League Draft. The Intra-League Draft, which later became the Waiver Draft, was an attempt to maintain a competitive balance among NHL teams, allowing the NHL teams with the poorest records the first opportunity to draft players not on the protected lists from one of the teams with a better record.

If Imlach had chosen to protect Bower and Cheevers, it would have made Terry Sawchuk available for the last-place Bruins. It was well known that the Bruins had no interest in Sawchuk because of his age (36), his health, and the fact that he would have been unlikely to report.

When Imlach chose to protect both Bower and Sawchuk, the Bruins leaped at the opportunity to select the 25-year-old Cheevers as their goaltender of the future. This Leafs-aided opportunity for the Bruins didn't require nearly as much time and effort as the aggressive pursuit of the young Bobby Orr, but the addition of Cheevers paid significant dividends as well.

The last key piece of the championship puzzle for the Boston Bruins would not come via Toronto but would be the result of the hard feelings felt in Chicago after their playoff exit to the Leafs in 1967. Chicago, as an organization that had been winning all season, took their first-round elimination extremely hard. As often happens with losing, fingers are pointed and blame is assigned. Many players on the Blackhawks were angered at management, and Chicago management took issue with the way many of their players had performed in the most important games of the season.

An emerging star of the future for the Blackhawks was 25-year-old Phil Esposito, who had recorded at least 20 goals in his first three NHL regular seasons. The final three years of the original six NHL teams were the last of an era where 20 goals were considered a significant offensive achievement. Esposito's early accomplishments with the Blackhawks had established him as a bona fide NHL-quality player in those difficult six-team days. Esposito did not, however, register a single point in Chicago's six playoff games against the Leafs, which drew the ire of Hawks management.

The playoffs ended for Chicago on April 18 in Toronto. A couple of days later, back in Chicago, they had the usual end-of-year team party that included a liberal consumption of alcohol. The party atmosphere could not dispel the foul mood that permeated the organization. Esposito was as unimpressed with Blackhawks management as they were with him and many of his teammates. A clearly over-served Esposito vented his frustration to veteran Bobby Hull. Included in his diatribe was the sentiment that the Hawks would never win with those "fucking guys in charge," this said as he pointed at General Manager Tommy Ivan and Coach Billy Reay. Feeling no pain himself, and in jest, Hull advised the young player to tell Ivan and Reay how he really felt about them. As we have come to know and love about Esposito over the years, he has never shied away from speaking his mind.

"I was just kidding him," Hull told me years later, "but when I looked around and then looked back, he had already stormed over to the two. It was too late." Needless to say, the old guard Blackhawks management was now even less impressed with their young star.

The next day, Esposito went into the Blackhawks office to make his travel arrangements home, and also hoping to get a chance to make amends of some sort with someone in management. Instead, Ivan remained behind his shut office door and just hollered at his secretary to "give him his money home and get him the hell out of the office."

It was soon after, on May 15, that Esposito, along with Ken Hodge and Fred Stanfield, were traded to Boston in exchange for Pit Martin, Jack Norris, and Gilles Marotte. In his eight full seasons with the Bruins he recorded 35, 49, 43, 76, 66, 55, 68, and 61 goals. He was selected to the NHL First All-Star team in six of those seasons. He won the Art Ross Trophy as the NHL's leading regular-season scorer on five occasions and twice, in 1969 and 1974, won the Hart Memorial Trophy as the NHL's Most Valuable Player.

The loss by the Blackhawks and gain by the Bruins wasn't just the play of Phil Esposito. Ken Hodge averaged scoring 33 goals per season in his nine full years in Boston, including hitting the 50-goal mark in 1973–74. Fred Stanfield scored at least 20 goals per season in his six years with the Bruins.

Rather than being the anchor of the Blackhawks' blue line, Gilles Marotte enjoyed a journeyman-type career in his three and a half years in Chicago. That didn't change the last seven and a half years of his career after leaving Chicago, with stops in Los Angeles, New York (Rangers), and St. Louis. Pit Martin was the one ex-Bruin who distinguished himself in his

10 seasons in Chicago, averaging 24 goals and 63 points per season. Jack Norris remained a career minor league goaltender who finished his career in the World Hockey Association. He played a total of just 10 games with the Blackhawks and, later, 25 games with the Los Angeles Kings.

Esposito, Orr, Cheevers, and the previously sad-sack Bruins won Stanley Cups in 1970 and 1972. The Blackhawks had to wait 43 years after the blockbuster trade with Boston until 2010 to do so. Phil's brother, Tony, remains a Blackhawks goaltending legend and was welcomed back with open arms as the franchise developed stronger ties with former Blackhawks greats over the past few years. It was the Blackhawks' first Stanley Cup victory since 1961.

Bobby Hull, who kidded the young Phil Esposito to speak his then inebriated mind to management, has also enjoyed an active role with the Blackhawks alumni. As an after-dinner speaker, Bobby Hull has been known to be engaging at times, while on other occasions he walks a fine line with stories or jokes that backfire. The team party of 1967 was one of those occasions things backfired on Hull, his actions helping to weaken the Blackhawks' Stanley Cup opportunity while strengthening the Bruins'.

Tommy Ivan's "Get him the hell out of my office" remains Phil Esposito's farewell from the Chicago organization.

For the first game of their Stanley Cup Final against Montreal on April 20, 1967, the Leafs took the midnight train from Toronto, arriving in Montreal in the early morning. They walked around the city a bit and then went to the forum to make sure all was well with their equipment.

Only then did they check in to their hotel. Whether this was a cost-saving measure by Imlach or he thought that the less time spent with distractions in Montreal would help his Leafs team, his plan backfired. The lack of a commonsensical travel plan likely was a factor in the Leafs' 6–2 loss at the forum to kick off that memorable series. Fortunately, a well-rested and no longer homeless Leafs team won the second game, 3–0. They went on to win four of their next five games—and no longer took the midnight train to Montreal.

The Leafs held a 2–1 lead and were 55 seconds away from winning the Stanley Cup in the sixth game of the finals against the Montreal Canadiens on May 2, 1967.

With a faceoff in the Leafs end, the Canadiens pulled goaltender Gump Worsley in favour of adding an extra attacker. "Kelly, Armstrong, Horton, and Pulford," Coach Punch Imlach bellowed from behind the home team bench at Maple Leaf Gardens, "and Stanley, you take the faceoff." This would be the last unforgettable moment for this collection of Leafs greats, and it seemed that Imlach grasped the significance of the occasion and chose to deploy his most loyal and longest-serving soldiers.

Unlike with their three consecutive Stanley Cup victories, from 1962 to 1964, these playoffs for the Leafs had not showcased these Leafs greats but, rather, the emerging younger Leafs who had made the difference. Dave Keon, Jim Pappin, Pete Stemkowski, Brian Conacher, and even Mike Walton had been the dominating forwards, while Larry Hillman and Marcel Pronovost had been outstanding on defence.

Of Imlach's final five, only Pulford had enjoyed what could be considered an outstanding playoff. "I think Imlach knew at that moment that was our swan song," Pulford recalled years later. "That was the swan song of his dynasty."

The most curious decision was to put Stanley at centre, which Stanley claimed hadn't occurred for several years. Feeling overmatched by Canadiens centre Jean Beliveau, Stanley chose to swipe at the puck and then charge directly into Beliveau as the puck was dropped in a play bordering on an interference infraction. Red Kelly swooped in to grab the loose puck and tapped it ahead to Pulford. Beliveau could be seen arguing about Stanley's actions with referee John Ashley as Pulford made the cross-ice pass to Armstrong. Armstrong skated over centre and fired in the empty net insurance goal with 25 seconds remaining.

Although Stanley remembers it differently, Imlach had actually used his defenceman on a number of occasions throughout that playoff to take the faceoffs in their own end. They almost always lost the draw through this unusual strategy. Even though Stanley's memory of how often he was called upon to take a faceoff might not be entirely accurate, the result of this last call can't be disputed. Alan Stanley came up with his best career faceoff win in this unorthodox strategy when it really counted.

Money, or the unwillingness to part with it, reared its ugly head immediately after the Leafs Stanley Cup victory, and would be a prevailing theme among Leafs ownership and management for most of the next 30 years. It could be seen not just during the well-documented Harold Ballard era but also with Steve Stavro's unwillingness to meet Wayne Gretzky's "modest" demands in 1996 and John Ferguson's election to not meet the demands of Gary Roberts and Joe Nieuwendyk in 2005.

There were various reasons why the Leafs would soon plummet from being Stanley Cup champions to being NHL doormats. Seeing players like Orr and Cheevers on the Boston Bruins while the Leafs lacked the young talent to adequately replace their veteran group from 1967 was likely the main reason. Money would certainly continue to contribute to the Leafs' on-ice demise.

Some would argue that Jim Pappin, not Dave Keon, deserved the Conn Smythe Trophy as the most valuable player in the 1967 playoffs. Pappin told me his mother believed this until her dying day. He led the Leafs in playoff scoring with 23 points. His salary was $14,500 that year, with a bonus of $1,000 for scoring 20 goals and another $1,000 for scoring 25 goals. He had scored 21 goals for the Leafs and 4 while in Rochester in the American Hockey League, which he thought would earn him the second $1,000 bonus given his outstanding playoff performance. The Leafs, however, gave him only the first $1,000 bonus.

Pappin asked for $22,000 in salary for the next season and reluctantly settled for less. This soured Pappin even more on the Punch Imlach style of management. Viewed by Imlach as somewhat of a malcontent, Pappin would be traded a year later by Imlach to the Chicago Blackhawks in exchange for Pierre Pilote. Over his seven full seasons in Chicago, Pappin would have one 40-goal, three 30-goal, and three 20-goal seasons. Pilote retired after one ordinary year on the Leafs' blue line. This is just one example of where bitter feelings fuelled a money-guided Imlach to make poor trades for the Leafs.

No player other than goaltenders played more minutes in the 1967 playoffs than Larry Hillman, who would immediately realize how little credit he was to receive. Making a $15,000 salary for the Stanley Cup year, Hillman asked for $21,000 for the next season. Imlach countered with an offer of $19,000. Hillman was armed with the knowledge that his brother Wayne had signed that summer with the New York Rangers for $21,000. With the first year of NHL expansion about to begin, Bob Baun, an extra defenceman for the Leafs during the playoffs, had signed the previous spring with the Oakland Seals for $35,000, while Al Arbour, who had played with the Leafs' American Hockey League team in Rochester, had signed with the St. Louis Blues for $25,000.

Though disappointed with how he was being treated, Hillman reduced his salary demand to $20,000; Imlach went up to $19,500. That modest $500 proved to be an insurmountable chasm for the stubborn Imlach and Hillman. It was where Hillman chose to draw a line in the sand and held firm. He began the season in the American Hockey League feeling Imlach's wrath. When fines were deducted, Hillman made $18,300 that season but felt he retained his principles and sense of pride.

What would make things even stranger about Imlach's stinginess in 1967 was how he became a completely different type of general manager when he took over the expansion team the Buffalo Sabres just three years later, in 1970. Unlike his time in Toronto, Imlach had a great rapport with his players and earned their professional respect. He was also on the generous side many times when it came to contract negotiations. That Imlach had been an investor with the Leafs through his interests in Leafs minor league teams in Rochester and Vancouver may have clouded his judgment. With the Buffalo Sabres, he was spending someone else's money—that of the wealthy owners, the Knox family.

The new, more generous Punch Imlach in Buffalo in 1970 was three years too late for the likes of Pappin and Hillman. The ordeal that Hillman was forced to endure resulted in him casting the "Hillman Hex" on his unappreciative employers. The hex was that the Leafs would never win another Stanley Cup again after 1967. Though his hex isn't all that well known, Hillman chuckles as he says, "It still seems to be working after 44 years."

"It taught me to never lose again," Hall of Famer and Montreal Canadiens legend Yvan Cournoyer said, sharing his thoughts with me as we sat enjoying the sunshine at the beautiful El Senador Resort in Cayo Coco, Cuba. It was January 2003, and I had been fortunate to have been invited for a week of sun and fun along with my wife, Lisa, who was four months pregnant, and our 3-year-old daughter, Jesse.

Serge Savard was the head of a group of Canadian investors who owned 50 per cent of the resort, with the balance owned by the Cuban government. El Senador, the name of the resort, refers to Savard's nickname, The Senator, and pictures of Savard and Fidel Castro adorned the main lobby.

I don't quite know how my family lucked into the trip. I had connected with Savard at a Hall of Fame weekend the previous November. He was anxious to put together a Toronto-Montreal hockey-themed week at his resort during the slow month of January. Wendel Clark, another investor in the resort, was to head the Toronto contingent. When he had to cancel, the focus switched to the Montreal Canadiens alumni angle, except, that is, for the lucky Stellick family.

In all, seven Montreal Canadiens alumni, with an impressive total of 52 combined Stanley Cups, enjoyed the week of sun and fun courtesy of their old teammate and general manager. Besides Savard and Cournoyer, there were Henri Richard, Yvon Lambert, Pierre Bouchard, Rejean Houle, and Jean-Guy Talbot.

All of those Stanley Cup rings and it was still the one he didn't get in 1967 that visibly irked Cournoyer all these years later. The world had been coming to Montreal for Expo '67 and the Montreal Canadiens and their fans were preparing for a celebration unlike any other in their history.

The Toronto Maple Leafs ruined the party. Also, as time passed, they ruined the true legacy of what really was a great Montreal Canadiens dynasty, on a par with the teams that won the Stanley Cup in the 1950s and the 1970s. That team won the Stanley Cup the two years before the Leafs victory in 1965 and 1966, as well as the two years following (1968 and 1969). Four Stanley Cups in five years and the focus on that last Leafs Stanley Cup victory detracts from what the Canadiens accomplished. The Oilers won four Stanley Cups in five years in the 1980s, and they are perceived as a greater dynasty than this Montreal team. For Cournoyer, although he won 10 Stanley Cups with the Montreal Canadiens, 1967 was the only occasion he played on a Montreal team that lost in the Stanley Cup Final. "It taught me to never lose again," he said. Cournoyer learned his lesson well.

There were several particularly interesting moments that enjoyable week at El Senador in Cuba. One was with El Senador himself. I was in the process of researching and writing the book that I co-authored with Damien Cox about the last Leafs team to win the Stanley Cup, in 1967, *'67: The Maple Leafs, Their Sensational Victory, and the End of an Empire*. It was what I had been discussing with Cournoyer and what evoked such vivid and somewhat painful memories for him.

Serge Savard spent the 1966–67 season with the Canadiens' Central Hockey League farm team in Houston before breaking into the NHL full-time the following season, so he hadn't been an active participant in the playoffs in the centennial year. I was more curious about what Savard thought about another well-known sports book, Ken Dryden's legendary *The Game*, which is recognized by many as the most insightful book written about hockey by an NHL player. It recounts the Montreal Canadiens team in the 1970s, giving both a public and behind-the-scenes perspective.

Savard featured largely in that book, as befitted his stature as a big cog in that Montreal team. I assumed he had read it and so was curious about what he thought of Dryden's work. "I did not read the book," he said as he took a long drag on his ever-present cigar. "Ken Dryden was a different kind of teammate." Different? Not sure what he meant, I inferred from

Savard's demeanour that he thought that anybody who played goal behind Savard, Larry Robinson, and Guy Lapointe was bound to have a great NHL career. Savard seemed definitely unimpressed by anything Dryden had written.

Another vivid El Senador memory is of a few days later, the last night of our stay there. A dinner had been organized for our party of Montreal Canadiens alumni and their families, the tag-along Stellick family, and former NHL referee Bruce Hood and his wife, Daphne. It had been a wonderful week and it was a fun and fabulous dinner. The Montreal group spoke mostly French and, not being bilingual, the rest of us felt a bit like outsiders. So it was classy and much appreciated when Savard and Bouchard made a point of breaking away from their larger group and shared a table with my family and the Hoods.

Later in the evening, Rejean Houle rose to make an impromptu speech and to thank our host. Houle was the consummate corporate-type spokesman, a little slick, savvy about personal politics, and comfortable behind the microphone. He called Savard up to join him so he could be acknowledged by our appreciative group. As he continued speaking to the group, Bouchard served as interpreter back at our table. "Oh, this is interesting," said a clearly bemused Bouchard. Bouchard gave us a play-by-play interpretation as Houle extended an olive branch to Savard. "There remained some bad feelings between Serge and Reggie because of things Reggie had said after taking over as GM for Savard," Bouchard explained.

I remembered how out of character it had been for the Montreal Canadiens to fire both a coach and general manager just a few games into a regular season, as they had done with Savard and coach Jacques Demers in 1995. Houle became the new general manager and former Canadiens' player Mario

Tremblay the new head coach. They were full of brash and bravado, and oozed with cockiness out of the gate. Whether obvious or more subtle, Savard's tenure was quickly viewed as old and outdated; the organization was set on bringing in a "new and improved" environment, to bring the Canadiens back to glory. That didn't happen, and Houle and Tremblay held their general manager and coach positions for a considerably shorter time than did Savard and Demers. The signature moment came when Patrick Roy was traded to the Colorado Avalanche on December 6, 1996.

The trade was necessary because of Roy's inability to get along with Coach Tremblay. It was Houle who then brokered the one-sided deal that sent Roy and Mike Keane to Colorado for Andrei Kovalenko, Martin Rucinsky, and Jocelyn Thibault.

Back in Cuba, as Houle paid homage to fellow ex–Montreal Canadiens general manager, a pleased Bouchard added, "Good, this brings it around full circle." No one broke out singing "We Are the World," but it was still nice to see a mending of any hard feelings. The general manager's job wasn't Serge Savard's or Rejean Houle's worry anymore; Andre Savard now held that position, though a few months later he would be out and another Montreal Hall of Famer, Bob Gainey, would be in.

The immediate post–Stanley Cup era would have been a lot less painful and dragged out for Toronto Maple Leafs fans had the World Hockey Association not begun as a rival professional league in 1972. The players welcomed the competition for their services and the vastly increased player salaries, but NHL owners felt otherwise, and had to make hard decisions about whether to compete with the upstart league when it came to player salaries.

The bombshell signing that proved that the World Hockey Association was for real was that of Blackhawks superstar Bobby Hull to the Winnipeg Jets. Other notable defections to the new league included Bruins goaltender Gerry Cheevers to the Cleveland Crusaders, Montreal defenceman J.C. Tremblay to the Quebec Nordiques, and the flamboyant and popular Derek Sanderson leaving the Bruins for a far richer deal with the Philadelphia Blazers. These were all significant losses and certainly hurt the calibre of the line-up of the NHL teams they left behind. But, in the bigger picture, no team would be harder hit by defections to the rival league than the Toronto Maple Leafs.

Rather than being successful in regenerating the Toronto Maple Leafs roster, Punch Imlach ended up totally dismantling the 1967 Stanley Cup champions and seeing them fall further down the NHL standings. Imlach would pay the ultimate price by being fired as both general manager and coach after the 1969 playoffs.

After the disastrous dismantling of the 1967 Stanley Cup championship team, new Leafs general manager Jim Gregory did a masterful and underrated job in his first few years by rebuilding a Leafs team that was well on its way back to respectability and possibly being a league contender.

Great drafting had procured the likes of Darryl Sittler, Lanny McDonald, Errol Thompson, Tiger Williams, and Ian Turnbull. Gregory and his staff were scouting pioneers in the Swedish hockey market, landing free agents Borje Salming, and Inge Hammarstrom. Solid hockey trades added the likes of Bernie Parent and Jim Harrison.

But as the WHA counted down the final weeks to its debut in the summer of 1972, the Leafs were heading toward a significant blow to Gregory's rebuilding of the roster. The team wasn't in need of total renovation, as it had been after Imlach's final two seasons at the helm, but it needed significant, unexpected work. It wasn't just that new Leafs owner Harold Ballard was somewhat unable and certainly unwilling to ante up the cash in a market where the average NHL player could easily double or triple his salary, citing the possibility of a move to the WHA as leverage. Though that in itself created a big challenge for Gregory, it was also Ballard's respect for NHL president Clarence Campbell, which he used to justify his fiscal stinginess and lead the Leafs team down the wrong path.

Campbell made it clear to NHL owners that, in his opinion, the WHA was not a serious threat and would be a short-lived competitive nuisance, and encouraged team owners to stick to their financial guns during contract negotiations. Most teams ignored Campbell's advice to some degree. The New York Rangers, for example, dug deep to keep their talented team intact, and the Chicago Blackhawks did the same after they suffered the major blow of seeing their superstar Bobby Hull sign with the Winnipeg Jets.

Ballard backed Campbell's edict to its fullest and a mass exodus left the blue and white for the new rival league. Three young defencemen who were emerging as a solid core after a few years on the Leafs' blue line all signed with the New England Whalers. They were 25-year-old Jim Dorey, 24-year-old Rick Ley, and 24-year-old Brad Selwood. At least in Dorey's case, anticipating salary difficulties and his likely jump to the WHA, Gregory had managed to swing a trade to the New York Rangers in exchange for Pierre Jarry, near the end of the 1971–72 season.

Twenty-five-year-old Jim Harrison was a great presence as the Leafs' third line centre and scored a career high of 19 goals. He joined the Alberta Oilers after Gregory thought he had a deal that would keep him in the Leafs fold. And 31-year-old journeyman Guy Trottier signed with the Ottawa Nationals, who, a year later, became the Toronto Toros.

Bobby Hull joining the Winnipeg Jets was the marquee signing by the new rival league. Meanwhile, his old Blackhawks team continued in the upper echelon of the NHL standings. The most debilitating blow of all to any of the NHL teams was the defection of 27-year-old Leafs goaltender Bernie Parent. Gregory had masterfully acquired Parent in a trade from the Philadelphia Flyers less than two years earlier. And it looked like the Leafs were set in goal for the next decade, with Parent in his prime and entrenched in the elite class among the top three or so goaltenders in the league. After posting a 2–0 shutout over Pittsburgh on the Wednesday, and a 7–1 win over Vancouver on the Saturday, Parent used a day off on Sunday, February 27, in the 1971–72 season to fly to Miami to make his announcement that he would be playing in the WHA the next season with the Miami Screaming Eagles.

With no Sunday newspapers published in Toronto to give Leafs fans any hint of Parent's plans for that day, Leafs fans got their first news of it reading the Monday morning *Globe and Mail*. With a short report of the Leafs win two days earlier, most were surprised by the picture bursting from the sports pages of their smiling star goaltender: Bernie Parent sporting the unfamiliar Miami Screaming Eagles red jersey with a white eagle logo and silver lines from the armpits down to convey

an eagle in flight. While the new jersey was a curiosity for
Leafs fans, a sickening feeling gave them less appetite for their
morning coffee, toast, and eggs. It wasn't the new jersey that
Parent was modelling that upset fans, it was the grim realization that he would be wearing the Leafs blue and white for
only a few more weeks.

Although the Miami Screaming Eagles never got out of
their nest, Parent's flight from the Leafs was a *fait accompli*. The
Miami Screaming Eagles became the Philadelphia Blazers, and
that is where Parent demonstrated his outstanding goaltending skills in the inaugural 1972–73 season to lead the upstart
WHA in wins with 33.

Meanwhile, the Leafs dropped 16 points in the regular-
season NHL standings, from 80 in 1971–72 to 64 in 1972–73.
Veteran Leafs like Paul Henderson, Norm Ullman, and, arguably the greatest Leafs of all time, Dave Keon, would leave the
team for the WHA over the next three years. To Jim Gregory's
credit, although his Leafs team took a tangible hit that season,
he was able to continue with another phase of his rebuilding.
However, in the summer of 1972, for the sake of a few dollars
and thanks to the unenlightened views of the NHL president,
the Toronto Maple Leafs took a step back in a rebuilding plan
from which they would never fully recover.

The Bernie Parent saga with the Toronto Maple Leafs had one
final chapter and one more missed opportunity for the organization and Leafs fans. And once again, an NHL president, this
time a future president, would play a role.

A substantial increase to his salary was really all Parent appreciated about his year in the WHA. The new owner of the Philadelphia Blazers, Bernard Brown, was not happy to have to live up to some of the contracts he had acquired, like the one Parent had signed. The owner had already said good riddance to Derek Sanderson just eight games into his 10-year contract, settling on a $1.1 million payment rather than the $2.5 million in the original contract and having to spend 10 years together.

So, although he had three years left on his deal with the Blazers, Parent knew he was free to move to an NHL team should he wish. Parent was enthused at the thought of returning to the NHL. He had enjoyed playing for Toronto but had really enjoyed playing in Philadelphia for the Flyers, for whom he played almost four years as one of the emerging Broad Street Bullies before being traded to the Leafs. Even more enthused was Parent's wife, who was from the Philadelphia area. She had no split loyalties: Philadelphia was where her heart was and where she wanted to be. The City of Brotherly Love was their chosen city of hockey love.

The problem for Parent was that he wasn't free when it came to choosing his NHL team. He had another problem too: the Philadelphia Blazers were likely on the move, to relocate somewhere after their one disappointing year both on and off the ice in Philadelphia. His NHL rights still belonged to the Toronto Maple Leafs, and in the off-season in 1973, Jim Gregory was intent on using that leverage to have his star goaltender return to the fold. Gregory knew that Parent, especially after a year in an inferior professional league, aspired to play in the only professional league that mattered: the NHL. Thus, Parent would have had no option but to rejoin the Leafs.

Gregory also knew that it was unlikely that the WHA would return to Philadelphia for a second season, which gave the Leafs leverage in any negotiations. And finally, fully aware that Parent wanted to go to the Flyers, Gregory was ready to be patient, knowing Parent's professional pride involved playing with and against the best of the best. Gregory was confident in his strategy and felt that the Leafs holding their ground was pivotal in this next rebuilding stage.

The problem for Gregory was that Leafs owner Harold Ballard never exhibited patience. As well, Ballard lacked respect for his general manager. He had reluctantly gone along with Gregory's plan but was anxious to trade Parent and get something back. At an NHL board of governors meeting during the 1973 playoffs, Ballard engaged in casual conversation with Flyers' alternate governor and legal counsel Gil Stein. From the Flyers' perspective, Stein played the Leafs owner perfectly as he agreed with Ballard that he couldn't understand why the Leafs were looking to move forward with "nothing" when they could get "something" of value for Bernie Parent from the Philadelphia Flyers. "Better than nothing," was what Stein subtly conveyed to Ballard.

That was the catalyst the Leafs owner needed to order Gregory to abandon his plan and get "something" for Parent. Of course, the leverage reverted to Philadelphia, as the team was aware of Ballard's orders and the new pressure on Gregory. They were also the only NHL organization Parent was interested in playing for. He claimed to be quite prepared to return to the WHA Philadelphia team whether it remained in Philadelphia or not and to fulfill his contract there should the Flyers not be able to acquire his NHL rights.

The deal was made on May 15, 1973, with the Leafs acquiring goaltender Doug Favell, long Parent's backup in Philadelphia, and a first-round selection in the 1973 Entry Draft (Bob Neely) and a second-round selection in the 1973 Entry Draft (Larry Goodenough). Six weeks later, the Philadelphia Blazers announced they were relocating to Vancouver. They became the Vancouver Blazers, and lasted just one season there as well.

Gregory proved that he knew what he was talking about, as Parent soon paid big dividends for the Flyers. He would be the Vezina Trophy winner, the Conn Smythe Trophy winner, and a First Team All-Star in both 1974 and 1975. Parent's regular-season goals-against-averages were a microscopic 1.89 in 1973–74 and 2.03 in 1974–75. Gregory has held a grudge against Stein since that day for his counterproductive coercion of the Leafs owner.

Gil Stein's power grew beyond being legal counsel for the Flyers and he was named NHL president in 1991. Many hockey fans take issue with Harold Ballard being enshrined in the Hockey Hall of Fame as a Builder. Yet it was Gil Stein who was in for the briefest of times, as it was ultimately ruled that he had circumvented the rules to get himself inducted. He left the Hall in shame, independent arbitrators ruling that Stein's orchestrated induction was to be reversed. Ballard's remains.

The truest Hall of Famer through all of this is Jim Gregory, who was inducted into the Hall of Fame in 2007: a true respected Builder of the NHL and the game of hockey in every sense of the word.

The end of the Original Six era in 1967 meant the end of many things in what had been an intimate six-team professional hockey league. It is said that Leafs broadcast legend Foster Hewitt never needed or relied on a line-up sheet when he was broadcasting a game, and began using one only when the league doubled to 12 teams. Players from the six-team NHL look back and kid that they thought there were only five other players in the league because they were usually matched against the same player on the five other teams in the 14 games they played against each other in the regular season.

The introduction of new teams brought an end to one informal act of collusion that had existed among Original Six players. The end of their 70-game regular season usually concluded with three home-and-home series on a weekend in late March or early April. In all three situations, a team would host an opponent at home on that final Saturday and then would travel to face that same opponent on the road on the Sunday. An informal arrangement existed for that final weekend whereby a team representative would alert the opposing team to which players were close to a personal bonus for an achievement, usually for scoring a certain number of goals. A player one goal shy of a cash bonus might play a more forgiving opponent those final two games to enhance his chances of cashing in on his $500 bonus, and his team would do the same for a player on the opposing team in a comparable situation. They certainly never did anything intentional to alter the result of the game, and, with two games left, the playoffs were usually set. It was just an understood arrangement.

The entertaining and witty Dennis Hull kids that in one situation, the goaltender kept giving the opposing player in question more and more of the net to shoot at, but each time he kept firing it directly at the goaltender. The goaltender yelled, "I'm going to get myself killed the more that I'm trying to help you get that goal for your bonus."

Even after the mass defection of players to the WHA, Jim Gregory was able to build a team that made it to the semifinals in 1978 and quarter-finals in 1979, though both times they were eliminated by the powerhouse Montreal Canadiens, the eventual Stanley Cup champions those years.

This was not enough to satisfy the Leafs owner, and Gregory was fired after the 1979 season. Actually, as was often his style, Ballard never actually informed Gregory that he was fired. In early July 1979, Gregory was relaxing at his cottage in Haliburton, north of Toronto. He interrupted his solitude to take a call from Brian O'Neill, an NHL vice-president from its Montreal offices.

Gregory was curious as to why O'Neill would track him down while on vacation. O'Neill had good news for Gregory— he was offering him a job to head up the NHL Central Scouting Bureau. A surprised and puzzled Gregory told O'Neill that he was appreciative of his offer, but he already had a job as Leafs general manager. "I just talked to Harold a few hours ago," a slightly chagrined O'Neill said, "and he told me that he had fired you and was bringing back Punch Imlach." And so Jim Gregory learned that his 10-year run as Leafs general manager and almost 30-year connection with the Leafs organization was over. Gregory accepted O'Neill's offer and remains a valued executive in the NHL offices today.

So, for the second time, George Punch Imlach took charge of the Leafs. In a matter of months, the team Gregory built was dismantled. After months spent at odds with many of the veteran players, Imlach pulled the trigger on his signature trade on December 29, 1979. Lanny McDonald and Joel Quenneville went to the Colorado Rockies for Wilf Paiement and Pat Hickey—a move that would set the Leafs organization back a number of years.

Not only did the Leafs lose the best player in the trade in McDonald, Imlach also managed to arouse bitter feelings in Imlach's chief adversary, the team captain and McDonald's best friend, Darryl Sittler. A more disruptive outcome of the unpopular trade that caused hard feelings among Leafs players was that Paiement and Hickey arrived in Toronto on existing NHL contracts that made them the two highest-paid Leafs players.

Imlach's adversarial tactics with the players were one thing, seeing their team salary structure out of whack was another. Jim Gregory had done an excellent job keeping his players in Toronto at below league-wide market value, and as long as the structure was intact, the players felt comfortable knowing where they stood on the Leafs salary pecking order: Sittler followed by McDonald and Salming, and then the likes of Williams and Turnbull. Now, Paiement's and Hickey's salaries topped the Leafs list.

Although McDonald's departure from the Leafs in December 1979 was met with the outrage of Leafs fans, fans may be surprised to learn that at one time, the possibility that he might return to the Leafs did exist. And, unlike the Bernie Parent trade years earlier where Ballard lost patience with the efforts to bring Parent back, this time it was Ballard who enthusiastically advocated the return of McDonald to the blue and white.

Fast forward almost two years from McDonald being traded to Colorado to the fall of 1981. Ballard had tired of Imlach's second tenure as general manager and dismissed him after training camp in 1981. Leafs chief scout Gerry McNamara was promoted to interim general manager; he would get the job full-time the next summer.

That November, McNamara got a sense that the Colorado Rockies might entertain a trade for McDonald. This was in the era before networks like TSN and Sportsnet, and the extent of hockey coverage was nowhere near what it is today. There really weren't insiders in the sense that Bob McKenzie, Darren Dreger, Damien Cox, Elliotte Friedman, and Nick Kypreos are today, and there was a more informal exchange of information that moved communication forward. It was said that the three best ways to get your message out were telephone, telegram, or by telling a scout. Business gossip was a large part of the scouting fraternity, and the gossip had McNamara's ears burning.

When McNamara shared his information with Ballard and bounced the possibility of reacquiring McDonald off the Leafs owner, he was very keen. For the next few days, McNamara tried to track down Rockies general manager Bill MacMillan— not so easy in an age before cell phones, texting, and e-mail. McNamara left phone messages at MacMillan's office in Denver and at the hotel where he heard MacMillan was staying while on the road.

MacMillan had played for the Leafs the first two seasons (1970 to 1972) of his seven-year NHL career, and McNamara was looking forward to their chat. Lanny McDonald had been a favourite of not only the Leafs owner but also McNamara and everyone else in the organization. The possibility that he could return was a huge boon for the team, both on and off the ice. Obviously, given Ballard's enthusiasm, McNamara was prepared to pay a significant price in any trade negotiations.

McNamara began to get a little concerned when MacMillan did not return his repeated phone calls on the second day and then the third day. He also had an enthusiastic and demanding Ballard asking for updates, and McNamara was getting annoyed that he had nothing to report to the Leafs owner. McNamara's worst fears were realized on November 25, 1981, with the breaking news that Lanny McDonald (and a fourth-round pick in the 1983 Entry Draft) had been traded to the Calgary Flames for Don Lever and Bob MacMillan, the brother of the Rockies' general manager.

McNamara always felt that Bill MacMillan must have been anxious to give his brother Bob a fresh start with the Colorado team after Bob had a slow start that season with the Flames. Otherwise it made no sense that he wouldn't return at least one message from Toronto and see what they had to offer. Anyone who understands the art of the deal, the art of negotiation, the art of the trade understands that the more teams interested in a player, the more leverage the trading team had. The Leafs would have been a significant card for MacMillan to use as leverage with Calgary and any other team.

I remember McNamara talking over the phone to MacMillan a day after the trade was announced. "What if we were going to offer you Vaive and Salming?" McNamara threw at the Rockies' GM. "There is no way you would have offered that," countered MacMillan. "Of course not, but you never know what kind of offer we could have made because you never gave us the chance to discuss it, but we were really keen to get Lanny back," an annoyed McNamara finished the conversation.

As we well know, McDonald would continue to play his Hall of Fame style in Calgary for the next eight years, including a 66-goal season in 1982–83. There is no question that because of the pressure from Harold Ballard, as well as his keen interest in the trade, McNamara would likely have made an offer superior to Calgary's offer and all other comers. Whether it was a case of blood being thicker than water, a Leafs prodigal son of the 1970s was unable to return. Somehow I think that McDonald, long entrenched in Calgary both on and off the ice and inducted into the Hockey Hall of Fame in 1992, is content with the way things worked out and happy that MacMillan didn't return McNamara's calls.

He would have been especially content as he sipped out of the Stanley Cup along with his Calgary Flames teammates in 1989. He thought of great teammates like Darryl Sittler and Borje Salming, who never got that opportunity.

When Wayne Gretzky played his final game in 1999, among his many honours was one from NHL commissioner Gary Bettman who decreed that no NHL player shall ever wear the number 99 again. In some ways, that seemed a bit of an empty honour, as the hockey world has a general understanding of what the number 99 symbolizes.

No other player wore that number during the Gretzky era, with one exception: Wilf Paiement after he came to Toronto in the Lanny McDonald trade. Since then, no other player has had the "audacity" to give the impression that they consider themselves in the same class as arguably the greatest NHL player of all time.

So why Paiement? It wasn't an arrogant move by Paiement, as some have speculated. Paiement arrived in Toronto early in the 1979–80 season, which was also Gretzky's first season in the National Hockey League. And while number 99's greatness was soon apparent, he wasn't yet universally acclaimed "the Great One."

It was Leafs general manager Punch Imlach who encouraged Paiement to wear 99. He had worn number 9 in Colorado, but that number in Toronto was already taken by Dan Maloney. Imlach felt pressure (whatever pressure Imlach could actually allow himself to feel) for Paiement to make Leafs fans forget about Lanny McDonald's skills. He thought Paiement wearing 99 would help accomplish that. However, Leafs fans remained more aggrieved that Paiement had cost them Lanny McDonald in a trade. To Leafs fans, he never replaced McDonald's contribution on or off the ice. It seemed like his wearing 99 was almost incidental.

More importantly, Wilf Paiement was never under the illusion that he was as good as Wayne Gretzky.

May 15, 1993 . . . doesn't it seem like all of the best Leafs playoff memories since 1967 revolve around that memorable six-week run in the spring of 1993? The Leafs had already pulled off their biggest upset in the first round of the playoffs when they eliminated the Detroit Red Wings in seven games, with memorable overtime goals by Mike Foligno in Game 5 and Nikolai Borschevsky in Game 7 at Joe Louis Arena.

Now, the Leafs were getting set for another Game 7 against the St. Louis Blues, but this time it was on home ice because the Leafs had finished the regular season 14 points ahead of the Blues. Reading the press notes and statistics before the game as I prepped for my role as colour commentator on the radio broadcast, one note jumped out at me. This would be the first Game 7 the Leafs would play on home ice in 29 years.

April 25, 1964, two days after Bobby Baun had scored his memorable overtime goal in Detroit playing with a broken ankle, the Leafs would win the Stanley Cup on home ice with Johnny Bower posting a shutout in a 4–0 win over Detroit. Twenty-nine years later, Felix Potvin would match power with a 6–0 shutout as the Leafs eliminated the Blues and headed to Los Angeles the next afternoon for their memorable show-down with the Kings.

To go almost three decades without a seventh and deciding playoff game being played on Maple Leaf Gardens ice, to me, summed up all those years of playoff futility.

I started working full-time for the Toronto Maple Leafs in 1979. This was the first year that four WHA teams joined the NHL, and so there were 21 teams altogether.

Thirteen of those 21 teams have won the Stanley Cup at least once since then: Boston, Colorado (which became New Jersey), Detroit, Edmonton, Minnesota (which became Dallas), Chicago, Calgary, New York Rangers, New York Islanders,

Hartford (which became Carolina), Quebec (which became Colorado), Pittsburgh, and Montreal.

The Toronto Maple Leafs are one of eighth teams to not win the Stanley Cup over that period. However, they are one of only three (the Winnipeg Jets/Phoenix Coyotes and St. Louis Blues are the others) to not make it to a Stanley Cup Final since 1979. Both St. Louis and Phoenix have faced bankruptcy issues over the period, unlike the Toronto Maple Leafs.

It is a depressing list for Leafs fans to be subjected to but it shows the extent and uniqueness of how they have supported a team that is in a class by itself with lack of playoff success. Of the 12 NHL teams that were members of the league after the Leafs' last Stanley Cup victory in 1967, all of the other 11 teams have at least been to a Stanley Cup Final since 1967. The other five Original Six teams have also won Stanley Cups since 1967. Pittsburgh and Philadelphia as well. Oakland switched cities once and merged with the Minnesota North Stars, who won after they moved to Dallas, as did the Hartford Whalers after they became the Carolina Hurricanes. The St. Louis Blues made it to the Stanley Cup Final their first three seasons in the league (1967 to 1969). The Los Angeles Kings never won the Cup but made it to the final in 1993 (after eliminating the Leafs).

The Buffalo Sabres and Vancouver Canucks were added in 1970. Both have made it to the Stanley Cup Final. The New York Islanders and Atlanta Flames were added in 1972, and both have won Stanley Cups (Atlanta after moving to Calgary).

Even teams added from 1990 onward have had success in making it to the Stanley Cup Final and even in winning the Cup. The Anaheim Ducks and Tampa Bay Lightning have been Stanley Cup champions, and the Florida Panthers and Ottawa Senators have made it to the final.

The saying that misery loves company confirms what Leafs fans feel and believe, but they don't have any company. Their team not even playing for the Stanley Cup is something that Leafs fans suffer alone.

The positive upside is enormous when they get that opportunity. Witness the first Stanley Cup in Boston in 2011 after 39 years, the recent Chicago Stanley Cup win in 2010, their first in 49 years, the New York Ranger Stanley Cup win in 1994 after a 44-year drought. Another comparable is the Boston Red Sox winning their first of two recent World Series in 2004, their first since 1918.

Toronto Maple Leafs fans, like Chicago Cubs baseball fans, (the Cubs last played in a World Series in 1945 and last won the World Series in 1908) feel that the opportunity to celebrate their next run at playoff greatness will be well worth the wait. They just wonder when the wait will end.

9   LIFE BEHIND THE MICROPHONE

I gave a lot of interviews over my career with the Toronto Maple Leafs, and in 1991 I moved to the other side of the microphone. Several interviews in particular stand out.

"Gord, remember what we have talked about? Well . . . I'm making that call." The voice on my answering machine was that of Allan Davis of the Telemedia Radio Network. It operated a network of radio stations across Canada that broadcast all the Toronto Blue Jays games and all the Toronto Maple Leafs games. That call marked my official change of careers, on Halloween 1991.

The Leafs radio broadcast crew consisted of play-by-play man Joe Bowen and former player agent Bill Watters. Watters had just advised Allan Davis that day that he had been hired by Cliff Fletcher to be the assistant general manager of the Toronto Maple Leafs. They needed a colour commentator to be in Washington the next night for the Leafs' game against the Capitals.

Allan Davis had been a friend of mine when I had worked in the Leafs front office, and I had kept in touch with him for more than a year about media possibilities. I had been out of hockey for about a year since being fired by the New York Rangers as their assistant general manager, and had dabbled in the various media opportunities that came my way. Jim Tatti had used me for a segment on *Sportsline* on Global TV after about 30 Leafs games aired on their station. I had begun co-hosting a syndicated magazine television show called *Rinkside*, which covered the American Hockey League on a weekly basis.

The message from Allan Davis was music to my ears, probably the most exciting message I have ever received. It allowed me to be involved with an NHL team on a daily basis once again, filling the huge void I felt after being fired in New York. I flew to Washington the next day to start my new career. As colour commentator, I needed a guest for the second inter-mission. Still nervous about that element of the show, I asked if it was okay to pre-tape someone. David Poile, then the Washington Capitals general manager, was my first guest and ended up being my only pre-taped guest ever. I dropped by his office about 90 minutes before the game. He was pleased about my new job, and I appreciated that he accommodated my pre-tape request and made it a relatively first interview with some-one in the business who I considered a friend.

When I listen to a tape of my first game, or any of my first few games for that matter, I shudder to hear how bad I was. I spoke too quickly and tried to force in too much informa-tion. Allan Davis, Joe Bowen, Ken Daniels, Nelson Millman, and others were invaluable in their assistance. I used to gather short notes, facts, pieces of information, and statistics as part of my game preparation. Early on, I would try to get all of those points into the broadcast. I soon came to realize, though, that the better game broadcasts were usually those where fewer notes were used, as it meant that I was playing off what was going on in the game rather than referring to my research.

The call from Allan Davis that launched my new career also was my way of notifying the hockey world that I didn't get the job as assistant general manager to Fletcher. I had had a very good interview with him the previous July and was on the shortlist. It took him a few months to get things settled and approved by new Leafs president Steve Stavro before he could make the hire. Whether I came 2nd in the running or 100th, it doesn't really matter. Bill Watters was an excellent choice. And, his selection gave me the opportunity at an excellent consolation prize.

The next fall, in September 1992, The Fan launched as Canada's first all-sports radio station. With my now being involved with the Leafs broadcasts, for which The Fan was the Toronto-area affiliate, I liked my chances of being one of the stable of broadcasters on their opening day line-up. I was one of two guys who were really disappointed. The other was a rather new friend of mine named Damien Cox, from the *Toronto Star*. Like me, he had been doing a bit of radio work on The Fan, and we both hoped that bigger things were in the offing. We were wrong.

The opening-day radio line-up included the *Morning Show* with Mike Inglis, Joe Bowen, and Stephanie Smythe. Sports

columnists Steve Simmons and Mary Ormsby then moon-
lit for two hours each, from 10:00 a.m. to 12:00 noon. Next
was Dan Shulman from noon until 4 p.m., followed by Bob
McCown and Jim Hunt with *Prime Time Sports*. Jim Richards
and Stormin' Norman Rumack hosted the evening shows.

Damien Cox and I did get a chance to do a three-hour
morning show every Sunday. That was probably the right
speed for us at that point, to gain some experience and skills.
The show got better each week and we really connected as a
radio team. The following August, in 1993, Allan Davis (now
the first-ever program director of The Fan) hired Damien and
me to co-host an afternoon show.

My first foray into live NHL television broadcasting was working for three years on the Leafs broadcasts on CHCH-TV from
1995 to 1997. I was paired with Paul Hendrick on the dozen
or more broadcasts each year for which CHCH-TV had the
Toronto Maple Leafs rights.

Both Paul and I have vivid memories of an unusual 15 or
so minutes before a Leafs game in Anaheim on November 13,
1996. Being the on-air talent for a broadcast meant getting
to the game three hours early for a production meeting with
the entire crew. After that, there were about 90 minutes to kill
while the technical team, including the producer and director,
got things ready before the opening puck drop. For Paul and
me, especially for games on the road, it was just the two of us
going over the press notes and statistics and enjoying a conversation about the upcoming game, or life in general.

That late afternoon in Anaheim there was a third individual with us in the rather rudimentary press room at the Anaheim Duck Pond. He had his white dress-shirt sleeves rolled up to give the impression of a boss who likes to get involved. Since Paul and I were the only two others in the press room, we were the only ones he could engage in a conversation.

The gentleman certainly had something on his mind. Apparently, his head coach had missed much of the training camp and pre-season to coach the American team in an international tournament a couple of months earlier. Maybe it was because we were media associated with a Canadian-based NHL team or because we were from Toronto, where the media coverage was far more extensive than what he was used to in Anaheim, I don't know, but this guy went to great lengths to make sure that he made his point to us.

His coach was Ron Wilson, the first coach in Anaheim Mighty Ducks history, and the man we were talking to was Tony Tavares, the president of the Ducks. The tournament he was annoyed about was the 1996 World Cup, which was a huge victory for U.S. hockey, the biggest win since the Miracle on Ice in 1980. Canadian hockey fans had taken the loss hard, especially taking issue with Brett Hull's key goal being counted when all of Canada felt it was knocked in with a high stick.

We knew that in the United States this win wasn't met with the kind of national excitement or pride as it would have been in Canada. But we were certainly surprised to hear Wilson's boss lament that his head coach had missed time to coach the American national team to victory.

Brett Hull kids that the U.S. World Cup victory in 1996 has caused his popularity to wane the farther northeast he travels. Buffalo Sabres fans take issue with his Stanley Cup–clinching overtime goal when his skate was in the crease, and a few miles farther north, Canadian fans take issue with his high stick goal at the 1996 World Cup.

Fourteen years later, Wilson would be behind the American bench for the 2010 Winter Olympics in Vancouver. He certainly knew this time that he had the full support of his boss— Brian Burke, his boss with the Leafs, was the Team USA general manager. All of Canada held their collective breath as the Americans rallied to tie the game from two goals down, until Sidney Crosby scored the golden goal in overtime and won the gold medal for Canada.

Despite a lack of appreciation from Tavares, Wilson has had an outstanding NHL career, with stops in Washington, San Jose, and Toronto, picking up his 600th career NHL coaching victory in 2011. And despite his questionable perspective on Wilson's national team stint in 1996, Tavares has also had a solid career as a sports executive. His latest role is to help keep the Dallas Stars afloat despite their myriad financial issues.

I have been fortunate to have interviewed thousands of people over the past two decades on radio and it is hard to pick out who were the funniest, the most interesting, the most compelling. Needless to say, I do have a couple of stories.

February 7, 1981. I was the host of my regular afternoon show, *The Big Show*, on The Fan radio station and was also doing hockey analysis on television for *The Score*. My good friend Brian Spear was one of the producers at *The Score*. He had previously worked with me at The Fan as well.

He was the one who came up with an idea for the 25th anniversary of Darryl Sittler's six-goal, 10-point night. Why not try to get Sittler and Bruins goaltender Dave Reece on at the same time to relive that game? After all, that night has remained an enduring memory for all Toronto Maple Leafs fans and an NHL record that has stood the test of time. I was one of a fortunate group who witnessed Sittler's achievement in person, as it was during my first year working part-time in the press box at Maple Leaf Gardens at Leafs games.

The Leafs won 11–4, and the game was never in doubt from a competitive point of view. This allowed the crowd to focus on Sittler's tremendous personal feat. There was a great energy in the building and it absolutely rocked with noise with each Sittler goal and point. The crowd wasn't aware of exactly just what NHL records Sittler was coming close to. We had that advantage in the press box, as did the television viewers at home watching *Hockey Night in Canada*.

In the third period as he closed in on the six goals and 10 points, things became almost comical. He could do no wrong, and Reece seemed unable to stop any kind of shot. To add insult to injury, Reece wasn't getting any breaks, while luck seemed to be on Sittler's side too. Sittler even kids that one of the goals basically went in off a Bruins player's butt after he just threw it out in front of the net from behind it.

I left the building that night feeling as if on a cloud of energy and excitement, having witnessed that record-setting game. So, now, I looked forward to arranging a reunion of sorts. Sittler was an easy person to get for the radio show. He had become media savvy and was always accommodating when I had asked him to come on the radio with me. This record was obviously an achievement he remained proud of. Reece would take some digging, but my radio producer, Ian Cunningham, came up with a phone number for Reece in upstate New York. I was pleased when I was told that Reece gladly agreed to come on.

This was one of those talk show rarities. Basically, I introduced the two men and then let them run with it, while I sat back and became part of the audience. Unbelievably, they had never even spoken one word to each other over the 25 years. This was their first time reliving the night together.

I think Sittler was a little taken aback about how magnanimous and classy Reece was that day on the show. Reece took the bull by the horns and established a very comfortable environment for the discussion. He reflected on the game with a sense of humour and took nothing away from Sittler's achievement. He talked about how classy Sittler had been, how he had not been overly demonstrative, how he had just gone about his business, scored, and lined up again. In Reece's words, "A consummate professional through the entire game."

It was well known that Reece's teammates had shown him a great night out in Toronto the night before that infamous game. Gerry Cheevers had just returned to the Bruins organization after a time in the World Hockey Association. Boston coach Don Cherry realized that Cheevers was not yet in game shape so he wanted Reece to start two final games, the Saturday game in Toronto and a Sunday home game in Boston.

It is ironic that Cherry, recognized as one of the all-time greatest "player's coaches," would not make a goaltending substitution to relieve Reece from his horrible night in Toronto. Cherry just didn't feel he had a backup goalie ready yet to play in Cheevers. He changed his plans after the Leafs debacle and Cheevers started the next night's game at home in Boston.

Dave Reece never played another second in the National Hockey League after Sittler's record-breaking night.

Being an American, Reece was totally unaware of the magnitude of the media coverage of the game in Canada. It happened to be a rare Saturday night when the Montreal Canadiens were idle. In those days, the great Montreal teams usually played in the national game broadcast across most of the country, while the Leafs game would be the regional game broadcast in Ontario. With the Canadiens off that night, the Toronto-Boston game was the national broadcast right across Canada.

He chuckled about the magnitude of that evening and the dubious notoriety he attained. Those who know Reece are quick to point out his excellent record in the American Hockey League and how well he had played with the Bruins before Cheevers's return. Before the Toronto debacle, Reece had posted a respectable 2.68 goals-against-average in 13 Bruins starts, with a 7-4-2 record. The previous year he had posted a then outstanding 2.92 goals-against-average with the Bruins' American Hockey League affiliate, the Rochester Americans.

On my radio show on The Fan, Reese played down his record and remained humble, and talked about how he realized over the next few years after Sittler's record-setting night that he himself didn't have what it took to stay in the NHL so had begun another career in teaching.

We had slotted the interview for about a 10-minute period. We doubled that. I bumped the scheduled sports update back and we let the conversation flow. It was talk radio at its finest. It seemed like Darryl Sittler and Dave Reece were sitting having a beer together and me and our thousands of listeners were right there with them.

This started an enduring friendship between Sittler and Reece. Sittler's big night has been acknowledged from time to time by the Leafs organization, and Reece has been a part of the tribute on occasion.

But nothing matched that first interview. Sittler offered Reece as a memento a copy of the game sheet from that night. He made his offer with the best of intentions and Reece graciously accepted in that spirit. It was very apparent, even 25 years later, that while one man had established NHL records, two class acts were the central characters of the story.

Sittler's record-breaking night was a night that one young Leafs fan was very aware of: Wayne Gretzky would evolve from being a childhood Leafs fan into arguably the greatest NHL player of all time, with stops in Edmonton, Los Angeles, St. Louis, and New York. Though Gretzky set scores of NHL scoring records, Sittler's record was one that eluded Gretzky throughout his NHL career.

The Sittler record was among one of the many subjects I was able to discuss with Gretzky during an interview in December 2001, a few months before the Winter Olympics in Salt Lake City. Wayne Gretzky was the coach of the Canadian men's hockey team for the upcoming Games.

His handlers had arranged that weekday December morning as a dedicated period in which Gretzky was available to knock off a number of sit-down television appearance requests. Finding a date that worked was complicated by Gretzky having assumed duties as part of the management team of the Phoenix Coyotes a few months earlier. (A few years later, he would become the head coach of the Coyotes from 2005 to 2009.)

I was working that year at The Score television network, as well as keeping my regular radio duties at The Fan. On that particular morning, I was filling in on The Fan's *Morning Show*. I'd be finished by 10 a.m. and figured I'd be at Gretzky's restaurant, an appropriate venue for the series of interviews, in downtown Toronto, about a half hour later. I was assured that it would likely be around 11 a.m. that we would get our interview with the Great One; he was starting at 10 a.m. with interviews with the NBC and HBO television networks and those were expected to take about an hour.

I arrived as scheduled at 10:30 a.m. and parked in the outdoor lot beside the restaurant. I could see my producer, Brian Spear, looking out apprehensively from a side door. He met me halfway as I made the short walk from the parking lot. "We're ready to go—Wayne has been asking where you are." I picked up the pace and asked him why we were so ahead of schedule. It turned out that the NBC and HBO interviews had been quite short, shorter than Gretzky and his handlers had expected.

I sat down on my stool and was quickly having makeup applied. I had been there for a total of 30 seconds when, from behind a curtain, just like in the *Wizard of Oz*, came a voice saying, "Gordie Stellick," and in bounded Wayne Gretzky. He shook hands with me and quickly took his spot on the stool facing me. I could tell that he was enthused and energetic about doing the interview. Brian Spear told me later that he thought Gretzky had been a bit disappointed that the two earlier interviews had been so short.

There is the public "regular" media side of Wayne Gretzky—the class act who says all the right things and is friendly and personable but really gives very little substantive content. However, on other occasions, when he is in the appropriate frame of mind, he can give a compelling interview. A year earlier, I had experienced that side with Gretzky at the public Fan Forum on the Sunday morning of his Induction Weekend at the Hockey Hall of Fame. It was magical to see how he connected with the hundreds of fans at the question-and-answer session with the Great One, and I very much enjoyed moderating the discussion. I had a good feeling that this was going to be one of those days.

Making small talk as the last-minute preparations were made for the interview, Gretzky brought up his current NHL team: "How about those red-hot Phoenix Coyotes?" I was certainly aware of their recent hot streak and asked Gretzky what had been the key in the turnaround. He took a half-second pause before answering, "Goaltending [referring to Sean Burke], it's pretty well always goaltending." An interesting observation from a player who won four Stanley Cups in Edmonton with a team that could strike offensively like no other, and a common perception: playoff success in hockey comes down to goaltending; in baseball, to pitching.

We were getting close to starting the on-camera interview. I felt like we were changing on the fly, as this had all happened in a blur. But with still a few minutes before the camera began rolling, it was my turn to make small talk. I mentioned how Gretzky had struck an emotional chord with me and millions of others with an article he had written for *Sports Illustrated* a few weeks earlier about his great friend Garnet "Ace" Bailey, who had been on one of the planes that crashed into the Twin Towers on September 11, 2001. Bailey had been employed as a scout for the Los Angeles Kings and was on his way to the Kings' training camp. It had been a powerful article, written from the heart and full of raw emotion. Full of touching memories, it was a wonderful tribute.

I knew Bailey a little and I told Gretzky how much his article would have been appreciated by his friends and, especially, his family. "His family is really struggling with his death," he shared. Then his demeanour abruptly changed and he said, "The thing that haunts me is that I got him that job in Los Angeles in the first place." Talk about steering the conversation into a brick wall. Later, Spear would kid me, "Nice small talk, Gord!"

When the camera started rolling, we both were able to quickly move forward and what resulted was a compelling, engaging conversation—he brought the best of Wayne Gretzky to the interview that morning. He talked about Sittler's record and how in the third period of many games throughout his NHL career he strived to match or break the six goals and/ or 10 points. He smashed so many scoring records, but, for a single regular-season game, the Great One was no match for the "Great Darryl." Gretzky's career bests were five goals and eight points in a single NHL game.

Our discussion moved on to the subject of the upcoming Winter Olympics and Gretzky's role as the coach of the Canadian team. Naturally, in discussing Team Canada's disappointing exit from the 1998 Games in Nagano, Japan, the subject of the shootout against the Czech Republic came up and, specifically, Gretzky's reaction to not being included among the five shooters in the shootout loss.

Gretzky gave his usual well-rehearsed tactful answer, leery of criticizing Team Canada coach Marc Crawford or anyone else. I pressed him a bit more about the omission. One urban myth that had emerged was that Gretzky wasn't the best of scorers on clear-cut breakaways, that he had so many break-aways that the average hockey fan didn't realize he actually scored on a lower percentage of opportunities than most other NHL players.

Gretzky smiled diplomatically at the question. "I'm not sure if I was or wasn't one of the better players at scoring on a breakaway," he said. Then a sense of empowerment and pride seemed to come over him as he said, "All I know is when I had a breakaway and it really mattered, I didn't miss too many." He fixed me with a steely gaze that left no doubt that he was deadly serious—even though there was a twinkle in his eye. It was obvious Gretzky wasn't big on the urban myth. He had wanted to be at the shootout and he doubted that he would have missed his shot. To Gretzky, all theories to the contrary were absurd.

Ours took much longer than his first two interview com-mitments, and he seemed to enjoy talking hockey and life the longer we went on. The interview was an excellent two-part feature on our show *Ice Surfing*, which was then airing on The Score.

I had met Wayne Gretzky on a couple of occasions, and he was and still is one of the few sports figures I am somewhat in awe of, even though we have developed a friendly acquain-tanceship. My being in awe was never more evident than at our first meeting. It was May 1993 and Gretzky's restaurant in downtown Toronto was hosting an invitation-only party to celebrate the opening of its rooftop patio, The Oasis.

I was invited, along with my future wife, Lisa, to attend. We arrived and joined a table that included NHLPA director

Bob Goodenow, NHL senior vice-president and future Leafs general manager Brian Burke, star NHL player and friend of Gretzky's Brett Hull, media personality Christine Simpson, and a few others. All except Hull I had a personal friendship with.

It was a pleasant and warm Friday afternoon. It was also the day O.J. Simpson led Los Angeles police on that infamous slow-speed Bronco chase for hours. We were able to follow that on a television set up near our table.

About a half hour after Lisa and I had joined the table, three new guests arrived: Tom Bitove, the owner of Gretzky's and a friend of mine, and Wayne Gretzky himself and his wife, Janet. Goodenow, helping to make the introductions, said to Wayne, "You know Gord Stellick." Gretzky nodded as he reached over the table to shake my hand. I stood up slightly to be able to meet his hand. In the process I knocked over a full glass of water, much to the delight of the others at the table. I could just imagine Lisa shaking her head and rolling her eyes. I still joke about my lame move that day. Yes, I guess I was a little excited and a little in awe.

And that was one reason I was so pleased with the interview eight years later inside the same venue. Gretzky had been relaxed, which helped me relax. I made sure I drank water from a paper cup this time. I could tell he was engaged in our conversation and was willing to give more than his usual discreet responses. Somewhat arrogantly, I felt that it was one of my first notable pieces as an interviewer. I felt I had brought the best out of Wayne Gretzky the person. Of course, he being in the right mindset had allowed me to do it.

Gretzky was in no hurry to leave that day, and our conversation had flowed so well that we continued to talk for about another 10 minutes after the camera had been turned off. Usually someone like Gretzky is in a hurry to get somewhere else.

I had heard what a great sports fan Gretzky was, how he loved to follow all sports and loved to talk sports. When he lived in Edmonton, before sports networks like TSN and Sportsnet were up and running, he would watch via his own satellite dish the nightly *Sportsline* show out of Global TV in Toronto with Jim Tatti and Mark Hebscher.

This was illustrated to me first-hand a few weeks after Gretzky announced his retirement from the New York Rangers, in 1999. It was a Friday afternoon in April. Having finished my radio show at The Fan at 4 p.m., I quickly went home to get set for the NHL playoff action that evening. When I checked my work voice mail about an hour later, I heard a distinctive voice. "Gordie Stellick, this is Wayne Gretzky. I heard you chit-chatting on the radio and I wanted to get through to talk to you. But I guess you keep banker's hours." He was in Toronto and he had been listening to The Fan. He had called when I was on-air and had wanted to talk some hockey like any "regular" Fan listener.

A few weeks later, I was at the NHL awards, which were held in Toronto. Many of the nominees, and some of the successful award winners, were seated near me. The friend I was with tapped me on the shoulder at one point: Wayne Gretzky was trying to get my attention. He was one row in front of us and a few seats to our left. "I bet you were surprised when I called in and left you a message at your station," he said, smiling. Was I ever. Our receptionist at The Fan was a very sweet woman who knew absolutely nothing about sports. We would hear her pages over the intercom as she put through calls from people we didn't know and weren't really interested in talking to. And then when Wayne Gretzky calls, she puts him right through to my voice mail. Go figure!

The Great One on the ice is a regular sports fan off the ice, his appetite to talk about whatever is topical in the world of sports almost insatiable.

Through my years in broadcasting I have learned the perils of doing live shows on both radio and television. And they are heightened when we welcome callers to phone in to the show. I find that the callers can be either compelling, which helps make for enjoyable talk radio, or pedestrian, and the show subsequently suffers. That's why it's important that a competent producer screens the calls off-air first.

The dump button is located near the microphone on and off switches. The radio station goes into delay when it has callers, meaning that there is about an eight-second gap between the actual conversation and what is heard over the airwaves. If an inappropriate comment is made, the host simply pushes the dump button. To listeners, it merely sounds like a glitch that the conversation ends so abruptly, and it saves whatever inappropriate comments were made from being broadcast.

We are told as hosts to not react to the callers but to just keep things moving forward. Pretty well all callers have figured it out that the good old days when they could sneak a crank call through are gone. Some, unfortunately, still try.

It was February 1989, and as general manager of the Toronto Maple Leafs I had been invited to field calls from viewers on a TSN show titled *It's Your Call*. TSN was a growing all-sports station at the time but still in its infancy. It wasn't yet available on basic cable packages in and around Toronto, though that would all change soon after.

Pat Marsden was the host of the show. I grew up watching Pat Marsden as a dinner-hour staple delivering the day's sports on CFTO-TV, which was a Toronto CTV affiliate. Engaging and personable, Marsden gave me the scoop on what would happen when we hit the airwaves: the name of the caller would appear in bold letters on a screen and I was to look directly into the camera as if looking directly at the caller.

I did have one quick question before the show began: What type of delay was there for the callers? Marsden explained that this was an expensive proposition for television and that TSN didn't have it in place. He assured me that the screeners at TSN were excellent at their job.

Lights! Camera! Action! Well, it doesn't really work that way, but that's how it felt to me. It was a bad stretch during the Leafs season and I was expecting my fair share of critics and criticism. Marsden grilled me in the preamble to begin taking callers. I was ready to take on all comers. I just wasn't prepared for the first question.

The caller was Tim from Stouffville, a small community north of Toronto. I looked directly at the camera at Tim—and the rest of the viewing audience—as he asked his question: "Do you suck Harold Ballard's cock?" I thought this surreal situation might have been part of a practical joke, but Marsden quickly jumped in and took the caller to task. (Though years later he would kid me, "You never answered the question.")

All hell broke loose at the TSN studio once we went to commercial a few minutes later. Nothing as memorable happened the rest of the half hour, but we were all leery that Tim or one of his cronies would call back.

Returning home after the show, my answering machine had about five messages from friends identifying themselves as "Tim." The next day, a TSN publicist announced in the local Toronto sports sections that "due to lewd comments directed at Leafs general manager Gord Stellick," they were going to pay the thousands of dollars for the technology for a delay system.

Pat Marsden joined The Fan radio station as a co-host of the *Morning Show* in 1996. It was a pleasure to work with him from time to time. He left the station in 2004, and I was hired as his replacement about a month later.

Despite the Tim from Stouffville incident, Marsden had given me excellent advice that day I appeared with him on *It's Your Call*. He told me during a commercial break after I had taken issue with something he had said that I had reacted rather strongly. "That's great," he said, "you went back at me—that's what people want to see." It made me understand better how things operated on the other side of the microphone. The criticism (including from Marsden) wasn't personal, even though

I sometimes took it that way; it was just part of their mandate to create compelling television and radio.

During my time as general manager, I often appeared after a Leafs game when time permitted to be interviewed by Dave Hodge, long recognized as one of the best media personalities in Canada. It started as a one-time event, but the television people producing the local game broadcasts on Global TV were pleased with how it went and it became a somewhat regular feature called "Generally Speaking."

Friends will recall that I was almost 35 pounds heavier than I am today and that I would glisten with sweat a fair bit both because of my weight and my nervousness (which thankfully eased up with each appearance). Having no television makeup on didn't help either. My first interview or two, Hodge hit me with some tough questions and I was taken aback by the direction he was taking. What it did, though, was allow me to shine by giving good answers to those questions. I realized that as an interviewer, asking cream-puff questions will result in a lame interview—you're not giving your subject a chance to talk about what really matters. Both in life and in the media we often have a tendency not to ruffle feathers and so avoid addressing a topic that might be difficult for the interviewee. Through my experience with Dave Hodge, I learned that it was up to the interviewee to figure out which way he or she wanted to go. For the interviewer, the best interviews are those where you aren't afraid to ask the tough questions.

As I grew more comfortable with the media, I took on the challenge of being a host rather than exclusively a hockey expert in the passenger seat. Hosting required a whole different skill set that I had to develop. Doing even the simple parts of the job is incredibly difficult when you aren't used to them.

Ron MacLean of CBC's *Hockey Night in Canada* was a guest of mine in-studio at The Fan when I was new to my host job back in 1994. I remember asking him during a break, "Do you forget what you are going to ask somebody? Doesn't that ever happen to you?" "All the time" was his quick response. I felt better knowing that it happens to even the best of us. It also showed me how MacLean so capably covers for those moments when as a multitasking host he loses his train of thought.

Don Cherry said something to me that I choose to take as a compliment. "You're doing great, Gordie," he told me after I had been at my "new" profession for a few years. "Just be yourself, don't get all smooth like those other guys, just be yourself!"

Brian Williams, now of TSN after many years with CBC, is someone who makes a habit of making a supportive phone call out of the blue to less experienced sportscasters. He has done so with me on several occasions to give me his positive take and constructive comments on a particular interview.

Williams enjoys hearing me reminisce about when he was with CBC's Toronto station, CBLT-TV. He covered the Leafs beat on a daily basis and was often at Maple Leaf Gardens for practice. One morning in January 1981, he was part of a large media contingent waiting for the arrival of Leafs general manager Punch Imlach. Harold Ballard had flexed his muscle over Imlach and fired Joe Crozier as the coach a day earlier. Now it was Day 2 for the Leafs without a coach as they waited for Imlach to solve the predicament Ballard had created.

I could hear activity outside the door to our executive offices, on the concourse of the red seats, on the east side of Maple Leaf Gardens. It was the media descending on Imlach,

who had just arrived and was making his way through the concourse toward the offices. I was in the waiting area as Imlach
opened the door to enter. He was tight-lipped and reminded
the media to stay outside the offices. Then a final smart-aleck
shot as the door shut behind him: "You guys are such geniuses,
why don't you pick the next coach?"

Five seconds later, the door opened halfway and Brian
Williams popped his head in. In that distinctive voice that
has come to be synonymous with Canadian television coverage of both the Summer and Winter Olympics, Williams good-
naturedly hollered after Imlach, "Punch, when we've settled
on your choice, where can we get a hold of you?" Even the
beleaguered and prickly Imlach had to smile.

It had all the makings of a disaster, but it ended up being a great
memory. I had got a call from Dave Andrews, the president of
the American Hockey League, about a television opportunity.

It was the spring of 1997. While the National Hockey
League Stanley Cup Final was underway with Detroit against
Philadelphia, so was the American Hockey League final as the
Hershey Bears and Hamilton Bulldogs vied for the Calder Cup.

They had hastily put together a television network that
included the New England Sports Network (NESN) and a
couple of other local markets in the United States, including
Hershey. They needed a colour commentator for the three
games in Hamilton and Andrews had thought of me.

They had another commentator in the Hershey area who
would handle Games 1 and 2 and then 6 and 7 if they were

necessary. I would be part of the broadcast for Games 3 and 4 and then Game 5 if necessary.

It was a series dominated by Hershey. Their general manager Jay Feaster had that same role when Tampa Bay won the Stanley Cup in 2004 and their coach Bob Hartley held the same position with Colorado when they won the Stanley Cup in 2001.

The best the Hamilton Bulldogs were able to do was win the fourth game to avoid a four-game sweep and give me one more date as the colour commentator. As Hershey built up a big lead in the third period of Game 5, I was asked to leave the broadcast booth position and head to ice level to capture the post-game celebration.

I was excited and appreciative of the opportunity. I quickly found my contact at ice level from the television crew. He gave me an earpiece to go with my portable audio transmitter and I held one of those larger microphones, best for post-game interviews.

I quickly had one problem. The ear piece easily fell out of my ear. When I showed it to the technician, he asked where the piece that was supposed to be on the end of it was. I didn't know. When he uttered the words "holy shit," I figured my worst fear had been realized and that piece had remained in my ear.

I thought he had just disappeared but he soon returned with a pair of pliers. This big sweaty individual took the pliers to my eardrum area and successfully pulled out the long plastic piece that had been imbedded. Though getting very low marks for appearances, he had actually exhibited the skills of a surgeon.

My other fear had been a break in communication with the producers of the game who would think it was okay to throw the broadcast to me as I was on the ice and ready. Fortunately, I was repaired in the nick of time.

The Calder Cup is the American Hockey League equivalent to the Stanley Cup. The Hershey Bears celebrated as if it were the Stanley Cup. Joining the celebration on the ice, careful not to slip in my dress shoes, I put any immediate concerns about long-term hearing loss aside as I savoured the moment. The players were euphoric. The interviews were fun, the players on both teams were great. As I went about doing my work, I savoured the moment being with these people I really didn't know all that well personally. It was what we all dream about being kids—winning it all! The celebration seems to be in slower motion and it all seems so surreal and so wonderful.

The many great people, the many great experiences— I appreciate being involved in the greatest game in the world.

INDEX

'67: The Maple Leafs, Their Sensational Victory, and the End of an Empire (Cox, Stellick), 220